PENGUIN BOOKS

How Children Learn Mathem

Pamela Liebeck is Lecturer in Mathematical Education at Keele University. She was educated at Guildford County Grammar School, Somerville College, Oxford, and Cambridge University. At Oxford she graduated in mathematics and at Cambridge she gained a Teaching Certificate with distinction. She subsequently gained a Bachelor of Music degree.

She has taught in primary school, secondary school, university and teacher training, and was Head of Mathematical Education at North Staffordshire Polytechnic from 1979 to 1985. She has lectured on mathematical education in the USA, Australia and South Africa, is the author of *Vectors and Matrices* and has written articles on mathematics and mathematical education.

Pamela Liebeck is married to Hans Liebeck, Reader in Mathematics at Keele University. They have three children, of whom one is a Reader in Mathematics at London University and another a teacher of mathematics.

To Martin, Gillian and Helen,
whose mathematical development has been a joy to watch

Contents

Introduction

Progress may have been all right once, but it's gone on too long.

— Ogden Nash

Ever since mathematics has been taught in schools, there has been no lack of reformers advocating change. In the seventies, reformers laid great stress on the necessity for children to understand mathematical structure rather than become competent at routine calculations. The standard joke against these pioneers was that they insisted that children should understand that 5 × 3 = 3 × 5, but didn't care whether they also knew that five threes are fifteen. The emphasis was certainly on mathematical structure rather than calculating techniques. The reaction in the late seventies and eighties tended to tip the scales the other way. Employers complained that their young recruits were incompetent at calculations. Their prescription to schools was: 'Make children competent at calculating, and let their understanding take care of itself.'

Of course, what employers wanted was not mindless calculating techniques, but competence at using mathematics to solve real problems. However, you cannot get very far with real problems until you understand the relevant mathematical structure *as well as* knowing a relevant calculating technique. To find the area of a rectangle 5 cm long and 3 cm wide, it is no help to know that 5 × 3 = 15 and 5 + 3 = 8 if you do not know which of these is the relevant calculation: Again, you cannot decide to pay for five £3 garden plants with three £5 notes until you have understood that 5 × 3 = 3 × 5.

When we teach only for calculating competence, we get demands for understanding. When we teach only for understanding, we get demands for calculating competence. The real need is for both of these. It is through both of them that we are equipped to solve real problems. To solve real problems, we need to understand mathematics. Paradoxically, to understand mathematics, we need to explore real problems. When children learn mathematics, they need to play with real objects and explore real problems that interest them.

The 1988 Education Reform Act in Britain introduced a National Curriculum for schools. As far as mathematics is concerned, the

National Curriculum sets out to stabilize rather than reform current teaching. It lays down the core content of school mathematics, but refrains from prescribing *how* it should be taught. This book suggests how we can utilize the natural learning process of children to help them lay the important foundations of their mathematical development, step by step. It attempts to set up a proper balance between the needs for understanding and calculating competence.

Chapter 1 proposes a general strategy for introducing mathematical concepts to children. Chapters 2 to 7 and 9 to 20 present the mathematical content (which essentially covers levels 1 to 5 of Targets 1 to 13 of the National Curriculum), together with activities by which this content can be introduced. At the end of each of these chapters is a list of equipment needed for the activities and also suggestions for the reader. Chapters 8 and 21 summarize some contributions made by psychologists to the theory of child development and the theory of learning.

In writing this book I have been greatly helped by Gillian Liebeck, a practising mathematics teacher, Marion Jordan, an interested parent, and Hans Liebeck, a professional mathematician. All three of them read the manuscript with hawk-like eyes and pointed out irrelevancies, inconsistencies and points that required clarification. If any remain, the blame is of course attached to them! My gratitude goes to them, to Ruth Eagle, John Sloboda and John Armstrong, who read and criticised parts of the manuscript, and also to the members of staff of Penguin Books, who have been so obliging over the production of the book.

P.L.

January 1990

1   Six Questions on the Why and How of Learning Mathematics

Sometimes Eeyore thought sadly to himself 'Why?' and
sometimes he thought 'Wherefore?' and sometimes he
thought 'Inasmuch as which?'

– A. A. Milne

1. Why teach mathematics?

This is the initial question posed in the Cockcroft Report [1].[1] The
report gives the answer that mathematics is useful for everyday life, for
science, for commerce and for industry, because it provides a powerful,
concise and unambiguous means of communication and because it
provides means to explain and predict. It attains its power through its
symbols, which have their own 'grammar' and syntax. Also, the report
claims, it develops logical thinking, and it has aesthetic appeal.

2. Why do people enjoy mathematics?

Some people may enjoy mathematics because it is useful. But it is far
more likely that its appeal for us lies in the intellectual or aesthetic
satisfaction that we derive from it. This is particularly true of children.
So teachers must be constantly aware that, although the justification for
spending so much school time on mathematics is that it is useful, its
appeal for children is based on their intellectual or aesthetic response, in
much the same way as the appeal of music or art.

3. How can mathematics appeal to one aesthetically,
in a way similar to music or art?

We must first recognize that personal differences influence our response
to music or art. We do not all like the same sort of music, and we
certainly cannot expect everyone to like the same sort of mathematics.
However, a basis to our enjoyment of music or art is our response to

1. References are printed at the end of the chapter.

pattern, and the following little excursion appeals to that response in mathematics.

As you know, the numbers 1, 3, 5, 7 and so on are called odd numbers. Let us pose the problem of adding up the first *hundred* odd numbers. Even with a modern calculator, the task could prove very long and boring. We shall revolt against such a task. (Revolting against tedious calculation is a sign of promising mathematical ability!) Let us instead add the first *two* odd numbers:

$$1 + 3 = 4.$$

Next, let us add the first three, four and five odd numbers and then pause for reflection.

$$1 + 3 + 5 = 9,$$
$$1 + 3 + 5 + 7 = 16,$$
$$1 + 3 + 5 + 7 + 9 = 25.$$

Look at the answers to our additions, namely 4, 9, 16, 25. Knowing our multiplication tables, we can associate these numbers with 2×2, 3×3, 4×4 and 5×5. We notice a pattern:

The first two odd numbers add to 2×2,
the first three odd numbers add to 3×3,
the first four odd numbers add to 4×4,
the first five odd numbers add to 5×5.

Do you 'feel in your bones' that the first hundred odd numbers just *have* to add to 100×100? We haven't proved that this is so, but the power of pattern is such that you probably scarcely feel the need to check the fact. It is possible to show that 10,000 is the correct result by using algebra or by resorting to calculation. But we have predicted the result without either.

4. Mathematics is often called an 'abstract' subject. What is meant by this?

It is paradoxical that, although mathematics has enormous power to solve practical problems, it is yet regarded justifiably as an abstract subject. A mathematical calculation, or a formula such as $e^{i\pi} + 1 = 0$, does not of itself demonstrate any practical relevance. Yet the most complex mathematics has its feet firmly planted in the real world. It is rightly called an abstraction from the real world. Even 'two' is an abstract concept. You cannot understand 'two' until you have met many pairs (for example a pair of eyes, a pair of shoes, a pair of wings), and abstracted what all pairs have in common. You cannot understand what is meant by 'number' until you have understood 'two', 'three', 'four' and other similar concepts. 'Number' is an abstraction from a set of abstractions. The concept of 'addition of numbers' is an even higher abstraction than 'number'. Mathematics involves a hierarchy of abstractions, and we cannot understand any mathematical concept without also understanding the concepts on which it depends lower in the hierarchy.

Of course, language itself is abstract, and we communicate mathematics through language. But language in general does not involve this hierarchical structure to the degree that mathematics does. The teacher's task is to lead children through this hierarchy without losing the chain of connections with the real world.

5. How does my brain cope with this hierarchy? When I see the symbol '143', I do not imagine one hundred and forty-three objects set out before me. Have I then lost contact with the real world?

No, you haven't. Symbols are an essential ingredient of mathematics. They condense a hierarchy of concepts into 'manageable' form. You do not need to imagine one hundred and forty-three objects in order to understand the symbol '143', but you do need to have understood our very useful system of notation, whereby the '4' represents four groups of ten and the '1' represents a hundred, which is itself ten groups of ten. The Romans would have symbolized the same number by CXLIII. Such notation enforces a much more complex thought process than does our decimal notation. Symbols are a very important part of mathematics.

6. How does a child develop abstract thought?

A baby sees, feels and explores physical objects, such as his (or her) toys. It is not long before he recognizes words to represent them. (The spoken word is an abstraction from reality.) Later he will recognize pictures of them (another abstraction). And much later, he will associate written symbols with them. His mathematical experience, like all his experience, must progress through this sequence of abstraction. We shall categorize the sequence by:

> E – *experience* with physical objects,
> L – spoken *language* that describes that experience,
> P – *pictures* that represent the experience,
> S – written *symbols* that generalize the experience.

Let us trace this sequence for a child's learning about the concept 'ball':

E – He sees, feels, tastes, holds, rolls and drops his ball. He has 'fun', and learns about many of its properties.

L – He associates the sound of the word 'ball' with his toy. This is useful. If he says the word, he may be given the ball to play with. He will soon associate 'ball' with other objects that have the same rolling property as his ball.

P – He recognizes a picture of a ball. The picture is very different from the ball itself. The picture does not roll, or feel like a ball. But the child sees that it has enough in common with his own ball to be called 'ball'.

S – Much later, he learns the symbol that we write to represent the sound 'ball'. This is sophisticated. The symbol has no properties at all in common with a real ball, and it is only artificially associated with the sounds that we utter in saying the word 'ball'.

As we proceed to analyse the stages that children need to progress through in attaining mathematical understanding and competence, we shall often refer to the sequence of abstraction, E–L–P–S. A mathematics textbook for children, however carefully prepared, can be concerned *only* with the last two items of the sequence, pictures and symbols. No book for young children can start where they need to start, namely with experience and spoken language.

References

1. *Mathematics Counts*, HMSO, 1981 (Cockcroft Report)

2 Concept Formation

A child of four would understand this!
Send somebody to fetch a child of four.

– *Groucho Marx (Duck Soup)*

They're the same but different.

– *Primary-school child*

As we saw in Chapter 1, mathematics is an abstraction from reality. We summarized the sequence E–L–P–S that leads to mathematical abstraction. In this chapter we shall be concerned with only the first two of this sequence: E (experience) and L (spoken language that describes that experience).

We mentioned in Chapter 1 that you cannot understand 'two' until you have met many pairs of objects and abstracted what all pairs have in common. In the process of learning language, children utter words (such as 'green') in imitation of what they hear, and they gradually associate words with concepts (such as the concept of what 'green' is). Some important early mathematical concepts include 'many', 'few', 'as many as', 'more than', 'fewer than', 'long', 'short', 'as long as', 'longer than', 'shorter than', 'round', 'flat', 'straight', 'curved'. How do children form such concepts? And how can we find out whether their concepts of these terms are the same as ours? To answer these questions, we must describe four basic activities: matching, sorting, pairing and ordering.

1. Matching

At the age of sixteen months, Helen learnt that 'bath' named the object where she sat in water and played. For a while, she called every container of water 'bath'. This showed that she had perceived a common property of these objects, but that her concept of 'bath' differed from convention. Later, she learnt that there were other names (such as 'sink', 'bowl') associated with water containers, and she gradually refined her concept of 'bath' to fit convention. At the age of two and a half, Martin called holly berries 'peas', showing that he had perceived a common property of holly berries and peas. But did he have a concept of 'green'? He did not use the word, but he did have a concept of 'green' that will never fit convention, for he is red–green colour blind, and his concepts of red and green are identical.

Children, then, develop concepts spontaneously, by perceiving and selecting properties that are common to a range of their experience. The word that we normally use to describe the selection of common properties is 'matching'. If your skirt has the same colour as your jumper, you say that the colours match. When you say, 'I can match that performance', you mean that you can give one of the same calibre. *Matching* is the way that children learn to use language correctly – in particular, the language of mathematics. In any matching process, you are selecting experiences that have the property that you are seeking and discarding those that do not. To have a concept of 'green', you must know what is *not* green as well as what is green. A fish, I fear, will never have a concept of water!

Matching Activities for Children

To enable children to form concepts, we must provide them with suitable experiences to foster their impulse to perform matching. We must also provide them with suitable language to describe the common properties that they perceive. The initial matching activities that we encourage in school should be concerned with concepts that children have already formed, or are likely to be able to form immediately. For instance, we might ask them to pick out the conkers from a box containing conkers, shells and fir cones, and to put all the conkers together. Or we might ask them to pick out the spoons from a collection of cutlery. The purpose of such activities is to make children aware that in matching activities we are looking for a common property. After a matching activity, we should talk about this common property.

For some children, matching for colour will be of the above nature. Children in a reception class usually have clear concepts of colours, but not necessarily the appropriate language to describe those colours. Matching for colour will help children to consolidate their concepts of colours and to use the appropriate words (red, yellow, blue, green, pink etc.) to describe those concepts. We cannot teach them what blue is; we can only provide them with matching activities so that they will learn for themselves. Let us consider some matching activities that might be organized to introduce mathematical concepts to children. We shall focus on concepts concerned with length – 'long', 'short', 'as long as', 'longer than' – and with shape – 'round', 'flat', 'congruent to'.

'*Long*' *and* '*short*'. The word 'long' is imprecise. It suggests that one has a standard of length, and that a length described as 'long' is considerably longer than that standard. Nevertheless, children learn to use the word 'long' before the more precise term 'longer than'. Their use of the words 'long' and 'short' should indicate that they are applying some sort of visual comparison between contrasting lengths. They should be invited to make a long train of bricks and a short train, to thread a long row of beads, or to find a short ribbon from a box of ribbons. Children who show that they appreciate the comparative meanings of 'long' and 'short' can proceed to the matching activity that follows, introducing the concept 'as long as'.

'*As long as.*' We assemble a collection of sticks that have been previously cut to several different lengths. We pick out a long one and say to a group of children, 'Here is a long stick. I am going to try to find one as long as my stick.' We pick a shorter stick and hold it against the long one. 'No, that stick is not as long as my stick.' We pick a long one and say, 'Yes, this stick is as long as my stick. John, can you find a stick that is as long as my stick?'

My stick:	My stick:
Not as long as my stick:	As long as my stick:

John picks a stick and tests, as we did, whether his stick is as long as ours. Together the children assemble a set of sticks that are as long as the original stick. Following this activity, each child can select a stick and assemble for himself a set of sticks that are as long as his stick.

'*Longer than.*' In the activity for introducing 'as long as', we encounter sticks that do not match for length. We can now focus on such sticks to

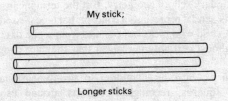

My stick;

Longer sticks

introduce the concept of 'longer than'. We can say, 'This stick is longer than my stick; find some more sticks that are longer than my stick.'

'Round.' We assemble a collection of shapes, such as boxes, tins, balls, cones. From it we pick out shapes that roll. 'The ball rolls because it is round,' we say, 'and the tin rolls because it has a round part.'

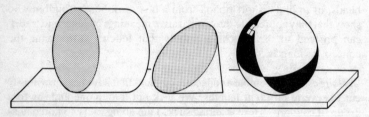

'Flat.' From the same collection of shapes, we pick out those that will stand firmly on a table without rolling or tending to roll. 'The tin stands still because it has a flat part,' we say, indicating the surface of the tin in contact with the table.

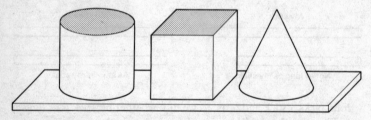

The concepts of 'round' and 'flat' will help children later to form concepts of 'cylinder' and 'cone'. Cylinders do not all have the same shape; but they all have a round part and two flat parts. Cones all have a round part and one flat part.

'Congruent to.' Adults tend to associate the term 'congruent to' with formal secondary-school geometry. But the term means 'the same size and shape as', and it represents a concept that is possessed by very young children. A child who picks out pennies from a pile of coins and stacks them has almost certainly perceived that they are congruent to each other.

How can we introduce children to two-dimensional shapes such as circles, squares, rectangles? Objects around us are not two-dimensional, but three-dimensional. You cannot pick up a circle. But the activity described to introduce the concept of 'flat' has focused attention on the faces of solids, which are two-dimensional. We can follow that activity by putting paint on a flat part of a solid and letting children make prints on paper. The prints are congruent to the faces that made them.

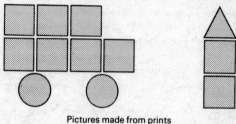

Pictures made from prints

We shall return to the subject of congruence in Chapter 6.

Open-ended matching activities. Matching activities can develop into a guessing game. A child who matches a blue lorry with a red fire engine probably has a common property other than colour in mind. Other children can be invited to guess this property.

2. Sorting

Matching activities involve picking out individuals with some common property. Sorting involves breaking up a set into new sets of matching individuals. It is slightly more complex than matching, and it grows from matching. All the activities that we described under 'Matching' can be

Sticks sorted by length

extended to sorting activities. Children who have matched for colour can progress to sorting for colour, to consolidate their understanding of the concept of 'colour'. Children who have matched sticks for length can progress to sorting sticks by length, as a step towards understanding the concept of 'length'.

Like matching, sorting is an activity that often arises in free play and in tidying up after play. ('The dolls' clothes go in that box, the cars go in this one', and so on.) The activity can also develop into a guessing game. The 'objects' shown below have been sorted for some criterion. Guess what it is! (If you can't guess, be patient, and wait for a hint in section 5.)

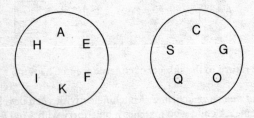

3. Pairing

We now come to some activities that are important for introducing concepts concerning number. Just as 'long' and 'short' are imprecise terms suggesting comparison of contrasting lengths, so 'many' and 'few' are imprecise terms suggesting comparison of contrasting numbers. The more precise terms relating to number are 'as many as', 'more than' and 'fewer than'.

Look around a room where people are sitting. Does the room contain more chairs, or more people? You will not need to count in order to answer the question. You will mentally 'pair' each person with the chair that he or she is occupying, and observe whether there are extra chairs or extra people. You have attempted to set up what is called mathematically a 'one-to-one correspondence' between people and chairs. Such an activity is basic to the concept of number, and it is much simpler than counting. The term 'one-to-one correspondence' is rather a long mouthful for a child. An alternative term is 'pairing', and we shall use this word to describe the activity. Some books for teachers and children call the activity 'one-to-one matching', but it seems inadvisable to use the same word 'matching' to describe two such different activities. In a pairing activity, such as pairing people and chairs, it is of no consequence which person is sitting on a particular chair. We do not say, 'Pam matches the green chair.' (She doesn't!)

Let us see how the activity of pairing can introduce the concepts of 'as many as' and 'more than'.

'As many as.' We put out a row of 'sweets' for Teddy. We do not count them, but we explain that they are Teddy's sweets. Then we suggest that Action Man would like some sweets too, and we invite a child to put out a row of sweets for Action Man, encouraging the child to arrange Action Man's sweets as illustrated, so that children will be invited visually to pair the two sets of sweets. We say that Action Man wants as many sweets as Teddy, and when the two rows of sweets exhibit pairing, we say, 'Now Action Man has as many as Teddy.'

Teddy's sweets

Action Man's sweets

Opportunities for pairing arise constantly in play (putting a rider on each horse, a car in each garage), in stories ('a chair for Daddy Bear, a chair for Mummy Bear, a chair for Baby Bear'), and in everyday activities (a drink for each person, a pencil for each child). Whenever pairing has been performed, we have the opportunity to say 'There are as many cars as garages', 'There are as many pencils as children' and so on.

'More than.' When it is impossible to pair people with chairs because there are some chairs without people on them, we say that there are *more* chairs than people. Pairing 'failure' leads to the concept 'more than'. Activities designed to illustrate the concept 'as many as' can be easily adapted to illustrate 'more than'; and opportunities for pairing 'failures' occur as often in play and everyday activities as opportunities for pairing.

'Fewer than.' The concept of 'fewer than' occurs less spontaneously to children than the concept of 'more than'. The English language is peculiar in that it has one word to apply to both larger number and larger

quantity (*more* eggs, *more* milk) but two words to apply to smaller number and smaller quantity (*fewer* eggs, but *less* milk). The situation is complicated by the fact that usage is changing. So many people nowadays say '*less* eggs' that it may be only a matter of time before it is considered quite proper to do so.

4. Ordering

Ordering a set of objects by no particular rule invites the concepts of 'first', 'next to', 'last', 'between'. Children might copy a row of toys, or a string of beads made by the teacher or another child. The activity itself will focus their attention on 'first' and 'next to'. After such an activity, children can discuss the arrangements that they have made ('The car is next to the doll', 'The doll is between the car and the ball' and so on).

Some ordering can be introduced in pattern form, where the question 'What comes next?' is answered not by reference to a model row, but by the pattern itself. We might ask children to continue threading a string of beads that exhibits a pattern, or to copy and continue a pattern of pencil marks which have been selected to prepare children for forming letters or numerals.

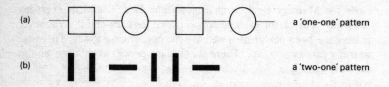

(a)   a 'one-one' pattern

(b)   a 'two-one' pattern

Pattern-making can involve shape (as in (a)), orientation (as in (b)), size or colour.

Concepts involving comparisons such as 'bigger than', 'longer than', 'wider than' can be deepened by the activity of ordering. Arranging the sticks A, B, C, D in order of length is quite a complicated process. Children who initially arrange A next to C are faced with the problem of what to do with B. They will have to perceive that B is longer than C and shorter than A, before placing B *between* A and C. Ordering a set by 'longer than' invites the rather sophisticated concept called *transitivity* – in this case, the deduction that since A is longer than B, and B is longer

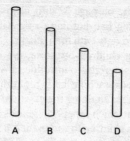

than C, then it must be true that A is longer than C. (Children who have ordered the sticks and can say that A is longer than C are not necessarily making this deduction, for they can use visual clues to reach this conclusion. We can only say that *asking* them which is longer, A or C, invites them to make this deduction.) Ordering a set by 'longer than' also enables us to introduce the concepts and words of 'longest' and 'shortest'.

Like matching, sorting and pairing, ordering often arises in play ('The big Teddy goes in bed first, then the little one'), in stories ('The first little pig built his house of straw, the second little pig built his house of sticks' and so on), and in everyday activities (stacking a pile of books for carrying). Ordering by size deepens the concepts 'bigger than' and 'smaller than', and invites the concepts of 'biggest' and 'smallest'.

5. 'Noise'

We have argued that the teacher who designs suitable matching, sorting, pairing and ordering activities for children can help them to form concepts that are basic to mathematics. Through those activities, the teacher can also introduce appropriate language to represent those concepts. In designing activities, it is advisable to be aware of the possibility that children might be misled into selecting common properties other than those that truly identify the concepts under consideration. For example, in the matching activity for 'as long as', described in section 1, suppose that all the sticks of the same length as the one selected by the teacher happened to be red. It is conceivable that a child may perform the activity correctly, while supposing that the concept 'as long as' is connected with 'red'. Colour is irrelevant in this activity, and it is an example of what is called in psychological terms 'noise'. If you found the guessing game on page 22 difficult, it was because of noise. The criterion for sorting had nothing to do with the meaning of the letters; it was concerned only with their shape.

To avoid misleading children by noise, we need to devise varied activities, with varied materials, to introduce any one concept. The key to successful mathematics teaching lies in repetition, varying activities as much as possible while maintaining the essential ingredient that invites the concept to be learnt. Such repetition guards against noise, acts as a memory aid and invites children to widen their horizons by applying the new concept to unfamiliar situations. The child who says correctly, 'My liquorice is longer than yours,' when he or she has not performed an ordering activity involving liquorice, has truly absorbed the concept 'longer than'.

Equipment Useful for Early Matching, Sorting, Pairing and Ordering

Environmental objects such as conkers, fir cones, shells, leaves, pebbles, flowers, buttons, bottle tops, cotton reels, corks, matchboxes, old keys.

Set of sticks of at least four differing lengths.

Solid shapes, such as boxes, tins, sweet cartons, balls, cone-shaped drinking cups, commercially made spheres, cylinders, cuboids, pyramids and cubes.

Piping cord or plastic loops for surrounding sets.

Boxes and tins for sorting into.

Large beads and plastic thread.

Dolls, toy animals, cars, lorries and boats.

Dolls' clothes, furniture, crockery and cutlery.

Building blocks.

Simple shape puzzles with shapes that go with holes.

Nesting boxes, Russian dolls.

Cups, mugs, jugs, jars, bowls, spoons, buckets, funnels, for sand and water play. (Some containers should match for shape and size; that is, they should be congruent.)

Suggestions for the Reader

1. (Matching) Put yourself in the place of a child learning a new concept. Play the 'Concept Game' with a friend. You think of a concept that applies to more than one of the objects illustrated below. (Your concept might be 'animate', for example, or 'made of wood'.)

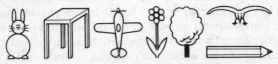

Give a name to the objects fitting your concept, such as 'splog'. Select one of these objects and tell your friend, 'This is a splog.' Your friend's task is to find out what a splog is. We give an example of how the game might proceed.

You say, 'This is a splog' (pointing to the bird).

Your friend thinks that splogs might be objects with wings. He says, 'Is this a splog?' (pointing to the aeroplane). You say, 'No.'

Your friend then thinks that splogs might be animate. He asks, 'Is this a splog?' (pointing to the tree). You say, 'No.'

He decides that splogs must be animals, and he is right.

2. (Sorting) Do you still have problems solving the guessing game in section 2? If so, consider the criteria 'straight' and 'curved'!

3. (Sorting) Pick some buttercups, daisies, cow parsley and dandelions. Sort the flowers into white ones and yellow ones. Do you have a problem? Where will you put the daisies? The trouble is that they belong in *both* the sets you are making. (Young children should not be faced with this kind of problem!)

4. (Pairing) Test some five-year-olds to see whether they have the concepts of 'as many as', 'more than', 'fewer than'. If they have difficulty, is this due to noise, or language, or the concepts themselves?

5. (Ordering) Test some five-year-olds on their ability to order objects such as pencils, toy cars, lollipops, according to length. Do they understand the terms 'longer than', 'longest', 'next to', 'between'?

3 Counting

MORIARTY: How are you at Mathematics?
HARRY SECOMBE: I speak it like a native.

– *Spike Milligan* (The Goon Show)

In many ways it is harder to analyse the process of learning mathematics in the early stages than in later stages. For example, counting, a seemingly simple process, is really a most complex one. We are going to analyse the process of counting, step by step, and we shall see that it involves all the basic activities that we described in Chapter 2. To help in this analysis, you should, ideally, be going through the process yourself as we proceed. You should imagine, or better still have, a large bag of boiled sweets, of which you are going to count the red ones.

1. Do you know which sweets you are going to count? You know that the red ones *match* in colour, and you will mentally pick them out.
2. You will *sort* the sweets into two sets: those that are red, and those that are not red.
3. You will study the red sweets. Are they in a suitable arrangement for counting? Perhaps some overlap others, or are concealed from view. You will want to *order* them in a row, so that you will not leave one out, or count one twice.
4. Now you have an ordered row of sweets. To count them, you will say some words: 'one', 'two', 'three' and so on. It is essential that you know these words in the conventional order. (Have you ever heard a child recite 'one', 'two', 'five', 'six'?) You must know enough *number names in order* before you can count your sweets.
5. What will you do as you recite these number names? You will touch one sweet as you say each name. You will leave no sweet untouched, and you will touch each sweet exactly once. You will *pair* some number names with the sweets, saying as many number names as there are sweets. (Some children try to count a set of objects without pairing them with the number names; they touch the objects faster than they can say the number names, so that by the time they touch the fifth object, they are saying 'four'.)
6. You will find yourself saying a word as you touch the last sweet. Suppose this word is 'twelve'. You will then say that there are twelve

sweets in your set. You have selected the final number name that you recited, and associated it with the whole set. 'Twelve', which you used as a 'label' for the last sweet that you touched, has changed its role, and is now used to describe *all* the red sweets. How very strange!

You have used 'twelve' in two ways in your counting process. In your pairing activity, you used it in what is called its *ordinal* sense. It labelled the twelfth sweet that you counted. But when you say that there are twelve sweets, you are using 'twelve' in another sense. This sense is called its *cardinal* sense.

What a complex process you have been through! You have performed, mentally or physically, six different processes in order to count your sweets. They were: (1) matching objects for a common property; (2) sorting them into those that have this property and those that do not; (3) ordering the relevant set in some way; (4) recalling the number names in conventional order; (5) pairing the ordered objects with some number names in order; and (6) using the final number name, in its cardinal sense, to describe the whole set of objects that you counted.

You will notice that the activities of matching, sorting, ordering and pairing, described in Chapter 2, have arisen as essential steps in the process of counting. No wonder that these activities are fundamentally important for mathematics! Furthermore, before children are able to count a set of objects, they must know some number names in conventional order, without necessarily understanding what those names mean. And finally, they must learn to select the final number name that they have used, and associate it with the whole set of objects that they have counted. They need activities to assist these two processes.

1. Learning Number Names in Order

Children do not need to know *all* the number names before they can begin to count, but they cannot start counting before they know some of them. Children enjoy reciting 'One, two, three, four' and so on, and they should be encouraged to recite the sequence as often as they like. There are rhymes that underline this learning, such as, 'One, two, buckle my shoe', 'One, two three, four, Mary at the cottage door', and 'One, two, three, four, five, once I caught a fish alive'.

There is no reason to terminate the reciting of number names at any particular point. Let children continue as far as they can. Although they may have no practical use for a number such as 'twenty-nine', the knowledge that it comes after 'twenty-eight' will stand children in good stead later.

2. Linking Ordinal and Cardinal Number

We have seen that when we pair objects with number names, we are using the number names in their ordinal sense, as temporary labels for the objects. The car in the set below has nothing in common with 'three'; it is just the third toy in the ordered row of toys.

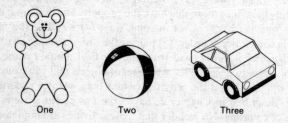

One   Two   Three

But when we say, 'There are three toys', we should have mentally dissociated the label 'three' from the car, and reassociated it with the whole set of toys, using 'three' in its cardinal sense. Martin, aged three, when asked to count these toys, paired them correctly with the number names 'one, two, three'. But when asked to give me three toys, he handed me the car. He had not yet learnt the cardinal sense of 'three'. Children learn this cardinal sense of 'three' by counting three toys arranged in varying orders, and by perceiving sets of three in differing situations, such as three traffic lights, three wheels of a tricycle, the three bears. Children who have learnt the cardinal sense of 'three' will need to repeat the activities appropriate to learning the cardinal sense of 'four' and 'five'.

The 'Money Box' game is a suitable one to help establish the link between ordinal and cardinal number. Children drop pennies into the box, one at a time, counting as they do so: 'One, two, three, four.' They then are asked how many pennies are in the box. Children who have established the link will answer 'four', while those who have not yet established it will open the box and count the pennies. Children who answer confidently when four pennies are dropped may still need the experience of opening the box and counting the pennies when five or six pennies are involved.

3. Recognizing Cardinal Number by Sight

It is quite common for a five-year-old to be able to recognize by sight, without counting, a set of three or even four objects. You may like to try your own skill at recognizing a set by sight. Drop a few buttons or smarties at random and try to estimate instantly, without counting (or adding!) how many you have dropped. You should find that you can instantly recognize up to seven objects.

Children who can recognize by sight that a set contains four objects show that they have understood the cardinal number four, but they have not necessarily grasped the link between ordinal and cardinal number. A game that encourages the recognition of cardinal number by sight, while linking it with ordinal number, is 'Guess How Many'. For this game, eight small buttons are provided. One child in a group takes all the buttons. He selects a few to display on the palm of one hand, keeping the remainder in his other hand. Other children guess how many buttons are displayed. Then they all count the buttons together, and see whose guesses were right. In this game, a number of buttons may be displayed in several different arrangements, so children are gaining the experience of seeing, for instance, several different arrangements of five buttons.

Dice games, using normal spotted dice, involve recognizing by sight (or counting) cardinal numbers up to six, and counting up to six to move a counter the appropriate number of steps. We can prepare a simple track consisting of a chain of about twenty-four squares, with a picture of a 'treasure' at its end. The winner is the first child to reach the treasure (or beyond).

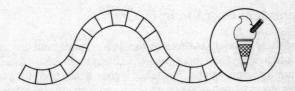

4. 'One More'

Another important concept concerning cardinal number is the *relation* between successive cardinal numbers. It is important for children to realize not only the 'fourness of four', but also that a set of four objects contains *one more* than a set of three objects. A display of objects or pictures could be a starting-point for a story, or a rhyme like the following:

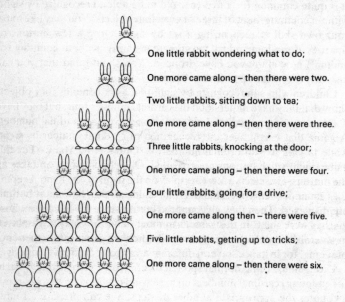

One little rabbit wondering what to do;

One more came along – then there were two.

Two little rabbits, sitting down to tea;

One more came along – then there were three.

Three little rabbits, knocking at the door;

One more came along – then there were four.

Four little rabbits, going for a drive;

One more came along then – there were five.

Five little rabbits, getting up to tricks;

One more came along – then there were six.

Children can 'act' the rabbit rhyme, or use their own toys to make the growing collection.

5. Representation of Sorting by Graphs

Suppose there are eight children on the 'yellow' table, and they can be sorted into five boys and three girls. The children can record these facts by a primitive form of graph. Each child is given a matchbox (or a cube); each boy places his matchbox on one pile, and each girl places hers on a neighbouring pile. If the children's names are written on their matchboxes, and they can identify their own written names, then the pairing between children and matchboxes is highlighted. The graph that they have made *represents* the children in the group. They should count the boys and the pile of boys' boxes, count the girls and the pile of girls' boxes, count the children and all the boxes. As in any sorting situation, they are very near addition when they do this counting. The graph illustrates that there are more boys than girls, and also the important fact that 'five' is more than 'three'.

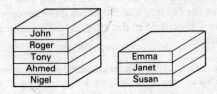

The children can use the same matchboxes to make other sorting graphs about themselves, for instance those who stay to lunch and those who go home, or those who have pets and those who do not. Each graph should involve a small group of children only, so that counting is restricted to manageable numbers.

The teacher may wish to extend the concept that 'five' is more than 'three' by referring to other situations involving 'five' and 'three'. In a football match, if our team scores five goals and the other team scores three, who wins? If Jane is five and her sister is three, who is older? (Although young children do not really understand the meaning of 'I'm five and she's three' or 'I'm older than her', they will say both of these sentences.)

6. Conservation of Number

Suppose that Roger has counted a row of seven conkers correctly, and he can say, 'There are seven conkers.' Somehow, the conkers become disarrayed. 'Oh dear,' we say, 'how many conkers are there now?' If Roger repeats his counting activity to find the answer, he shows that he does not have the concept that is called *conservation of number*. A child who has this concept will answer the question by saying in effect, 'Seven, of course', because he sees that however the conkers are rearranged they will not change in number. Until children have understood conservation of number, they have not grasped the significance of counting. It is important to know how far children are on the road to number conservation. We end this chapter with a description of three simple tests that can be administered quickly on an an individual basis, and the results easily recorded. They test whether the child has grasped the significance of pairing, the significance of cardinal number and the significance of linking pairing and cardinal number. In each test, the hypothetical child A shows that he or she has the concept, and child B shows that he or she has not. Child B needs more practice in the sort of activities we have described in this chapter, accompanied by plenty of talking about them.

1. *Pairing.* Put out a row of cups, and ask the child to put a spoon into each cup. Ask him if there are as many spoons as cups. He should say yes.

Remove each spoon and put the spoons in a small pile beside the cups. Ask him if there are now as many spoons as cups.

Child A answers, 'Yes' (because there are as many as before).
Child B answers, 'No' (because the spoons take up less space).

2. *Cardinal number (five).* Put out five pencils and ask the child to count them. He should say that there are five pencils.

Pick up the pencils and put them into an empty box. Ask him how many pencils are in the box.

Child A answers, without looking, 'Five, of course!'
Child B looks in box and counts, 'One, two, three, four, five.'

3. *Linking pairing and cardinal number (five).* Put out five cups and ask the child to count them. He should say there are five cups. Ask him to put a spoon into each cup. Ask him how many spoons he has used.

Child A answers, 'Five, of course!'
Child B counts the spoons: 'One, two, three, four, five.'

It is quite possible that a child who shows understanding of the cardinal number 'five' and of linking pairing with the cardinal number 'five' will not show similar understanding when these tests involve the cardinal number 'six'. It is therefore advisable to repeat these two tests using several different cardinal numbers before claiming that a child has attained number conservation.

Equipment Needed for the Activities in This Chapter

All the equipment listed at the end of Chapter 2.
Dice and race tracks.
Matchboxes.
Moneybox and pennies (imitation or real).

Suggestions for the Reader

1. (Counting) Although many five-year-olds can successfully count a set of six sweets, very few can count the six faces of a cube. Try them! If a child has a problem, is it concerned with matching, sorting, ordering, knowing number names in order, or using 'six' in its cardinal sense?

2. (Number names) Pretend that the number names are 'a, b, c' and so on. Count the number of fingers that you have. Set yourself a few problems, such as 'What number is f more than c?' (Try not to 'translate' the letters into conventional number names.) Why is it hard?

3. The English language has a set of words to describe ordinal numbers: *first*, *second*, *third* and so on. In spite of this, we often use the words *one*, *two*, *three* and so on as ordinal numbers. Decide whether the following sentences use numbers in their ordinal or cardinal sense:
(a) You have just read Chapter 3.
(b) The chapter covered sixteen pages.
(c) I'm twenty-one today!
(d) A waltz is in $\frac{3}{4}$ time.
(Answers at the end of Chapter 4, page 43.)

4. ('More than') Ask some five-year-olds the following questions in the order that they appear here:
(a) If you had six sweets and I had four sweets, who would have more sweets?
(b) Here are six sweets for you and four for me. (Count out the sweets into two piles, but do not arrange them in rows.) Who has more sweets?
You should find some children who can answer both questions and some who can answer (b) only. Why should there be no child who answers (a) but not (b)?

5. Play the 'Money Box' game with some five-year-olds, and note their response. Test the same children for conservation of number.

4 Numerals

Numeration is the representation of numbers by figures.
This is done by means of ten figures as here shown: 1, 2, 3,
4, 5, 6, 7, 8, 9, 0. Of these, the first figure, 1, is not called a
number but the source of number.

> – The Treviso Arithmetic *(the earliest known printed
> arithmetic)*, *1478*

We are now ready to consider the introduction of pictures and symbols
into children's mathematics (the 'P, S' of the sequence E–L–P–S).
Although the text of Chapters 2 and 3 has been illustrated with pictures,
those pictures served only to describe for you the activities that children
might engage in while forming concepts, and while learning the
appropriate language in which to express those concepts. As children
become familiar with mathematical concepts, however, it is appropriate
for them (or the teacher) to draw pictures as a record of some of their
activities. When the objects are cleared away, the pictures remain to
remind children of what they have done, and to form a basis for
discussion on what they have done in the past. Such discussion recalls for
them the language that they have learnt through their activities. All the
activities that we have introduced so far can be recorded in picture form.
For instance, the graph of Chapter 3, section 5, is just as easy to
understand in terms of pictures as in terms of matchboxes. It is beneficial
for children to make the graph in both ways.

The *symbols* that we use to represent number names are called
numerals. Children see numerals around them constantly – on house
doors, buses, car number plates, clocks. But numerals are more abstract
than quantities. When we use numerals, we imply that we are using

numbers 'in the abstract'. Six kittens can be seen and counted, but '6' is a numeral that does not stand for six kittens or six anything else. Young children think not in terms of the abstract number 'six', but in terms of the physical concept 'six kittens'.

1. Reading Numerals

We can certainly teach children to recognize numerals as representing number names. We can display a large *number strip* on the wall. We would display only the numerals 1 to 5 at first, and extend the list gradually to 10. Children can read the strip from left to right, pointing at the numerals as they say the number names in order. This is an exercise in reading numerals, and it needs consolidating. We give some suggestions for doing so.

1	2	3	4	5	6

(a) Draw a large number strip in paint or chalk out of doors. Children will walk or jump along it, and invent games to play on it. Leave them to it!

(b) Prepare individual number strips and sets of cards marked with the numerals 1 to 5, each card congruent to one square of the number strips. Invite children to match the cards with the appropriate squares of their number strips.

   Introduce a matching game for two children using two strips and two sets of cards. The cards are placed face down on the table, in random order. One child turns over a card. If the numeral on the card matches an uncovered numeral on his strip, he says aloud the corresponding number name and places the card over the appropriate numeral on his strip. It is then the second child's turn. If a child at any stage turns a card labelled with a numeral that is already covered on his strip, he turns that card back and his turn is over. The winner is the child who first covers his strip.

(c) Prepare some large duplicated sheets for 'Join the dots' games. You need simple pictures that require fewer than ten dots to be joined.

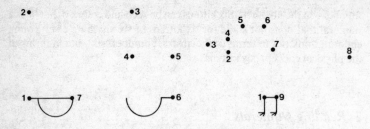

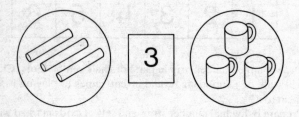

2. Linking Numerals with Counting

Some methods of teaching reading have been denigrated as merely 'barking at print'. The activities described in section 1 could be similarly criticized unless they were accompanied by activities linking the reading of numerals to children's experience of counting. For instance, the numeral cards described in 1(b) above can be used to label sets of objects that children have counted. Other suggestions follow.

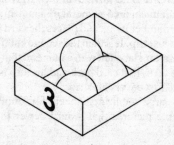

(a) Introduce dice games, using a die marked with numerals rather than dots. (One can be made using an unmarked cube.)

(b) Prepare *number trays* labelled with numerals, for putting sets of objects in. (Use tops of shoe boxes or the 'box' parts of kitchen-size matchboxes.)

(c) Make a 'shop'. Children can make plasticine 'fruit' and 'food' for it, and it can also be stocked with used sweet-packets and grocery cartons. Goods are labelled with their prices, which range from 1p to 10p (they need not be realistic). For a shopping expedition, a few children are each given ten plastic (or real) 1p coins to 'spend'. One child is the shopkeeper, and he must see that his customers exchange the correct number of coins for the goods that they buy. The activity involves matching the correct number of pennies with the numeral displayed on the article for sale.

(d) Use number strips to accompany counting activities. This will link numerals with both ordinal and cardinal number. Objects are paired with the numerals displayed on the strip and counted twice: once by touching the objects as they are counted and once by touching the numerals on the strip.

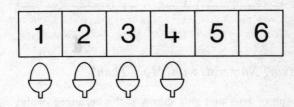

3. Writing Numerals

To write numerals correctly requires considerable control and coordination. Children could practise 'making a two in the air' with their fingers before trying to write '2' with a pencil. Finger painting is a useful transition stage. Apart from '1', each numeral presents its own complexity in writing. Children need to learn to form each symbol starting at the appropriate point. Early habits become ingrained; we are teaching them for life.

Start at the dot for each numeral. These numerals are conventionally formed without taking the pencil off the paper:

1 2 3 6 7 8 9

These numerals are formed with two pencil strokes:

Children can make rows of '2's, patterns of '2's and '3's (for example '2 3 2 3 2 3' or '2 2 3 3 3 2 2 3 3 3'), patterns of '6's and '9's, and so on. They should learn to form one numeral correctly and use it to record counting before progressing to another. They can also be reminded of the order of numerals by filling in missing numerals on a number strip, such as

| 1 | 2 | | 4 | 5 |

| 1 | | 3 | | 5 |

4. Linking Numerals with 'More Than'

The graph of boys and girls shown at the beginning of this chapter illustrates two important facts: (a) there are more boys than girls, i.e. five children are more than three children; (b) 'five' is more than 'three'. Notice that we say that five objects *are* more than three objects, but that 'five' *is* more than 'three'. The first sentence is about a 'real life' situation and the second is an abstract mathematical sentence. The second sentence is meaningless to children until they have realized that it stands for a host of 'real life' sentences, such as, 'Five children are more than three children', 'Five goals are more than three goals', and so on.

'Is more than' is an abstract mathematical concept. The three words can be abbreviated by using the mathematical symbol $>$. Pairing 'failures' can be recorded by children by writing the abstract number sentence '5 is more than 3', or the number sentence '5 $>$ 3'. Some teachers prefer to write the words 'is more than' rather than introduce the symbol $>$ as well as the words. If you decide to introduce the symbol, you can describe it as a bird's beak that is opened towards the larger number.

Here is an example of a worksheet that might be presented by a teacher to children who have learnt the words 'is more than' and also the symbol $>$. The task for children is to fill the boxes with appropriate symbols corresponding to the pictures. A few boxes are filled in by the teacher to help children on their way.

When children have completed such a worksheet, they should read aloud to the teacher some of the number sentences that they have made, and make up a 'story' about one of them (for instance, 'There were four dolls and two cakes, so there were not enough cakes for them all'), before their work is ticked and praised.

Stories. Young children often find it difficult to invent stories to illustrate number sentences. Their first attempts will probably be closely related to the activities that led to the number sentences, or to stories that the teacher has invented. An 'original' story indicates that a child has begun to see the general applicability of the number sentence involved.

5. Linking Numerals with 'One More'

The 'natural' order of numbers and numerals is basically linked with the concept 'one more than'. The numeral 4 comes next after 3 because 'four' means 'one more than three'. The 'rabbit rhyme' of Chapter 3, section 4, links the concept of 'one more' with the number names in order. Children can build a 'staircase'-type display of sets of toys, cubes or pegs in a pegboard and label the sets with numerals, to underline the link between 'one more' and the numerals in order.

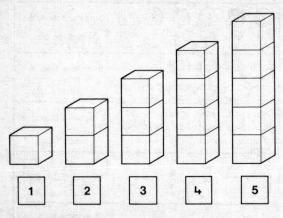

By referring to such a display, children can learn to arrange in order a set of numerals, such as 4, 1, 3, writing the ordering as 1, 3, 4, and reading aloud what they have written. They can also complete worksheets on 'one more' similar to the following:

One more
2 and 1 more is 3
1 and 1 more is ☐
4 and 1 more is ☐
3 and 1 more is ☐

After completing such a worksheet, children should read aloud some of the number sentences that they have completed and make up a story about one of them (for instance, 'There were three cars in the garage and one more drove in, so there were four cars in the garage').

6. Number Competence

Children who have not mastered all the tests on number conservation that were described in section 6 of Chapter 3 need not be precluded from the activities that have been described in this chapter. Learning to talk, read and write about numerals is a useful experience for them, even if they may not fully understand the significance of a sentence such as 'Six is more than four'. However, it is not until they have understood number conservation and are familiar with the numerals up to 10 that they should be allowed to proceed to the adventure of adding and subtracting.

Equipment Needed for Early Work with Numerals

Equipment as listed after Chapters 2 and 3.
Gummed shapes of animals, cars, children, geometric shapes.
Large number strip for wall display.
Duplicated sheets of 'Join the dots' numerals.
Dice marked with numerals.
Old clocks with numerals on the dial, for play (they need not be in working order).
Small number strips for individual use.
Numeral cards of suitable size for matching with number strips.
Picture cards for matching with numeral cards and number strips.
Articles for a shop.
Large self-adhesive labels marked with prices from 1p to 10p.
Toy telephone with numerals on the dial, for play.
Worksheets on 'count and compare', 'one more'.

Exercises for the Reader

1. For the activities suggested in sections 1 and 2 of this chapter, decide whether children who participate will be using numbers in their ordinal or cardinal sense.

2. The sentence, 'My stick is longer than yours', can be alternatively expressed, 'Your stick is shorter than mine'. Give similar alternatives for the following sentences:
(a) I am older than you.
(b) Six apples are more than four apples.
(c) Six is more than four.
(d) $6 > 4$.

Answers to question 3, page 35
(a) Ordinal; (b) cardinal; (c) ordinal; (d) cardinal.

5   Steps to Addition and Subtraction

There is no process in arithmetic which does not consist
entirely in the increase or diminution of numbers.

– Professor A. De Morgan, 1830

In Chapter 4, we pointed out that number sentences are different from
'real life' sentences, but they are related to such sentences. 'There are
three black kittens and two tabby ones, so there are five kittens' is a 'real
life' sentence. The corresponding number sentence is '3 + 2 = 5'.
Gillian, aged four, could work out with delight, 'If I have three sweets
and I get two more sweets, then I have five sweets'; but she could not
work out that 'Three and two more is five'. Such a sentence seemed
meaningless to her. Roger, aged five, was proud of being able to do
'adding sums'. If you asked him, 'What is five add three?', he would
manipulate his fingers and triumphantly shout, 'Eight!'. But if you asked
him which was more, five or eight, he could not tell you. His concept of
addition had not been built on the fundamental concept of 'more'; he
had learnt a trick to perform addition. Whereas Gillian was on the right
road towards understanding addition, Roger's trick was not helping him
towards such understanding.

What children understand by a number sentence is very important.
We must think very carefully about the way we introduce children to
number sentences such as '3 + 2 = 5'. The language used by their
teachers stays with them for life.

1. Addition

To understand the number sentence '3 + 2 = 5', children need to have
met a host of real situations that show that three objects and two more
objects together form five objects. For each situation, it is important
that children can use suitable words to describe not only the two sets to
be combined, but the set that is formed when they are combined. For
example, three red cars and two blue cars are five *cars*; three sweets in

my pocket and two more in my hand are five *sweets*; three dogs and two cats are five *animals*. Eventually, we shall pick out what is common to all these situations and record it as '3 + 2 = 5'.

How are children to be told to read the number sentence '3 + 2 = 5'? It involves two new symbols, '+' and '='.

The symbol +. An adult would read this symbol as 'plus'. 'Plus' is a Latin word meaning 'more'; our use of the word carries over from the time when all mathematics texts in Europe were written in Latin. So '3 + 2' means, roughly, 'three and two more'. We may choose to tell children to read '3 + 2' as 'three plus two', or 'three and two', or 'three add two', or 'three and two more'. Eventually they will learn to accept any of these, but initially they need a unique interpretation for the new symbol. In this chapter, we shall choose to read '3 + 2' as 'three and two more'.

The symbol =. An adult would read this symbol as 'equals', or 'is equal to'. The symbol was invented by an Englishman, Robert Recorde, in 1557, to save him from the tedium of writing the word 'equals'. Recorde said, 'I cannot think of two more equal things than two straight lines of the same length placed side by side.' We may choose to tell children to read the symbol as 'equals', or 'is equal to', or 'is', or 'is the same number as' or 'is as many as', or 'makes'. 'Makes' is not strictly accurate, because the function of 'makes' in normal sentences is different from '=' in number sentences. The sentences '3 + 2 = 5' and '5 = 3 + 2' carry the same meaning; but 'Susan makes cakes' and 'Cakes make Susan' do not. In this chapter, we shall choose to read '=' as 'is the same number as'.

Let us summarize the sequence E–L–P–S by which we arrive at the point where children are invited to record and read addition sentences:

E – Putting three red cars and two blue cars together in a set; putting out three sweets and adding two more sweets; making a tower of three bricks and adding two more to the tower; and many more similar experiences.

L – We say, or the children say, 'There are three red cars and two blue cars, so there are five cars,' 'There were three sweets and I added two more sweets, so there are five sweets,' and so on.

P – We draw pictures to record some of our experiences.

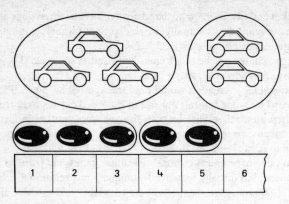

s – We put out numeral and symbol cards to show the number sentence:

3 + 2 = 5

Or we write

3 + 2 = 5

and we read what we have written as, 'Three and two more is the same number as five.'

After recording a number sentence such as '3 + 2 = 5', children should be invited to make up a story about the sentence, to reinforce the awareness that it applies not only to the activity that they have done, but to a host of real-life situations, such as, 'Three children were playing, and two more came to play, so there were five children.'

Note on Alternative Notation

Some texts for children suggest that the best initial way of recording the number sentence '3 + 2 = 5' is '(3, 2) $\overset{\text{add}}{\rightarrow}$ 5'. This is not a helpful way of recording, because the sophisticated symbols do not relate to the children's experience and language. Young children are unable to conceptualize brackets and commas, because in reading them one *says* no words to represent them. They are punctuation marks that teachers are advised to avoid using in children's early reading experiences. Children who copy writing that includes commas usually ignore them as irrelevant 'smudges' on the paper. I have seen countless children copy (3, 2) $\overset{\text{add}}{\rightarrow}$ 5 as 32 $\overset{\text{add}}{\rightarrow}$ 5. They will see no point in the comma or brackets, even if they obediently learn to copy them.

2. Partitioning

Addition involves combining two separate (or disjoint) sets to form one new one. Partitioning involves splitting up a set to form separate or disjoint sets. It is like 'undoing' addition. In adding three and two, we put a set of three and a set of two together and form a set of five; in partitioning five, we can split up a set of five to form a set of three and a set of two. It is a useful activity for children to take a set of, say, five cakes and see how many ways they can split it into two sets for two dolls.

How should children record such activities in symbols? Suppose we start with a set of five objects and split it into a set of three objects and a set of two objects. The logical way to record the activity is by the number sentence '5 = 3 + 2', which is read as 'five is the same number as three and two more'. We mentioned earlier that the sentences '3 + 2 = 5' and '5 = 3 + 2' have the same meaning; but for children at these early stages, they will suggest different activities: combining three and two to make five, and splitting up five to make three and two. Unlike addition, partitioning is an open-ended activity. Through partitioning five, children will discover for themselves a set of number sentences which they will record as '5 = 3 + 2, 5 = 4 + 1, 5 = 1 + 4, 5 = 2 + 1 + 1 + 1' and so on. After such recording, children should be encouraged to make up a story that corresponds to one of the sentences, to reinforce the awareness that the sentence applies not only to the activity that they have done, but to a host of real-life situations, such as 'There were five kittens; three were asleep and two were playing'.

After a full experience of partitioning five, children's ability to recognize a set of five objects by sight should be improved. When you drop five buttons at random, they are quite likely to fall into clusters of three and two or of four and one. Try it!

Children should be encouraged to see the *link* between addition and partitioning. You might call addition 'doing up a parcel' and partitioning 'opening up the parcel'.

The Commutativity of Addition

Experience in partitioning will lead children towards the realization that addition is commutative. When you partition a set of five into sets of four and one, it doesn't matter whether you record the set of four first or the set of one first; $5 = 4 + 1$ and also $5 = 1 + 4$. Most children will observe this useful property of addition for themselves, especially if addition exercises are also set in a form that emphasizes it, such as 'Fill the boxes' for

3+2= ☐   2+3= ☐

2+4= ☐   4+2= ☐   etc.

3. Comparison

In section 4 of Chapter 4, on page 41, we gave a specimen worksheet linking 'more than' with numerals, entitled 'Count and compare'. Children who have had experience in seeing, saying and recording that five is more than three can progress to seeing, saying and recording *by how many* five is more than three. We can repeat the activities involving pairing failures, focusing attention on the unpaired items. We record our findings in pictures and symbols in the following way.

5=3+2

We read the number sentence as, 'Five is the same number as three and two more.'

Worksheets on comparison might invite children to fill boxes with appropriate symbols or to draw appropriate pictures for given number sentences. A few boxes are usually filled by the teacher to help them on their way. When children have completed a worksheet like the following, they should read aloud one of their number sentences, and make up a story about it, such as, 'I've read five books and John has read two, so I've read three more books than John has.'

Count and compare

| ○○○○○ | 5 > 3 |
| △△△ | 5 = 3 + 2 |

| 👝👝👝 | □ > □ |
| ◎◎◎◎◎ | □ = □ + □ |

| △△△△△ | □□□ |
| 😣 😖 | □□□□□ |

| | 6 > 4 |
| | 6 = 4 + 2 |

'*Difference*'. Instead of saying, 'Five is three and two more', some texts for children say, 'The difference between five and three is two', and record this sentence as '5 − 3 = 2'. The danger of this approach is that since the difference between three and five is also two, children might logically but incorrectly record '3 − 5 = 2'.

4. Subtraction

The word 'subtract' means literally 'take away'. An adult would read '5 − 3' as 'five minus three'. 'Minus' is a Latin word meaning 'less', so that 'five minus three' means roughly 'five lessened by three', or 'three less than five'. We may choose to tell children to read the symbol '−' as 'minus', 'take away' or 'lessened by'. What is important is that children learn to associate the concept 'more' with '+' and the concept 'less' with '−'. In this chapter, we shall read '−' as 'take away'.

Children will approach the subtraction '5 − 3' through a host of activities (E–L) involving taking away three members of a set of five objects and counting the remaining members. Put out five spoons and take away three, leaving two spoons; give a doll five sweets and let him 'eat' three, leaving two sweets; go shopping with five pennies and spend three, having two left. When we record such activities in pictures, we shall have to resort to crossing out the pictures of the items that have been taken away.

$$5 - 3 = 2$$

We read the symbols that form the number sentence as, 'Five take away three is the same number as two.' Some teachers teach children to read $5 - 3 = 2$ as 'Five take away three leaves two'. These words describe the activity well, but unfortunately the word 'leaves' does not interpret the symbol '=' well. Eventually, children will come to see that the sentences $5 - 3 = 2$ and $2 = 5 - 3$ have the same meaning. But the sentences 'Five take away two leaves three' and 'Two leaves five take away three' obviously do not!

Children who have been through the E–L–P–S sequence, as described above, can progress to completing worksheets similar to the following.

Take away					
⌀⌀⌀○○	5	−	3	=	2
○○○○○	5	−	2	=	☐
⌂⌂⌂⌂	4	−	2	=	☐
	5	−	4	=	☐
⌀⌀⌀○○○	☐☐☐☐☐				

When children have completed a worksheet like this, they should read aloud one of their number sentences and make up a story about it, such as, 'There were five apples on the tree and three fell off, so there were two apples left on the tree.' Children can be encouraged to see the link between subtraction and partitioning. There is very little difference between taking three away from five and partitioning five into a set of three and a remainder set.

Some texts for children give *two* meanings to the number sentence '5 − 3 = 2': first, 'Five take away three is two'; and second, 'The difference between five and three is two' (meaning 'five is three and two more'). It is unlikely that young children will understand why the same equation can record two such different situations as subtraction and comparison. Therefore it seems unwise to record both situations by the same number sentence until children have come to understand the link between subtraction and comparison.

While children are at these early stages, we should concentrate on helping them to see the link between *partitioning* and each of the other operations, addition, comparison and subtraction. Their common link with partitioning is going to help children gradually grow towards the realization that the number sentences

$$3 + 2 = 5, \qquad 5 = 3 + 2, \qquad 5 - 3 = 2,$$
$$2 + 3 = 5, \qquad 5 = 2 + 3, \qquad 5 - 2 = 3,$$

are different ways of expressing the same mathematical fact.

5. The Symbol for Zero

It is not always easy for children to see the need for a symbol to represent zero, or 'nothing'. If you have nothing, why write down anything? Zero is not a counting number; we start the counting process with 'one'. Humans were using symbols for the counting numbers long before a symbol for zero was invented. The word 'zero' is derived from the Arabic word *ṣifr*, and so is the word 'cipher'. A cipher is a mysterious or magic symbol, and this is how a symbol for 'zero' was first regarded. To a child, '0' may seem a mysterious symbol too.

 Symbol for zero used by the Mayans

Until children are competent at counting, they need not be introduced to the number zero. Because it is not a counting number, it should certainly *never* be included on a number strip. The need for a symbol for zero might arise spontaneously during a partitioning activity. Children who are partitioning a set of five cakes into two sets for two dolls might decide to give five cakes to one doll and none to the other. They can be shown how to record this partitioning as '5 = 5 + 0', or '5 = 0 + 5'.

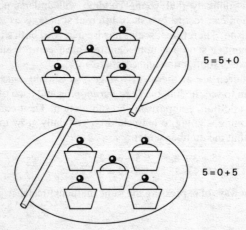

$$5 = 5 + 0$$

$$5 = 0 + 5$$

We can create the need for the symbol by introducing subtraction activities of the type '5 − 5 = □'. We may choose to read the symbol as 'zero' or 'nought'.

Equipment Needed for the Activities in This Chapter

All equipment mentioned previously in Chapters 2 to 4.
Numeral and symbol cards.

Suggestions for the Reader

1. Ask some five-year-olds to add five and three. Observe how they tackle the problem. Do they use objects or their fingers? Do they count on three beyond five? Do they know the result without seeming to go through any mental process? Do they know that eight is more than five?

2. Ask the same children 'What is eight take away three?', observing how they tackle the problem. Invite them to make up a story about 'eight take away three'.

3. Think of some unnecessary and undesirable problems that could arise for children by including the symbol for zero on a number strip like this:

| 0 | 1 | 2 | 3 | 4 | 5 | 6 | 7 |

4. The sentence 'Six apples are more than four apples' can be alternatively expressed: 'Four apples are fewer than six apples.' Give similar alternatives for the following sentences:

(a) Six is more than four.

(b) $6 > 4$.

(c) Four apples and two more are six apples.

(d) $4 + 2 = 6$.

6 Shape and Length

What she wants in up and down she hath in round about.

– J. Ray

In Chapter 2 we outlined activities concerned with early concepts and language in connection with shape and length. This chapter describes some activities that can introduce further important concepts relevant to shape and length, and language in which to describe those concepts.

1. Solid Shapes

Children are concerned from babyhood with feeling, observing and arranging solid shapes. They are interested in properties of solid shapes long before they are ready to consider plane shapes. Free play and building with solids, and junk modelling, involve children in stacking and packing shapes, seeing how they fit or do not fit together, how the same box can represent either the body of a lorry or a tower, how the same cylinder can represent either a wheel or a ship's funnel, and so on.

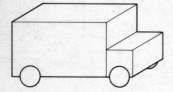 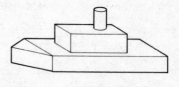

These activities and other more structured matching activities can be used to introduce the concepts and words for 'round', 'flat', 'face', 'edge', 'straight', 'curved', 'corner'. Objects that roll have a *round* part. Objects that stand firmly have a *flat* part, and that flat part is called a *face*. (We could *draw* a human face on it.) A face is surrounded by *edges*

that can be seen and felt. They may be *straight* or *curved*. Edges meet each other at *corners*. Everyday objects, such as boxes, tins, packets, balls, toilet-roll holders, are just as useful as commercially produced solid shapes for introducing these concepts.

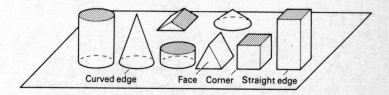

Curved edge   Face Corner Straight edge

The language introduced above can be reinforced by a matching game of the following nature. For the game, you need two identical sets of solid shapes, one set on display, the other in a box hidden from view. The teacher picks one shape from the box and gives it to a child to feel behind his back, so that no one can see the shape. The child must describe what he can feel – a round part, perhaps, or only flat parts, some edges, some corners. Other children must try to guess from the description which shape is 'just like' or 'congruent to' the shape this child is feeling. Lastly, the child who was feeling the shape tries to identify a shape from the display that is congruent to it.

Before children can use with understanding the names that we give to solid shapes (such as cylinder, cone, cube) they need experience with plane shapes. We shall see why this is so at the end of section 2 of this chapter. By building with solids, children's attention will be drawn to their faces, which are plane shapes. They can make paint prints of these faces or draw round them on card and cut them out. They are ready to explore some properties of plane shapes.

2. Plane Shapes

The plane shapes that we shall introduce are circles, squares, rectangles and triangles. For the activities that follow, a selection of plane shapes is needed. A possible set is illustrated overleaf; the number suggested of each shape is indicated in brackets by the illustration (for example, one large circle, two medium-sized circles, two small circles and so on). It is desirable that some of the plane shapes are congruent to some faces of

the solids that have already been used. The plane shapes can be cut out
from card and covered with adhesive film for protection.

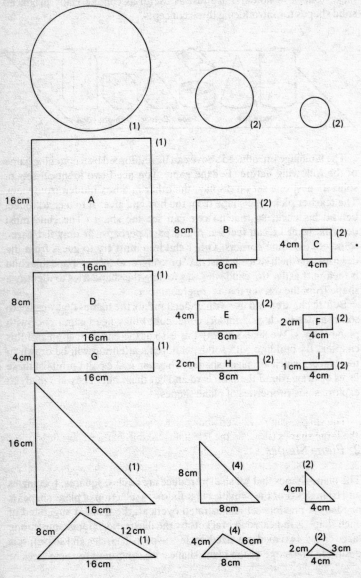

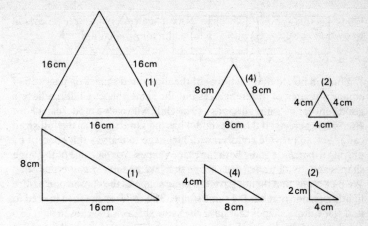

A person who only sees squares orientated as those shown in the group illustrated above will not readily call the figure below a square; he is likely to call it a diamond. Children need to handle and *reorientate* plane shapes just as much as solid shapes. Building pictures with the plane shapes will help children to discover some of their properties.

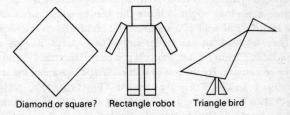

Diamond or square?   Rectangle robot   Triangle bird

The shapes can be named and used for a matching game. Remove all the large shapes (those in the left-hand column of the groups illustrated above). From the remaining shapes, let one child choose a shape and name it; let another child find a shape that is *congruent* to it, superimposing the two shapes to check whether they are congruent. The game continues until the collection is exhausted.

Restore the large shapes to the collection and try a more demanding matching game. Choose one of the large shapes. Children must try to build a shape that is congruent to it. We give two examples. Children will soon learn that it is impossible to build with the circles.

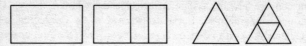

You will notice that each row of the illustrated shapes on pages 56–7 contains figures of different sizes but the same shape. Children have a good concept of 'same shape as'. (The child who calls a model car a *Ford Escort* has perceived that the model has the same shape as the full-sized car.) We can provide children with language to express this concept by playing a *matching* game with the plane shapes. We pick one of the large shapes and say, 'I want a little shape that has the *same shape as* this one.' We pick a few that do not have the same shape as the chosen one before lighting on one that has the same shape. The children are then invited to find some more shapes that have the same shape as the chosen one. (To check for 'same shape as', you can close one eye and move the smaller shape until it 'blots out' the larger, further one.)

A set of shapes that match for 'same shape as' can be ordered for 'bigger than'. The ordered row will resemble a row of the illustrated shapes on pages 56–7.

Rectangles and length concepts. The collection of rectangles in the illustration on page 56 includes some squares. A square is a special type of rectangle, and we might indicate this fact by sometimes calling it a *square rectangle* as well as a square. The rectangles in the illustration have been lettered for easy reference. The concept 'as long as' was introduced in Chapter 2, section 1. It can be reintroduced in connection with the rectangles. By the *length* of a rectangle, we mean the length of the longer of its sides, if they are unequal. Thus, on page 56, rectangle D is longer than E, but *as long as* G or A. By the *width* of a rectangle, we mean the length of the shorter of its sides, if they are unequal. Rectangles that have been matched for length (such as D, G and A) can then be ordered to introduce the concept 'wider than'.

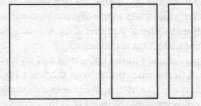

Rectangles (of the same length) ordered for 'wider than'

The concept 'as wide as' can be introduced in terms of the rectangles. Rectangle E is wider than F, but *as wide as* C or G. The rectangles E, C and G, having been matched for 'as wide as', can then be ordered for 'longer than'.

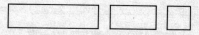

Rectangles (of the same width) ordered for 'longer than'

These activities are a valuable preparation for measuring the length and width of objects, which we shall discuss in section 3 of this chapter.

Linking solid and plane shapes. If some of the plane shapes in the collection are congruent to various faces of the solids that were used previously, they can be placed on the appropriate faces to show this, focusing attention back to the solids and to the shape of their faces, which can be named as circles, rectangles, squares or triangles. A further game can be played with the solids. The teacher describes a shape, and children try to identify it by such clues as, 'It has a round part, a corner, and one face that is a circle.' This description fits any cone in the set of shapes. Now the children will be able to use the term *cone* with understanding. Through the matching game, all the solids can be identified and named. Those with only a round part are *spheres*. Those whose faces are all squares are *cubes*. Those whose faces are all rectangles are *cuboids*. Those with two congruent circular faces and a round part are *cylinders*. Those with two congruent triangular faces and three rectangular faces are *triangular prisms*.

The activities that we have described for this introduction to shape concepts will naturally span a long period of time. Not more than two or three of them will be organized on any one day, and they all need continual repetition.

3. Measuring Length with Physical Units

In Chapter 2 we described matching, sorting and ordering activities that introduced the concepts 'as long as', 'longer than' and 'shorter than'. When these concepts are firmly established, we can introduce numbers into children's activities concerned with comparison of lengths.

Children can collect a set of sticks of the same length and make straight lines with these sticks. (The illustrations that follow show gaps between the sticks, but in reality sticks should be placed end to end without gaps.)

Ravi's line of 3 sticks

Sarah's line of 4 sticks

Sarah's line is longer than Ravi's line

They can compare one stick with a truck. Suppose the truck is longer than the stick. Is it longer than a line of two sticks? Yes. Is it longer than a line of three sticks? No. It is as long as three sticks.

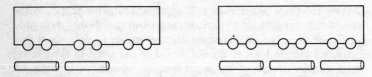

The sticks are now serving as *units* of length. We call them physical units, because they can be seen, touched and counted. Children need the experience of measuring lengths of objects using a variety of physical units, for example matchboxes, pencils of uniform length, metre sticks or garden canes of uniform length, paper-clips.

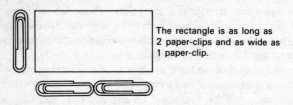

The rectangle is as long as 2 paper-clips and as wide as 1 paper-clip.

Teachers who wish to introduce units that are personal to children such as 'my hand span' or 'my foot' should let children cut out several copies of their own hand span or footprint to use, before they use their body measurements directly (by placing one hand or foot after another along the length to be measured and counting as they do so).

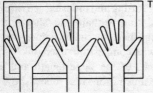

The cupboard is as long as 3 handspans

Length and number work. We can gradually link children's measuring of length to the number work in which they are involved. Suppose the engine is as long as two sticks. If the truck and the engine are lined up, they are seen to be as long as five sticks. We have performed an activity that can be recorded in symbols by $3 + 2 = 5$.

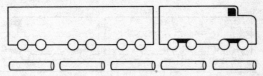

Comparison. We can find out *how much longer* the truck is than the engine by placing each of them alongside a line of sticks. We see that the truck is *one stick* longer than the engine. The activity can be recorded in symbols by $3 = 2 + 1$.

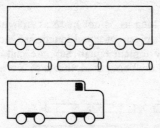

Subtraction. Cut a paper ribbon as long as six sticks. If we cut off a piece of it as long as four sticks, how long is the piece that is left? We see that it is two sticks long. The activity can be recorded in symbols by $6 - 4 = 2$.

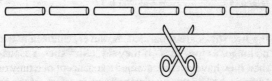

It is advisable to prepare carefully the measuring activities involved with number work. For these activities, it is important to choose objects that are as long as a *whole number* of the physical units used. All measurement is approximate. A child might say that the truck overleaf is as long as three sticks, and the engine is as long as two sticks. But look what can happen when we line up the truck and the engine – they are as long as six sticks! (A child who spontaneously wishes to measure the length of this engine should be encouraged to say that it is a bit longer than two sticks.)

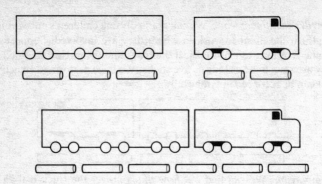

4. Conservation of Length

The concept of 'as long as' is not quite as straightforward as it may appear. When two objects of equal length are moved, children may doubt whether they remain equal. Suppose children say, correctly, when sticks X and Y are juxtaposed, that stick X is as long as stick Y.

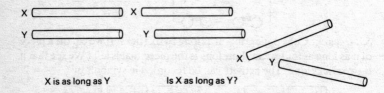

X is as long as Y   Is X as long as Y?

When the two sticks are separated, however, children may consider that X is no longer as long as Y. If they say, 'Now stick Y is longer than stick X,' then they have not yet attained the concept of 'conservation of length'. A child who has this concept will say, in effect, of the separated sticks, 'Of course X is as long as Y,' because he knows that moving the sticks does not alter their length. Children who do not have the concept of conservation of length will not fully understand in terms of length the activities described in section 3. However, the activities will be meaningful to them in terms of number. In Chapter 8 we shall return to the subject of length conservation.

Equipment Needed for the Activities in This Chapter

Everyday or commercially made solids, including a variety of cylinders, cones, spheres, cubes, cuboids, triangular prisms. Some should match for congruence.

Plane shapes cut from card, as shown in the illustrations on pages 56–7.

Sticks cut to three or four different lengths.

Matchboxes, pencils of uniform length, metre sticks or garden canes of uniform length, paper-clips.

Several cut-outs of each child's hand span and footprint.

Suggestions for the Reader

1. Test some five-year-olds on the concepts they have formed in connection with shape. Do they understand such concepts as 'round', 'flat', 'face', 'edge', 'straight', 'curved', 'corner'? Do they use conventional language for these concepts?

Do they have concepts of 'congruent to', 'same shape as', 'bigger than'? Do they use conventional language for these concepts?

What do they understand by the terms *circle*, *square*, *triangle*, *rectangle*?

2. Test yourself for conservation of length. Which is the longer line, AB or CD? How did you find out?

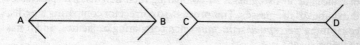

3. Test some five-year-olds to see if they understand 'longer than' and 'as long as'. Then test them for conservation of length. If they fail, try to find out why.

7 Capacity, Weight and Time

A study of visual perception serves as a useful introduction
to understanding how information is gained by other
means.

> — *M. L. Johnson Abercrombie*
> (The Anatomy of Judgement)

Children develop reliable concepts concerning length long before they
reach similar stages in terms of capacity, weight or time. Length is
perceived by the eye. As you will have seen in the optical illusion on
page 63, our eyes may give us one clue when our reasoning would give us
another. Our perception can *seduce* our reasoning. Whereas we can
compare two lengths by juxtaposing them, the situation is more complicated in the case of capacity. The capacity of a container is a measure of
the amount of fluid that it will hold, such as liquid, salt or sand. A given
amount of fluid can take many shapes. A child who has learnt to
compare lengths by juxtaposing them will want to compare the amounts
of lemonade in two glasses by comparing their heights, irrespective of
the shapes of the glasses. This process, so correct for comparing lengths,
constitutes *perceptual seduction* when comparing capacities, and it has
to be unlearnt.

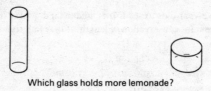

Which glass holds more lemonade?

1. Early Experience of Capacity

Through free play with sand and water and a variety of containers,
children will develop concepts concerned with capacity. The sight of
liquid pouring fascinates them. The shape taken up by liquid or sand can
change constantly. Cups that are filled will spill over, and sand can be
built to a shape and crumbled out of shape. Children will learn some

language concerned with capacity, such as *pour*, *full*, *empty*, *a lot*, *a little*.

Children's first structured activities concerned with capacity should involve containers that are either obviously congruent or obviously different in size. A cup should be filled with water, and the water poured to fill another identical cup. The cups *match* in capacity, and we say that they *hold the same amount*. The pouring operation should be extended to several identical cups, avoiding spilling as much as is possible. (A sink is necessary!) An ordering activity can be organized using containers of obviously different sizes. Children fill a cup and pour its contents into an empty mug. The mug is not full; we say the mug can *hold more than* the cup. We fill the mug and try pouring its contents into the empty cup. Some of the contents spill over, confirming that the mug will hold more than the cup.

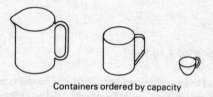

Containers ordered by capacity

Physical units of capacity. Pouring water from the cup to the mug told us that the mug will hold more than the cup. Will it hold more than two cups? We pour water from a second cup into the mug. If it fills the mug, we say the mug *holds the same amount* as two cups. To reinforce the fact, we pour the water from the mug back into the two cups. The cups have become *physical units* of capacity. We can record findings about the capacity of containers in pictorial or graphical form. Looking at the picture below, we can say the jug holds more than the mug, and the teapot will *hold most*.

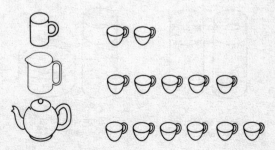

Such activities can be repeated with various physical units of measure, such as spoons, jugs, yoghurt cartons.

Capacity and number work. Activities using physical units can be linked with number work. If we want to know how many cups will fill both the mug and the jug, we have a situation that can be recorded in symbols by $2 + 5 = 7$. Comparing the teapot and the mug, we see that the pot will fill four more cups than the mug will, a situation that can be recorded in symbols by $6 = 2 + 4$. (The number sentence can be illustrated in another way; fill the pot and pour its contents into a mug and four cups.)

When preparing activities that are going to be linked with number work, it is advisable to choose the physical units to be used by children so that each container will hold a whole number of them. Yoghurt cartons are very adaptable physical units, as they can be cut to any desired size.

2. Conservation of Liquid

Children are said to have attained the concept of 'conservation of liquid' when they have learnt that an amount of liquid is independent of the shape that it takes up. Suppose we pour some water into a glass X and ask a child to pour some more water into an identical glass Y until he is satisfied that X and Y contain the same amount of water. We then pour the water from Y into a different shape container, Z, and we ask the child whether X and Z contain the same amount of water. The child who says in effect, 'Yes, of course; it's the same water,' has attained the concept of conservation of liquid. A child who says that there is more water in X than in Z has not attained the concept.

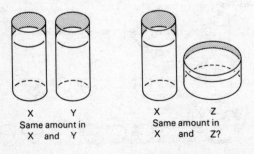

X   Y
Same amount in
X   and   Y

X   Z
Same amount in
X   and   Z?

Very few children understand conservation of liquid by the age of six (or even seven). Children without this concept will often experience perceptual seduction when performing activities such as we have described in section 1. However, the activities will be meaningful to them in terms of number work, and they will help them to progress towards an understanding of capacity. We shall return to the subject of conservation of liquid in Chapter 8.

3. Early Experience of Weight

Weight is the force exerted on an object by gravity. This force cannot be seen, but it can be felt when we lift the object. If it is hard to lift, we say that it is *heavy*. If we want to guess which is the *heavier* of two objects, we may hold one in each hand and try to decide which hand feels more force on it. Children who have developed the concept of 'larger than' by using their eyes will, however, readily be 'perceptually seduced' by the visual clues of size when asked to compare the weights of two objects. They have to learn to distinguish between size and weight. If two children are on opposite ends of a seesaw, the child who moves downwards is heavier than the child who moves upwards. If the seesaw remains horizontal, the children *balance* each other. Observations of the above nature, and free play with scale pans, are necessary to introduce children to this sophisticated way of recognizing 'heavier than', 'lighter than', 'balances'. It is quite remarkable that the scale pans tell us which is the heavier of two objects. There is no obvious reason why they do so; we learn it only from our experiences.

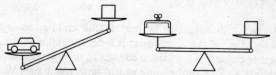

The car is heavier than the cube   The purse balances the cube

Before comparing the weights of two objects by using scale pans, children should feel both objects in their hands to guess which is heavier. The scale pans serve to check their guess. After considerable experience in using scale pans, ordering activities can be organized for 'heavier than' involving three objects such as a pebble, a sponge and a toy. If the pebble is heavier than the sponge, although it is smaller, it serves as a reminder that size is no indication of weight.

Objects ordered by weight

Physical units of weight. Prepare a collection of about twenty plasticine balls, ten weighing about 50 grams each, ten weighing about 100 grams each (100 grams is equivalent to about 3½ ounces). All the smaller balls should balance each other on the scale pans, and so should the larger balls. Give two children the collection of twenty balls and ask them to *sort* the balls into sets of balls that balance each other. The activity will take considerable time, but it is valuable. At the end the children have two sets of balls that can be used as physical units of weight.

Choose *one* of the sets of balls. Put a pebble on one scale pan and one of the balls on the other. Suppose the pebble is heavier than the ball. Is it heavier than two balls? If so, we continue to add balls to those in the pan until the pans balance. We count the balls in the pan. We have *weighed* the pebble.

Weight and number work. Suppose we find that the pebble balances eight balls and the sponge balances two balls. When we put the pebble and the sponge together in one pan, we shall find that they balance ten balls. Our activity can be recorded in symbols by $8 + 2 = 10$.

4. Conservation of Weight

For activities with weight to be meaningful, children must have the concept that the weight of an object is independent of its size. We can test whether children have gained conservation of weight by preparing three parcels X, Y, Z of the same weight but varying size. We place X and Y on the scale pans and the child agrees that X and Y balance each other. Next, we place Y and Z on the scale pans, so that the child will agree that Y and Z balance each other. Lastly, we ask the child which he or she thinks is heavier, X or Z. The child who has attained conservation of weight will say that X and Z must balance each other, because they both balance Y. But nearly all children of the age of six will say that Z is heavier than X, because it is bigger than X.

Very few children of six or even seven will understand conservation of

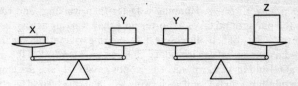

weight. However, the activities described in section 3 will be meaningful to them in terms of number and will help them to proceed towards an understanding of weight.

5. *Early Experience of Time*

Unlike length, capacity and weight, time can be neither seen nor felt. All timing devices measure time in terms of some quantity other than time. (In the case of a clock, this quantity is distance, or rotation; in the case of a sand timer, this quantity is volume.) A child who can tell the time from a clock face does not necessarily have a concept of the quantity that the clock is actually measuring, time. Young children have a poor concept of the rate at which time passes. An activity or game in which they are absorbed seems to take a short time, while a boring lesson seems to last an eternity. How can we make them aware that we can measure how long it takes to do something?

The first time-measuring device that we introduce to children should be one that measures small intervals of time audibly or visibly, such as a metronome, a swinging pendulum, or a loudly ticking clock. A simple pendulum can be made by attaching a lump of plasticine to the end of a string and suspending it freely from the other end. We can vary the pace at which the metronome ticks or at which the pendulum swings (by changing its length), and children can say that the ticks (or swings) are *fast* or *slow*. We should ask them to count in time with the ticks or swings and feel their rhythm. (Such experience will be of value to them in their musical learning.) We can time some activities by counting ticks or swings. How many ticks can we count while Jenny does up her shoes? While John does up his? If we counted twelve ticks for Jenny and ten for John, we say Jenny took a *longer time* than John, and John took a *shorter time* than Jenny. Notice that the words we use to describe time are borrowed from length, a quantity that can be *seen*. Children can time each other doing various activities such as drawing a house, walking across the playground, running across the playground. They can link *shorter time* with *faster*. Running is faster than walking, and running across the playground takes a shorter time than walking across.

After a variety of activities using different rates of metronome ticks or pendulum swings, we can introduce children to *seconds*. Set the metronome at 60 and its ticks will record seconds passing. Make the length of your pendulum 1 metre, and each swing will take one second. Activities will now be timed in seconds, instead of ticks. We can exploit the timing activities to promote a faster general response to tidying up or getting ready for a lesson. 'You took twenty-five seconds to get ready yesterday. See if you can do it faster today!'

For all the activities suggested in this chapter (and in Chapter 6), no recording in symbols is necessary. Occasional pictures drawn by the teacher or by the children will remind them of the activities, but most of the work should be oral.

Equipment for Measuring Capacity, Weight and Time

A sand tray, and a water trough or sink.
Many containers, some congruent (such as a set of matching cups).
Spoons, funnels.
Some transparent containers.
Scale pans, not too sensitive.
Various objects for weighing, including parcels.
Plasticine or matching cubes for physical units of weight.
A metronome (for children to see but not use).
Pendulums.
A stop clock that ticks loudly (for children to see and hear, but not use).
Old clocks with movable hands, for play.

Exercises for the Reader

1. Test some six- and seven-year-olds for conservation of capacity. Make notes on the language used by yourself and them. The notes will be useful for later reference (see Chapter 8).

2. Select a child who 'failed' the capacity-conservation test. Try to teach him or her the concept. Make notes on your own success or failure.

3. Test some seven-year-olds for conservation of weight. Make notes on the language used by yourself and them.

4. Select a child who has 'failed' the weight-conservation test, and try to teach him or her the concept. Make notes on your success or failure.

5. Ask some six-year-olds:
(a) Which is *faster*, running or walking?
(b) Which takes a *longer* time, running to school or walking to school?

8 Child Development

If all psychologists were laid end to end, they would not
reach a conclusion.

— (With apologies to George Bernard Shaw)

Psychological research into children's behaviour and thinking is naturally of importance to adults who are concerned with children. The single
psychologist who has contributed most to this type of research is Jean
Piaget. The enormous output of this Swiss psychologist began in the
1920s and by the time of his death, in 1979, it amounted to more than
1,500 publications. We shall taste a sample of his research and of the
theory that he wove around it.

1. Piaget's Interviews with Children

Piaget designed tests for conservation of number, length, capacity and
weight similar to those described earlier in this book. His tests took
the form of interviews conducted with individual children. Here is an
example of two interviews between Piaget and a child (M) of five and a
half. Piaget is testing her ability to link pairing and cardinal number. He
is pretending to buy sweets from her.

Piaget puts out five pennies.

P: How many pennies are there?

M: (*counting*): One, two, three, four, five. Five.

P: Put out a sweet for each penny. (M *does so*.) How many sweets are there?

M: Five.

Piaget puts out seven pennies.

P: How many pennies are there?

M: (*counting*): One, two, three, four, five, six, seven. Seven.

P: Put out a sweet for each penny. (M *does so*.) How many sweets are there?
(M *does not reply*.) How many sweets will you give me for one penny?

M: One.

P: And for two pennies?

M: Two.

P: And for three pennies?

M: Three.

P: How many pennies are there?

M: Seven.

P: How many sweets are there?

M (*counting*): One, two, three, four, five, six, seven. Seven.

Whereas M can link her pairing activity with cardinal number when that number is five, her number concepts are not firm enough for her to be able to form the link when the number is·seven.

Here is a record of Piaget's interviews with three children, to test their concepts of length conservation. Each child is first shown two sticks in configuration A, and agrees that the two sticks have the same length.

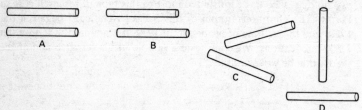

For S, aged six, Piaget moves the lower stick so as to obtain configuration B.

S: They're the same length. There's a little space there and the same little space there.

Piaget moves the sticks into configuration C.

S: They're still the same length.

Piaget moves the sticks into configuration D.

S: They're always the same length.

. . . .

For F, aged five, Piaget moves the lower stick so as to obtain configuration B.

F: They're the same size, I think. (F *puts the sticks back to configuration A for himself.*) Yes, the same.

Piaget moves the sticks into configuration C.

F: The same.

Piaget moves the sticks into configuration D.

F (*pointing to the upper stick*): No, that one is bigger.

. . . .

For K, aged five, Piaget moves the lower stick so as to obtain configuration B.

к (*pointing to the lower stick*): That one is bigger, because you pushed it.

Piaget moves the sticks into configuration C.

к: Now they're both bigger.

. . . .

As a result of these interviews, Piaget concludes that S has understood length conservation, K has not, and F is in a transitional stage.

2. Piaget's 'Immutable Sequence of Development'

As a result of his numerous interviews with children concerning a vast range of concepts, Piaget built a theory of cognitive development, that is, the development of knowledge by children. He maintained that all children pass through a sequence of stages in which they attain concepts such as number conservation, length conservation and so on, in a well-defined order. (There are many other concepts that he defined and listed in this sequence.) He grouped all these stages into four broad periods of development within a child's cognitive growth. During any one of these periods, said Piaget, children's learning is governed by the *mode* of learning that is characteristic of that period. The four periods are the following:

Period 1 (from birth to about eighteen months) – the sensori-motor period.
Period 2 (from about eighteen months to seven years) – the intuitive period.
Period 3 (from about seven years to twelve years) – the concrete operational period.
Period 4 (from about twelve years onwards) – the formal operational period.

We shall summarize the mode of thinking that, according to Piaget, is characteristic of each period.

Period 1 (from Birth to Eighteen Months)

Somehow, the infant has a propensity to attend selectively to certain aspects of his environment in preference to others. He learns, for instance, to associate *sensation* with *action*. He discovers that if he touches his beads, they move. He learns to grasp his rattle. If he shakes his hand there is a sound. If he shakes his hand when it is not holding a rattle, there is no sound. He learns the concept of *permanence* of objects. For the small baby, things exist only when he sees them or touches them. He will not cry out if you remove his toy when he is not holding it. But the maturer baby learns that the toy exists even when he cannot see it. If you hide it under a blanket, he will lift the blanket with delight to reveal it again.

The maturer baby also learns the important concept of *reversibility*. He picks up a toy and puts it down again. He puts a spoon into a saucepan and takes it out again. He will play endless games of handing someone a toy if they will hand it back to him.

Period 2 (from about Eighteen Months to Seven Years)

Piaget divides this period into two:

Period 2a (from about eighteen months to four years). This period is characterized by the child's growing power of *representation*. This is most strikingly evident in his use of words to represent objects (such as 'ball'), actions (such as 'go', 'make') and relations between objects (such as 'in', 'on'). His ability to represent is shown also in his play. He uses a block to represent a car; he will use several blocks to build a tower, a train or a house. He will draw a representation of a person. At the end of this period, said Piaget, the child's perception is well developed. (For instance, he can distinguish between two types of car as well as an adult can.)

Period 2b (from about four years to seven years). At the beginning of this period, the child is confident that the world is as he perceives it. Seven conkers when spread out look more numerous than when they are clustered together. To him, said Piaget, they *are* more numerous. He perceives that the water level in an upright jar is parallel to the base of the jar. But if he is asked to draw the water level in a tilted jar, or a chimney on a sloping roof, he will draw something like the following, because, said Piaget, he does not have a concept of 'horizontal'.

His perception of the world, as summed up by Piaget, is *egocentric*. He cannot imagine how a scene in front of him would be perceived from another viewpoint. He cannot imagine the feelings of other people. (He says it is wrong to steal because if he does so he will be punished.) He sees himself as causing things to happen. ('The bottle sank because I pushed it.') He will solve problems by empirical tests rather than by using logical relations, said Piaget. He can, for instance, discover by experiment that $8 - 3 = 5$, but he cannot yet see that *because* $5 + 3 = 8$, therefore $8 - 3$ must be 5.

Period 2b is marked by conflicts between the child's perception and his growing powers of reasoning, said Piaget. He gradually realizes, for instance, that the seven spread-out conkers are the identical conkers that were originally clustered. He argues, by *reversibility*, that they could be clustered together again. He has understood number conservation. By the end of this period, said Piaget, the child is able to think of two criteria simultaneously. He can sort a set of objects for two different criteria, such as colour and shape; he can recognize an array as being composed of rows and columns; he can use two numbers in differing senses (for example, he can arrange *three* sets with *four* objects in each set).

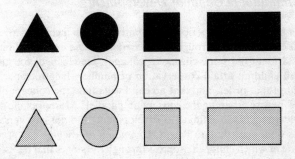

Period 3 (from About Seven Years to Twelve Years)

This period is characterized by the child's growing application of logic to physical situations, real or imaginary, said Piaget. He builds up mental structures to generalize physical situations involving number. (For instance, he understands the commutativity of addition.) His concept of *reversibility* deepens. He argues by reversibility that since adding three to five produces eight, then taking three away from eight must leave five again. (At a younger age, he may well have seen the link between partitioning and subtraction, because both apply to *splitting up*. This is not the same as seeing that subtraction is the reverse of addition.) His power of logical argument develops, said Piaget, and he begins to make *transitive inferences*. 'The discovery of transitivity at about 7 or 8 years permits deductions like the following:

$$A = B, \quad B = C, \quad \text{therefore} \quad A = C$$

or $A > B, \quad B > C, \quad \text{therefore} \quad A > C'$ [6].

You will see that there is not a sharp dividing line between Piaget's periods 2b and 3. In period 2b, the child is beginning to apply logic to physical situations, but his perception is predominant. In period 3, logic plays an ever-increasing role in his mode of thinking.

Period 4 – the Formal Operational Period

This final period is characterized by the ability to argue from abstract hypotheses and to make deductions solely on the basis of logic.

The Immutable Chain of Development

Piaget held that these periods of cognitive growth include many stages, which children pass through in *precisely the same order* (although not necessarily at the same chronological age). He claimed, for instance, that all children attain conservation of number, length, capacity and weight in that order, and that no child will attain the concept of 'horizontal' before attaining the concept of 'parallel'. Moreover, he claimed that 'learning is subordinate to development, and not vice versa'. This means that, according to Piaget, *no amount of teaching* can accelerate the rate at which children progress through the stages that he listed.

The influence of Piaget's work has been considerable, in spite of the fact that he never prescribed any course of action for teachers. However, his claims have not passed unchallenged. In the following section we shall look at some research that calls into question some of his tenets.

3. Challengers of Piaget's Theory

Piaget's theory has been challenged on four main grounds, namely:
(a) that the order of development is *not* invariant for every child;

(b) that development *can* be accelerated by teaching;
(c) that he severely underrates the powers of inference of young children; and
(d) that he pays insufficient attention to the way in which young children interpret language.

Order of Development

Piaget's claim that the order of development is invariant for every child has been challenged by many researchers. Of particular interest are studies showing that certain African children develop number concepts at a later stage than European children, but develop the concept of 'horizontal' much earlier. (These children are accustomed to helping their mothers to fetch water from wells.)

Accelerated Development

The claim that development can be accelerated comes from many researchers, in particular the US psychologist Jerome Bruner. Unlike Piaget, Bruner sees learning as a developing process that can indeed be influenced by teaching. We shall describe an experiment that he presents in support of his claim. It was motivated by Bruner's observations of children's reactions to Piaget's test for conservation of liquid. In Piaget's test, the child is asked to pour water into container Y until he feels that X and Y contain the same amount of water. The water is then poured from container Y to bowl Z and the child is asked if Z and X contain the same amount of water or not. Piaget maintained that the child who has recognized the *reversibility* of the pouring operation will argue that since the water in Z could be poured back into Y, therefore Z must contain the same amount of water as X. He called such a child a 'conserver'.

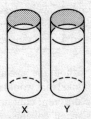
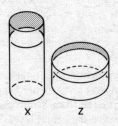

Bruner argues that reversibility is not the only principle involved here. Reversibility will enable the child to say that the water in Z is the *identical* water that was in Y. But, he says, the argument must continue from there; since Y held the *same amount* as X, therefore Z must contain the same amount as X. He found that many children who would be classified by the test as 'non-conservers' nevertheless agreed with the first part of this argument, namely that the water in Z is the identical water that was in Y. These children, Bruner claims, have the concept of reversibility, but instead of applying this concept to the problem, they rely on their perception, and say that the amounts of water in Z and X are different. One five-year-old, for instance, said that there is more water in X than in Z 'because it looks more and it is higher up'; but the same child agreed that when the water is poured back from Z to Y 'it will be the same again'.

Following these observations, an experiment was designed to try to teach children the concept of conservation by shielding them from perceptual seduction. Before the experiment, the children were given Piaget's test and were classified as conservers or non-conservers. In the first stage of teaching, the children were shown two identical containers, X and Y, X containing water and Y empty. Water was poured from X to Y behind a screen, so that the children could see the pouring operation but not the result. They were asked whether or not there was the same amount of water in Y as there had been in X. The process was repeated, replacing Y by containers of differing shapes. Each time the children were prevented from seeing the result of the pouring.

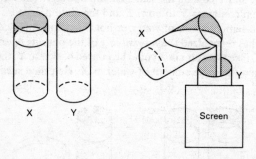

The experiment was then repeated, but without the screen. This time the children were asked to predict the water level that would result when water was poured from X into each of the different containers Y, and then to observe the actual level. They discussed possible reasons why their predictions did or did not accord with the actual observations. After a third stage of teaching, which does not concern us here, the children were again given Piaget's conservation test. The results were as follows:

| | | Age of children | | | |
		4	5	6	7
Percentage of conservers	Before teaching	0	20	50	50
	After teaching	0	75	90	90

Bruner claims that, even allowing that some of these children might have been on the verge of attaining the concept at the time of the experiment, the figures demonstrate that teaching must have been responsible for accelerating the progress of many of the children.

The above extract is paraphrased from Bruner [1].

Children's Powers of Inference

Piaget held that children are unable to make transitive inferences before they reach the concrete operational period, which begins at seven years or later. This seems wrong. I have often seen six-year-olds use transitive inference of the kind $A = B$, $B = C$, therefore $A = C$. I give one example. A six-year-old was tackling some addition problems that included '4 + 5'. She wrote '9' instantly as the 'answer' to this addition. I asked her if she knew that $4 + 5 = 9$ (as a number fact). 'No,' she replied, 'but I know that $4 + 4 = 8$.' Let us record in symbols the reasoning that she must have performed mentally, probably with some physical images in mind. (Of course, no one would expect a six-year-old to record such an argument in symbols.)

$$4 + 5 = 4 + 4 + 1, \qquad A = B,$$
$$4 + 4 + 1 = 8 + 1, \qquad B = C,$$
$$8 + 1 = 9, \qquad C = D,$$
$$\text{Therefore} \quad 4 + 5 = 9, \qquad \text{Therefore } A = D.$$

This is a sophisticated application of transitivity, and one that we can expect from children who understand what addition means.

Two psychologists, Bryant and Trabasso [2] performed an experiment to show that *four-year-olds* can make transitive inferences of the kind $A > B$, $B > C$, therefore $A > C$. The four-year-olds were shown five rods of different colours. They could not see the lengths of the rods, because only their ends were visible. They were told certain information, such as 'The red rod is longer than the blue rod' and 'The blue rod is longer than the yellow rod'. After receiving the information, the children were asked questions such as, 'Which is the longer, the red rod or the blue rod?' This question involves memory only, and the children got roughly 90 per cent of the 'memory' questions right. They were also asked questions like, 'Which is longer, the red rod or the yellow rod?' This question involves transitive inference, and the children got roughly 88 per cent of the 'inference' questions right. Bryant concludes that young children *can* make transitive inferences, although they may have difficulty in remembering the information on which the inferences should be based. He suggests that it is inference rather than egocentric perception that causes children to draw the water level parallel to the base of a jar even when the jar is tilted. They have noted that the water level is parallel to the base of the jar in the familiar case, and infer that the same rule will apply in the unfamiliar case. This explanation seems far more convincing than Piaget's. (Children who say 'catched' instead of 'caught' are using the same kind of inference; the rule that applies to 'walk', 'wash', 'push' and so on must, they infer, apply to 'catch'.)

Children's Interpretation of Language

In the view of the psychologist Margaret Donaldson, Piaget's tests are designed with insufficient attention to the way in which children interpret language. In her view, it is often the tester rather than the child who exhibits egocentricity. She points out that it is dangerous to assume that because children use certain words they therefore understand them in the same sense that adults do. Comprehension, she claims, comes *after* use. Children interpret the gist of what is said to them by the general context of the words and by the gestures and facial expressions that accompany them. They have a fundamental urge to 'make sense' of what other people do and say, and they have much greater powers of inference than Piaget claims. Their failure, when it occurs, is more likely to be one of interpretation than of reasoning.

Look again at the interview that Piaget conducted with K (page 73) testing this child for the conservation of length. K says that the stick that Piaget has moved is now 'bigger'. When Piaget moves both sticks, K says that they are *both* bigger. What can he mean by that? Bigger than what? Is he really suffering from perceptual seduction, or is he merely trying to show that he recognizes that Piaget has changed the configuration? Children will use the word 'bigger' in the way that they think respected adults require them to use it. Seven-year-olds have been known to participate in a serious discussion in response to an adult question, 'Is milk bigger than water?' [3]. Donaldson gives other instances where children try to interpret the language used by adults to 'make sense'. She quotes a story told to a group of three- to five-year-olds, which included various words whose sound can be interpreted in two ways (for instance 'a *hare* ran across the field', and 'they walked along the *quay*'). Many children interpreted these words wrongly, but accepted the context of the story. One child, when asked what a quay is for, said, 'for opening doors.' When asked if people could walk along a key, the child nodded. It had to be possible if the story was to make sense.

But let us see what happens when children are relating not to a respected adult, but to someone less knowledgeable than themselves. The psychologist James McGarrigle modified Piaget's standard test for conservation of length. Instead of the tester moving the sticks, a 'naughty teddy' interfered and pushed them around. McGarrigle found that many more children were classified as conservers using this version of the test than when Piaget's standard test was used. He concluded that some children must have interpreted the *same language* differently in the two test situations.

The above examples show that children use language as only one of many cues to assess other people's intentions. The mere fact that children try to assess others' intentions indicates that they are not as egocentric as Piaget claims. Their failures, when they occur, are not due to egocentricity, nor to poor powers of inference, but to an inability to abstract language from its context and analyse it *per se*. The ability to abstract language from context is precisely what is required in mathematics. It is with the conviction that such abstraction is difficult for children that we have so frequently in this book based the teaching of a new concept in the context of real physical experience (the E stages of our E–L–P–S sequences), and have introduced 'stories' that relate the abstract sentences of mathematics back to physical situations.

We shall return to Piaget in Chapter 21, when we shall consider theories of learning.

4. Conclusions

You may suspect that we have set Piaget up on a pedestal only to 'knock him down'. If so much of his theory has been challenged, how can it help us when we are dealing with children? The answer is that Piaget has drawn our attention to behaviour that is characteristic of child after child. No one denies that five-year-olds do indeed say that seven conkers are *more* when they are spread out than when they are clustered together. We cannot ignore such a situation; we cannot ask these children to add two *more* conkers to the pile of seven and expect them thereby to gain a concept of what is meant mathematically by *addition*. If they think that the seven conkers themselves become *more* by being spread out, they may well believe that in certain circumstances adding two more conkers to the pile might make them *fewer*! At a stage when children are 'failing' a conservation test, we have an excellent opportunity to decide for ourselves whether we accept Piaget's explanation that children do not believe in the permanence of the objects or the substances, that they believe that rearrangements can actually cause conkers to disappear, lemonade to vanish, or sticks to become longer. Alternatively, we may accept the explanation that children's interpretation of language (such as 'more', 'longer') is not the same as our own.

Piaget's tests are significant. It is up to us to put the interpretation on their results that seems most apt, and to deal with children accordingly.

References

1. Bruner, J., *et al.*, *Studies in Cognitive Growth*, Wiley, 1967
2. Bryant, P. E., and Trabasso, T., 'Transitive inferences and memory in young children', *Nature*, vol. 232, pp. 456–8, 1971
3. Donaldson, M., *Children's Minds*, Fontana, 1978
4. Piaget, J., *The Child's Conception of Number*, Kegan Paul, 1961
5. Piaget, J., and Inhelder, B., *The Child's Construction of Quantities*, Kegan Paul, 1974
6. Piaget, J., *Psychology of Intelligence*, Kegan Paul, 1950

Suggestions for the Reader

1. Have you found any evidence that challenges Piaget's assertion that his stages of development are followed in the same order by every child? For instance, when testing children for conservation, did you find any child who had attained conservation of weight but not conservation of capacity?

2. Have you found any evidence that challenges Piaget's assertion that no amount of teaching can accelerate the rate at which children develop concepts? For instance, were you able to teach any children who failed the conservation tests that you set them?

3. Examine the notes that you made when testing children for conservation. Do they suggest that children who 'failed' these tests did so because of perceptual seduction or because of failure to interpret language in an adult way?

4. The following example of everyday reasoning involves transitive inference:

'My carpet matches this cotton. The cotton matches the curtain material. Therefore the curtain material will match the carpet.'

Find another example!

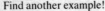

9 More Number

I cannot do it without counters.

– *Shakespeare (*The Winter's Tale*)*

In Chapter 5, we introduced the operations of addition, partitioning, comparison and subtraction, showing how each operation can be introduced to children through an E–L–P–S sequence. Pictures (P) were an essential part of the sequence. They are an important 'half-way house' between an activity (E) and its symbolic recording (S). It is advisable for pictures to accompany symbols until children show that they have realized that the symbols represent many real situations. A child who can produce several stories about a number sentence such as '7 − 2 = 5' shows that he or she has begun to understand the generality of this sentence. He or she probably no longer needs the reminders formed by the pictures. In this chapter, we are going to consider ways in which we can help children extend their understanding of the four operations listed above, and generally increase children's familiarity with numbers and their properties.

1. Addition Bonds

Part of our familiarity with the number 'six' is the knowledge that $4 + 2 = 6$ and that $3 + 3 = 6$. In this section we are going to consider ways of helping children to memorize useful number facts like these. All our illustrations will concern the number 'six'; but they can readily be adapted to concern other numbers.

The number sentence '$4 + 2 = 6$' is called one of the *addition bonds* of 'six'. Children can be encouraged to find further addition bonds of 'six' by a systematic partitioning of 'six'.

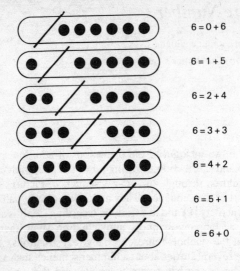

$6 = 0 + 6$

$6 = 1 + 5$

$6 = 2 + 4$

$6 = 3 + 3$

$6 = 4 + 2$

$6 = 5 + 1$

$6 = 6 + 0$

Note on reading number sentences. Previously, we have suggested that children read the symbol '=' in words as 'is the same number as'. At this stage, it might be safe to shorten these words to the conventional word 'equals' and to read '4 + 2' as 'four plus two' as an alternative to 'four and two more'.

Children will be interested in the pattern shown by the pictures and the number sentences. The pattern may well help them to memorize the bonds. There are many other activities and games that will help them.

Card Games

From an ordinary pack of cards, select twenty – the aces, twos, threes, fours and fives. (Each card is identified by a numeral and by the number of spots it carries, except the ace, which does not carry the numeral '1'.) Use the twenty cards for the following games.

'Sixes Pelmanism' (for two or three players). Put all the cards face down on a table. Children take it in turns to reverse two cards. If the spots on the two cards add to six, the child takes these two cards as a pair. If they do not add to six, they are both turned back, and it is the next child's turn. The winner is the child with the most pairs when all the cards have been taken. (Children's memory for the position of the cards will probably be better than adults'!)

'Sixes Rummy' (for two or three players). Four cards are dealt to each player, and the remainder are left in a pile, face downwards. The top card of the pile is turned and revealed on the table. The first child, if he can, puts a card from his hand to pair with the revealed card so that the spots on the two cards add to six. He then selects any other card from his hand and this becomes the new revealed card. If, however, he cannot put down an appropriate card to pair with the exposed card, he takes a card from the pile. It is then the next child's turn. The game continues until one child (the winner) has no cards left in his hand. The pairs remain on display throughout the game, serving as a reminder of the number facts that the children are being helped to memorize.

'Sixes Snap' (for two players). Ten cards are dealt to each child. The children play out their cards in turn, as in 'Snap'. When two cards show numbers of spots that add to six, the first child to call 'Six' takes both piles. The winner is the child who ends with all the cards. This game calls for speedy reactions, and sometimes emotions run high! The game can be heightened by allowing a call of 'Five' as well as 'Six', thus calling for even more speedy recall of addition bonds.

'Guess How Many'

For this game, six counters or small buttons are counted and given to a group of children. While the others close their eyes, one child removes some and hides them in his closed hand. The rest of the children then open their eyes and look at the remainder on the table. They must guess how many counters the first child is hiding in his hand. Then they count together the counters in his hand to see if they were right.

'Number Spiders'

For this game, we write the number '6' on a blackboard and encircle it to form the 'body' of a spider. We draw eight 'legs' radiating from the

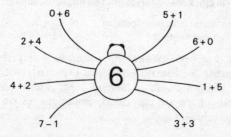

circle, and invite children in turn to give another way of writing '6'. Contributions should include addition bonds of six and one or two adventurous suggestions like '7 − 1' or '8 − 2'.

(This game needs to be run by an adult, because, unlike the other games, it provides no means of checking that contributions are correct.)

Linking Comparison with Addition Bonds

Comparison is very like partitioning. When comparing six dolls and four cakes, we partition the dolls into a set of four (to pair with the cakes), and a remainder set of dolls. Now we can ask children to compare sets mentally: If we have four cakes and six dolls, how many dolls will be without cakes? If we have six boys and three girls, how many more boys are there than girls?

Linking Subtraction with Addition Bonds

There is very little difference between taking two away from six and partitioning six into a set of two and a remainder set. Indeed, the game of 'Guess How Many' could be thought of as a subtraction game.

$$6 = 2 + 4 \qquad\qquad 6 - 2 = 4$$

When children have been reminded of this link, they can be invited to find mentally the answers to such problems as '6 − 4', '6 − 1' and so on.

Stories

Lastly, we should encourage children to invent stories about six that involve partitioning or subtraction. We might make each story start, 'There were six chickens'. Stories offered might include the following:

'Three were yellow and three were speckled' $(6 = 3 + 3)$
'Two ran away, so four were left.' $(6 − 2 = 4)$

When 'six' has been plugged *ad nauseam*, it is perhaps wise to intersperse other mathematics activities between repetitions of the routines for addition bonds of 'seven', 'eight', 'nine' and 'ten'. The addition bonds of *ten* are particularly important, as we shall see in section 4 of this chapter.

2. The Number Names 'Eleven' to 'Nineteen'

Children will, of course, have used number names beyond 'ten' in their counting activities. The counting of objects, or the reciting of number names in order, is a pleasurable activity for children, and they will do it spontaneously.

The 'teens' numbers are somewhat self-explanatory. 'Fourteen' means 'four and ten', 'fifteen' means 'five and ten', and so on. But why do we say 'eleven' and 'twelve' instead of 'oneteen' and 'twoteen'? The words 'eleven' and 'twelve' are derived from Old English: 'en lefan' ('one left') and 'twe lefan' ('two left'). We would probably not pass this information on to six-year-olds; but we shall help them to understand the 'teens' numbers if we stress the connection of each with 'ten'. We can initiate this connection by putting out a pile of ten books, letting children count the books as we make the pile. We then put out one more book beside the pile and ask how many books there are now. Children who have the concept of 'one more' linked to the order of the counting numbers will say 'eleven'; but some will need the reassurance of counting all the books. We tell the children that 'eleven' *means* 'ten and one more'. We add another book to the single book, so that the children can see ten books and two more books, and ask how many books there are now. When they decide that there are twelve books, we tell them that 'twelve' *means* 'ten and two more'. We continue the process until there are nineteen books on display.

We can follow this activity with oral work involving the 'teens' numbers. What number is the same as ten and six more? Ten and three? Would you rather have sixteen sweets or thirteen sweets? Which costs more, an ice-cream for thirteen pence or an ice-cream for sixteen pence? We can play 'Spot the Number'. We choose a 'secret' number and tell the children that it is more than ten. They are allowed to ask whether it is more than other numbers. Here is an example:

Is it more than fifteen?	No.
Is it more than twelve?	Yes.
Is it more than thirteen?	No.

These questions will reveal the secret number to bright children. After a few sessions, other children will learn to spot the number, and able children will be ready to take over the role of choosing a secret number. To consolidate the above work, children can be encouraged to count a number of objects (between ten and nineteen) by putting ten into a pile and counting the remainder. This is an appropriate point to introduce *structural apparatus*, for example congruent cubes of various colours that can easily be fitted together. Children can be asked to collect fifteen red cubes, for example, by building a 'train' of ten cubes and collecting five more. Alternatively, they can collect small counters, and put ten in a plastic bag (sealing the bag with a 'tie-band', and labelling the bag '10'). Or they can use sticks that can be tied into bundles of ten with the same tie-bands.

Structural apparatus representing 'fifteen'

3. Numerals for the 'Teens'

The 'teens' numerals present a particular reading and writing problem for English-speaking children. Many of them who can read and write '23' or '46' correctly will nevertheless read or write '41' to represent 'fourteen'. This is because they are learning to read and write from left to right; and although we say 'twenty' before 'three' for 'twenty-three', we say 'four' before 'teen' for 'fourteen'. For this reason (and others), it seems wiser *not* to explain at this stage the notation '14' in terms of *one* ten and *four* units, but merely as *ten* and four units. We can postpone further explanation until children are involved with numbers larger than twenty, when 23, for instance, will be considered as two tens and three units.

To introduce the 'teens' numerals, we can use a set of numeral cards labelled 1 to 9, and a larger card labelled 10, so that the '0' of the 10 can be completely covered by any one of the numeral cards, leaving the '1' of the 10 visible. We display the 10 card; children will read the numeral as 'ten'. We hold up the '1' card, and ask them what is ten and one more. When children say, 'Eleven', we pop the '1' card over the '0' on the 10 card, so that the numeral '11' is displayed. We continue showing similarly the numerals for 'ten and two' as '12', 'ten and three' as '13', and so on, up to 19.

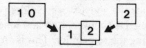

Children's number strips can now be extended as far as 19. (Each child can make one for himself on squared paper.) The games suggested in Chapter 4 (page 37) for reading numerals can be repeated for these new numerals. Children can refer to their number strips while doing mental work, such as, 'What is ten and two more? Ten and eight? Which is more, fourteen or sixteen?' They can be asked to find page 13 of a book and to say what the next page is and the previous page. They can do some written work, such as putting a set of numbers in order (for instance, the numbers 11, 7, 19, 15), or filling the boxes for such additions as $10 + 5 = \square$, $16 + 1 = \square$, $17 + 2 = \square$.

4. Operations in the 'Teens'

Addition in the 'Teens'

By 'Addition in the Teens' is meant adding a number to a 'teens' number, giving a sum less than twenty. The 'ε' for these activities can be provided by structural apparatus. To solve a problem such as, 'What number is twelve and five more?', children will put out twelve arranged as ten and two, add five, and see that there are ten and seven more.

  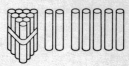

Worksheets can be designed to draw children's attention to a useful pattern:

$2 + 5 = \square$ $\quad$ $12 + 5 = \square$

$4 + 3 = \square$ $\quad$ $14 + 3 = \square$

$3 + 6 = \square$ $\quad$ $13 + 6 = \square$

Children will be excited to discover that if you know that $4 + 3 = 7$, you can immediately predict that $14 + 3 = 17$. To highlight this discovery, they can return to the number strip, cut it between 10 and 11, and place the second part of the strip below the first.

1	2	3	4	5	6	7	8	9	10
11	12	13	14	15	16	17	18	19	

The pattern of the numeral arrangement is obvious: 12 is below 2, 14 is below 4 and so on. If children have used number strips as addition aids before (as on page 46), the link between 4 + 3 and 14 + 3 is seen in another way; counting three beyond 4 leads to 7, and counting three beyond 14 leads to 17.

Complementary Addition

To solve the problem 17 = 14 + □, we can partition 17 into a set of 14 and a remainder set. The 'ε' for such a problem can be provided by structural apparatus. Children put out seventeen, arranged as ten and seven, partition off fourteen, and count the rest.

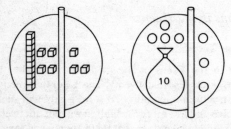

The link between addition bonds of seven and seventeen will be highlighted if worksheets are designed to draw children's attention to it:

7 = 4 + ☐   17 = 14 + ☐

7 = 1 + ☐   17 = 11 + ☐

7 = 5 + ☐   17 = 15 + ☐

After completing a worksheet, children should, as always, read aloud a few number sentences and make up a story about one of them. Stories might be about partitioning (for example, 'Simon had seventeen cars; he played with fourteen and left three in the cupboard'), or about comparison (for example, 'The table is seventeen sticks long and the train is fourteen sticks long, so the table is three sticks longer than the train').

Subtraction in the 'Teens'

Children who have seen the link between subtraction and partitioning can be reminded of this link, using structural apparatus.

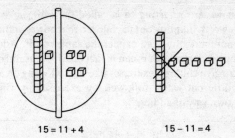

$$15 = 11 + 4 \qquad\qquad 15 - 11 = 4$$

Again, worksheets should be accompanied by reading aloud a few number sentences and making up stories. The work of this section should lead children to new powers of mental calculation. A session of 'Number Spiders' at this stage might lead to the following contributions. (We can always give the spider a few extra 'legs' if children wish to continue the game.)

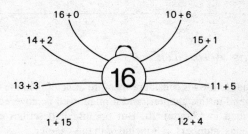

5. Adding Three Numbers

Consider the problem of finding the number that is $7 + 6 + 4$. We might perform the calculation in the following way:

$$7 + 6 + 4 = 13 + 4 = 17.$$

You may have considered an alternative way of calculating $7 + 6 + 4$, calculating $6 + 4$ first, and then adding 7. Why draw attention to this, when each calculation leads to the same result? Because it is very useful to know in advance that this is so. It does not take very long to verify that $(7 + 6) + 4 = 7 + (6 + 4)$. (The brackets show which part of the calculation is done first.) But imagine yourself trying to calculate $538 + 997 + 3$ without knowing that $(538 + 997) + 3 = 538 + (997 + 3)$! The property that we are referring to is called the *associative property of addition*. It is worth pointing out to children that however they choose to add a set of numbers, they can expect the same result. Adding a set of numbers in two different orders can in fact provide a useful check on the result. We can give children exercises like the following on adding three numbers in different ways, followed by exercises in which children choose their own way of adding:

Add in two ways

$5 + 6 + 4 = 11 + 4 = 15$	$5 + 6 + 4 = 5 + 10 = 15$
$3 + 7 + 6 =$	$3 + 7 + 6 =$
$6 + 5 + 5 =$	$6 + 5 + 5 =$

Look for the quick way

$4 + 3 + 7 =$	$4 + 6 + 2 =$
$5 + 2 + 8 =$	$7 + 8 + 2 =$

---

6. Counting 'Across Ten'

The work that follows is considerably more difficult than the rest of the work described in this chapter, and it might well be covered after the work described in Chapter 10. But because it describes operations involving 'teens' numbers, it is included in this chapter.

Addition Across Ten

By 'Addition Across Ten' is meant adding two numbers less than ten, whose sum is more than ten. There are several ways in which an adult might find the number that is $8 + 6$. Many *know* the result as an addition bond; some argue 'Eight and two is ten, and I must then add four more; so the answer is fourteen'; a few will resort to counting six beyond eight, to arrive at fourteen. There is no doubt that the first method leads most quickly to the result, and the third method most slowly. But we do not always help children most by teaching them quick methods first. The second method has much to recommend it, because it capitalizes on the structure of our number system, which is based on counting in tens. (If you wished to add 48 and 6, might you not build up 48 to 50 and add four more?) Although this method is widely used abroad, it is traditionally not often used in Britain. But it has the advantage of completing children's command of addition without necessitating their learning addition bonds extra to those up to ten.

If we choose to teach children the extra addition bonds up to nineteen, we will find, paradoxically, that it is easier to work 'downwards'. There are no addition bonds 'across ten' for nineteen, and only one for eighteen. The bonds to be learnt are set out below.

18 = 9 + 9	17 = 9 + 8	16 = 9 + 7	15 = 9 + 6
11 = 9 + 2	17 = 8 + 9	16 = 8 + 8	15 = 8 + 7
11 = 8 + 3	12 = 9 + 3	16 = 7 + 9	15 = 7 + 8
11 = 7 + 4	12 = 8 + 4	13 = 9 + 4	15 = 6 + 9
11 = 6 + 5	12 = 7 + 5	13 = 8 + 5	14 = 9 + 5
11 = 5 + 6	12 = 6 + 6	13 = 7 + 6	14 = 8 + 6
11 = 4 + 7	12 = 5 + 7	13 = 6 + 7	14 = 7 + 7
11 = 3 + 8	12 = 4 + 8	13 = 5 + 8	14 = 6 + 8
11 = 2 + 9	12 = 3 + 9	13 = 4 + 9	14 = 5 + 9

Subtraction 'Across Ten'

Most adults would perform a subtraction such as $15 - 8$ by solving the problem $15 = 8 + \square$. Some books for children suggest that the problem is solved by counting back from fifteen until eight numbers have been counted in this way. This is hard, and not a very practical help for such a subtraction as $72 - 63$!

Reminding children of the link between subtraction and partitioning is a good preparation for helping them to subtract 'across ten'. Work-sheets might contain examples as follows:

$$15 = 8 + \square \qquad \text{so } 15 - 8 = \square$$
$$16 = 7 + \square \qquad \text{so } 16 - 7 = \square$$

Children will solve $15 = 8 + \square$ either by using the addition bond stored in their memory, or by mentally adding to eight until they reach fifteen: 'Eight and two is ten, and five more is fifteen, so I have added seven.'

The process of growing familiar with numbers and operations is a very gradual one. The work described in this chapter needs to be spread over a long time, and interspersed with other mathematical work on shape and measurement. For instance, the work described in Chapters 6 and 7, using physical units of measurement, could well be extended to include numbers in the teens. However, by the age of seven, many children should be confident at tackling most of the problems discussed in this chapter, and they should be on the verge of seeing that number sentences like

$$9 + 8 = 17 \qquad 17 = 9 + 8 \qquad 17 - 9 = 8$$
$$8 + 9 = 17 \qquad 17 = 8 + 9 \qquad 17 - 8 = 9$$

are different ways of expressing the same mathematical fact.

Equipment Needed for the Work Described in This Chapter

Small objects for counting.
Unifix cubes, or other cubes that will fit together.
Plastic bags, that will contain ten counters, and tie bands to seal them.
Sticks and tie bands to secure bundles of ten.
Number strips for numerals 1 to 19.
Numeral cards labelled 1 to 9, and one larger card labelled 10.
Packs of ordinary cards for number games.
Duplicated worksheets.

Suggestions for the Reader

1. (Addition bonds) Test some six-year-olds to find out whether they know the addition bonds of seven. (You might play 'Guess How Many' with them.) (If they do not know the addition bonds, how do they calculate 4 + 3?)

2. (Number names) Test some six-year-olds on their understanding of the numbers eleven to nineteen. Do they think of these numbers as 'ten and one', 'ten and two' and so on, or do they think of them merely as an extension of the counting numbers on the 'one more' principle?

3. (Addition) Test some six-year-olds and seven-year-olds on their methods for adding (a) in the teens, (b) across ten. (You might play 'Number Spiders' with both groups, using 16 as the 'body'.) Compare the two groups of children.

4. (Links) Test some six-year-olds and seven-year-olds on their ability to link partitioning and subtraction. Ask them questions like 'What is eight and six?', 'Which is more, fourteen or eight? How much more?' and 'What is fourteen take away eight?' Find out how they calculate the answers.

10 Steps towards Multiplication and Division

We may say that 156 contains 12 thirteens; if we use signs,
we write 156 = 12 × 13. In *old* books, it is often found
written thus: 156 ÷ 13 = 12.

– Professor A. De Morgan, 1830

What is multiplication? If you were asked to demonstrate some arrangement of objects to show what you understand by 3 × 4, you might display something like this:

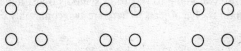

Your display would show that you had in mind three sets of four objects. To find out how many objects you had displayed, we would have to add four and four and four more. Without multiplication tables, multiplication involves adding together several (equal) numbers.

1. 'Primitive Multiplication'

In approaching multiplication, children are required to think of a pair of numbers describing two different quantities: the number of sets, and the number of objects in each set. It is advisable to give them practice in recognizing sets, each containing the same number of objects, and counting (a) the number of sets, and (b) the number of objects in each set, *before* proceeding to find the total number of objects by adding. Here are some examples:

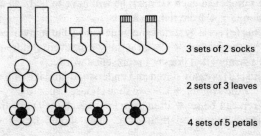

3 sets of 2 socks

2 sets of 3 leaves

4 sets of 5 petals

After such practice in identifying numbers of sets and the number in each set, children can be given exercises in putting out, for example, four sets of two buttons, or three sets of five sweets, and deciding each time on the total number of buttons (or sweets) that they have put out. Mental work can follow. 'If you have two cars, how many wheels will you have?' (This involves adding four and four, which children should know as an addition bond.) 'If you buy three cards of buttons with five buttons on each card, how many buttons will you have?' (This involves adding five and five and five, reasoning that five and five is ten, and ten and five is fifteen.)

Such mental work will be easy for some children, hard for others. After it, practical experience can be reintroduced to help with written work. How are we going to record in symbols that three sets of four objects contain twelve objects? There are two commonly used ways of recording:

$$3 \times 4 = 12$$
$$\text{and} \quad 3\,(4) \ = 12.$$

Both notations are useful, but only one will be chosen for the initial recording. We shall choose *3 × 4 = 12*. This sentence is commonly read in one of four ways:

(a) Three sets of four are twelve.
(b) Three multiplied by four is twelve.
(c) Three fours are twelve.
(d) Three times four is twelve.

Reading (a) is not strictly correct, because it is not the *sets* that are twelve, but the *number of members* of the sets.

Reading (b) means, strictly, 'Three repeated four times is the same as twelve.' That is, it means *four sets of three* contain twelve objects. Although mathematically sound, it necessitates an explanation that is rather complex for a child who has learnt to say the number of sets *first* and the number in each set *next*; he will have to learn to construe the expression '3 × 4' from right to left.

Reading (c) is easily stated and understood, but it involves no word to be said for the symbol '×'. Even at the age of seven, children may ignore or omit a symbol that does not represent a word.

Reading (d) is easily stated and understood, and it involves a word to be said for the symbol '×'. So we shall choose (d).

Children can be set written exercises, which they copy from a work-sheet and continue on their own. They should be allowed to use structural apparatus and draw pictures as they prefer, to illustrate their work. We give an example of a suitable worksheet.

Copy and continue

$3 \times 4 = 4 + 4 + 4 = 12$
$2 \times 5 = 5 + 5 =$
$4 \times 2 =$
$5 \times 3 =$
$3 \times 6 =$

After such an exercise, children should of course read aloud some of their number sentences, and make up a story about one of them.

2. The Table of Twos

Counting in twos is easy. We can arrange pairs of objects and record the results of our counting as our first table, the table of twos.

$1 \times 2 = 2$
$2 \times 2 = 4$
$3 \times 2 = 6$
$4 \times 2 = 8$
$5 \times 2 = 10$

We might choose to terminate the table after 5×2, and read it aloud together ('One times two is two, two times two is four' and so on). We can then refer to the table to solve problems such as 'Four children wore boots to school today; how many boots are there in the cloakroom?' or 'If you clean your teeth twice a day, how many times will you clean them in three days?'

Later, we can extend the table up to 9×2, and display it on the wall for children to read and use. At some stage, we can tell the children that the right-hand numbers of the table are called *even numbers*. Children can refer to the number strips that they have made for the 'teens' numbers, and colour in all the even numbers. The pattern will please them.

1	2	3	4	5	6	7	8	9	10
11	12	13	14	15	16	17	18	19	

We can introduce children to 2p coins, telling them that each 2p coin will buy as much as two 1p coins. Children tend to estimate the value of an amount of money by the number of coins present, and unless they are experienced shoppers, they will need practice in using 2p coins (plastic or real) in their shop play. They can be given up to nine 2p coins and asked how many pence they have to spend (referring to the table of twos if necessary). They can also play the 'Tenpence Game'. This is a simple game played with a track, coins and a die. The track resembles a clock face; children move counters round the track (clockwise) through a number of spaces corresponding to the numeral (or spots) shown on the die. When a counter lands on a space labelled 1p, the child takes a 1p coin from the central box; when it lands on a space labelled 2p, the child takes a 2p coin. The winner is the first child to collect 10p.

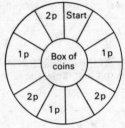

3. Equal Grouping

Think of a situation where you might wish to know how many sets of four can be made from twelve objects. You might have twelve pence and wish to buy some sweets costing fourpence each; or you might have twelve sticks of equal length and wish to build a number of squares with them. In each case, you will solve your problem by partitioning your set of twelve objects into sets of four.

Your activity is logically recorded in symbols by $12 = 3 \times 4$. We shall call this type of partitioning *equal grouping*. Children who before now have not met the word 'equal' must be told that it means 'having the same number'. (Later they will see that the word can be used in connection with length, capacity, weight and area.)

We can give children a certain number of objects, such as twelve, and invite them to find ways of grouping the objects into sets of two, sets of three and so on. They might record some of their findings by drawing pictures and writing symbols as follows:

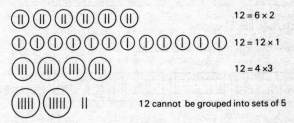

$12 = 6 \times 2$

$12 = 12 \times 1$

$12 = 4 \times 3$

12 cannot be grouped into sets of 5

You will recognize this activity as division; but at this stage, 'equal grouping' is a more appropriate term for children, focusing their attention on the new symbol '×'. In partitioning twelve in various ways, children will discover that $12 = 6 \times 2$ and $12 = 2 \times 6$, and that $12 = 3 \times 4$ and $12 = 4 \times 3$. They are on the way to discovering that multiplication is *commutative*. The discovery can be reinforced at this stage, or later, by pictures. (See page 173.)

4. Equal Sharing

Another type of partitioning concerns equal sharing. If you want to share some biscuits fairly between two people, you know that you want to build two sets containing an equal number of biscuits, but you may not know how many to put into each set. If you do not know, you will solve the problem by 'dealing out' the biscuits like cards in a card game: 'One for you, one for me; another for you, another for me,' and so on. Sharing 'fairly' is a common activity among children; for this reason, some teachers prefer to encourage and record equal sharing activities before equal-grouping activities. The decision as to which to cover first is not critical; but we should remember that whereas equal grouping is an important prerequisite for understanding numbers like twenty, thirty, forty and so on (see Chapter 11), equal sharing leads to fraction concepts, as we shall see later in this chapter. Children should perform their equal-sharing activities using real objects. We might provide them with 'sharing boxes' to 'deal' the objects into. They can record their results in pictures and symbols as follows.

Share six sweets equally between three children.

$6 = 3 \times 2$

Each child has ☐ sweets.

Deal sixteen cards to four children.

$16 = 4 \times 4$

Each child has ☐ cards.

Division. You will have recognized both equal grouping and equal sharing as division. There is really no advantage in teaching children to record these activities by using a conventional division symbol. Using only the symbol '×' at this stage will help them later to see the link between multiplication and division.

Children who have mastered confidently the two activities of equal grouping and equal sharing might be given a 'mixed bag' of problems such as the following:

$$8 = 4 \times \square \qquad\qquad 10 = \square \times 5$$
$$12 = \square \times 2 \qquad\qquad 16 = 2 \times \square$$

This will keep them 'on their toes'. To solve $8 = 4 \times \square$, they will have to share eight objects equally between four people; but in order to solve $12 = \square \times 2$, they will have to see how many sets of two they can make from twelve objects.

5. 'A Half' and 'a Quarter'

Equal sharing provides a golden opportunity to use the terms 'a half' and 'a quarter'. When we share biscuits equally between two people, each person gets *one half* of the biscuits. When we share them equally between four people, each person gets *one quarter* of them. Children hear the terms 'a half' and 'a quarter' constantly, and it is useful to be able to teach them to use the terms correctly. I do *not* suggest teaching children at this stage the strange symbols ('$\frac{1}{2}$' or '$\frac{1}{4}$') that we use to write 'a half' or 'a quarter'. If children wish to record their activities using fraction concepts, I would suggest that they write sentences like 'A half of 8 is 4', or 'A quarter of 8 is 2'.

6. Equal Grouping with Remainder

Children who have explored the possibility of grouping twelve objects into sets of five will have discovered that there are two left over that cannot be made part of a set of five. We may not initially ask them to record this discovery, but when they have had considerable experience of equal grouping, they could record it as follows: $12 = 2 \times 5 + 2$. This notation is perfectly acceptable; if you pressed the buttons of a pocket calculator in the order '2', '×', '5', '+', '2', '=', it would display the number '12'. However, at this stage, we might consider the graphical clarity of the notation $2(5) + 2$ (which might be read as 'two fives and two more').

We mentioned in Chapter 5 (page 46) that young children see no point in writing brackets in a number sentence such as $(3, 2) \rightarrow 5$, because in reading the brackets one says no words to represent them. But children can be shown the point of the brackets in $2(5)$ more easily than in $(3, 2)$. When children have had the experience of grouping into sets of five, it will not seem irrelevant to them to regard the brackets as symbolizing that grouping into sets, or the 'tying up' of sets, that they have made. However, the activity itself of drawing the brackets may still present some difficulties for children of limited manual dexterity.

The experience of seeing twelve as 'two sets of five and two more', and fifteen as 'two sets of six and three more' will be valuable for children's later understanding of numbers like 'twenty-three' (which is 'two sets of ten and three more'.) After much experience of equal grouping and equal sharing, children might try their mental powers on a new type of 'Number Spiders', where they are invited to suggest number combinations involving 'times' to supply the 'legs'. Contributions might include the following:

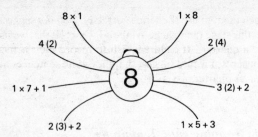

Equipment Needed for the Activities in This Chapter

Sticks, cubes, counters, tie bands, plastic bags.
Loops for surrounding sets.
Boxes for 'sharing' into.
Coins of value 1p and 2p.
Track for the 'Tenpence' game.
Pack of cards for 'equal sharing'.

Suggestions for the Reader

1. (Primitive multiplication) Invent a game for children where the scoring will involve some easy primitive multiplication (for example, 'Hoop-la' with two pegs, scoring '1' for hooping one peg, '2' for hooping the other). Try your game with some children.

2. (Vocabulary and symbols for multiplication) Find out from some six- and seven-year-olds the vocabulary and symbols that they use to express multiplication. (You could start by putting out three sets of two objects and asking them to describe what they see; then ask them how they would write down in symbols what they have said.)

3. (Even numbers) Test the same six- and seven-year-olds on their knowledge about even numbers. Do they know that *six* is an even number? Do they know why? Do they know that *seven* is an odd number?

4. (Equal grouping) Ask the same children to show you how they would find out how many squares they could build using twelve sticks. (Have the sticks available, but do not press the children to use them.) Note the language used by the children, and ask them how they would write down their result.

5. (Equal sharing) Ask the same children to tell you how they would share twelve sweets fairly between four people. (Have the sweets available, but do not press children to use them.) Note the language used by the children, and ask them how they would write down their result.

6. (Fractions) For children who have completed question 5 happily, ask them how many sweets make up *a quarter* of the sweets. If they do not know, try to teach them.

11   Tens and Units

An article is a number that is exactly divisible by ten, like
10, 20, 30 etc. A mixed number is one that exceeds ten but
cannot be divided by ten without a remainder, such as 11,
12, 13 etc.

– The Treviso Arithmetic, *1478*

In Chapter 9, we saw how children can be introduced to the numbers
eleven to nineteen. I suggested that our notation for the 'teens'
numerals should not be explicitly explained to children at this stage
(in terms of *one* ten and a number of units), but that the numbers should
be introduced by linking them strongly with *ten*. Children who are
introduced to sixteen as ten and six more will form an idea of why the
numeral 16 has 6 as one of its digits. This is a step towards understanding
place value, the system underlying our number notation. (We shall
discuss place value in section 3 of this chapter.)

In Chapter 10, we saw how children can be introduced to multiplication through their experiences of sets of two, sets of three and so on.
The concept of a number of sets containing equal numbers of members
is another important step towards understanding our number notation
for tens and units.

1. Sets of Ten

We can use *sets of ten* to introduce children to the numbers twenty, thirty
and forty. For appropriate experience (E) we can use structural apparatus as described in Chapter 9. Each child can be given one type of
apparatus and asked to make four sets of ten with it. We can ask each
child to put out *two* of his sets of ten, and to count the total number of
objects in his two sets. When it is agreed that each child has twenty, we
tell the children that twenty *means* two sets of ten (L).

We draw pictures (P) of the various representations of twenty that the
children have made.

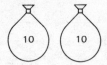

We can continue the lesson by introducing *thirty* as three sets of ten and *forty* as four sets of ten (using the language but not the symbols). Children can identify pictures of sets of ten, piles of exercise books stacked in tens, or fingers of several children who hold up ten fingers each. They count the pictures or objects in tens: 'Ten, twenty, thirty, forty.' Children can try some mental arithmetic, such as, 'What is twenty and ten more? What is ten more than thirty? If we have forty books and put ten away, how many are left?' We can introduce a story or rhyme involving twenty, thirty or forty, such as, 'Thirty days hath September, April, June and November.' (We would not go further with this rhyme at this stage.)

Children can play the 'Forty Game'. This is a game for two or three children, using a die and a box containing some sticks and some bundles of ten sticks. Children take it in turn to throw the die and collect from the box a number of sticks corresponding to the numeral thrown. As soon as a child has collected ten sticks he can exchange them for a bundle of ten. The winner is the first child to collect forty sticks.

The numerals 20, 30, 40 and 50 can be introduced in a lesson subsequent to the oral one just described. The same apparatus can be used, each child using a different type from the one that he used before. We have the chance to recapitulate the important facts that *twenty* means two sets of ten, *thirty* means three sets of ten and so on, by writing $20 = 2 \times 10$, $30 = 3 \times 10$, and so on. Children can be given practice in reading and writing the new numerals in exercises similar to the following.

$10 + 10 =$ $3 \times 10 =$ $20 = 10 + \square$
$20 + 10 =$ $4 \times 10 =$ $30 = 20 + \square$
$10 + 30 =$ $20 = 2 \times \square$ $20 - 10 =$
$20 + 30 =$ $50 = \square \times 10$ $50 - 20 =$

Children will be pleased at the ease with which they can operate with these 'large' numbers. They can be encouraged to make up stories about the number sentences that they write.

2. The Twenties

It takes time for the significance of our counting system to sink in. Helen, aged six, wanted to know from me one day what was twenty and four more. I made her find out by counting four beyond twenty – twenty-one, twenty-two, twenty-three, twenty-four. I told her that twenty-four *means* twenty and four more, and she seemed satisfied. But when I asked her 'What is twenty and seven more?', she proceeded to find out by counting seven beyond twenty; she could not deduce that twenty-seven must *mean* twenty and seven more. Children need a great deal of experience in building up and analysing sets of ten objects and single objects so that they may gradually learn that the *name* of a number between twenty and ninety-nine tells us how it is made up of tens and units.

For an activity (E) to introduce numbers in the twenties, each child can be given one type of structural apparatus, and be asked to put out two sets of ten and one more object. (Counters are laid out beside the bags that they will later be put in, and sticks are clustered in tens but not yet tied together.) Children count, one by one, the total number of objects that they have put out; it is twenty-one. Then the sets of ten are tied up and the total number is counted differently: 'Ten, twenty, twenty-one.' (This is the 'L' stage of learning.) We tell children that twenty-one *means* twenty and one more, and we draw pictures of the various representations of twenty-one that they have made (P):

 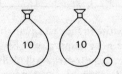 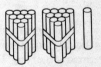

We repeat the activity for the numbers twenty-two and twenty-three. By the time we reach twenty-four, it should be enough to count the sets of ten as 'Ten, twenty' and omit the one-by-one counting of the first twenty objects, and we might terminate the counting process altogether by the time we have reached twenty-six. We now draw pictures for children to identify as two sets of ten and any number up to nine more; we produce two piles of ten exercise books and add more for children to identify the total number of books (up to twenty-nine); we ask three children between them to display a number of fingers between twenty and thirty. We do some mental arithmetic 'in the twenties': What is twenty and six more? What is six and twenty more? What is twenty-one and one? Twenty-three and one? Which is more, twenty-eight or twenty-five? We recall the nursery rhyme, 'Sing a Song of Sixpence', with its 'four and twenty blackbirds'. How many blackbirds were baked in the pie?

The *numerals* 21 to 29 can be introduced in a lesson subsequent to the oral one just described. The same apparatus can be used, each child using a different type from the one that he used before. We can introduce the numerals in a manner similar to that suggested for the 'teens' numerals (on page 88), using cards labelled 1 to 9 and a larger one labelled 20.

As each number is recalled, we pop the appropriate numeral card over the 0 on the 20 card, so that the corresponding numeral is seen (s). After this, each child can make his own *number array* for the numerals 1 to 29 on squared paper.

1	2	3	4	5	6	7	8	9	10
11	12	13	14	15	16	17	18	19	20
21	22	23	24	25	26	27	28	29	

What numeral shall we write in the last square of the array? Children should remember that the next numeral will be 30, because it means three sets of ten. The pattern in the array will please children. They can refer to their arrays while doing mental arithmetic: What is 10 and 2? 20 and 2? Point to 8, 18, 28. Which is more, 19 or 21? Count up in twos, starting '2, 4, 6, 8'. How many even numbers are there on our arrays? Do they occur in a pattern? Find page 28 in a book (using the number array if it helps). What is the next page? What is the page before?

The thirties and forties can be introduced in a similar way to the twenties, although progress can be faster for most children.

3. Place Value

Until now we have not needed to explain what *place value* is. The two digits in the numeral 22 have different values because of their *places*. The right-hand digit has a place value of *two*, whereas the left-hand digit has a place value of *two tens*. Our numeral system is *based* on the number ten. Using only ten digits (0 to 9), we can represent any number, however small or large. We say that our number system has *base* ten. The only reason for our counting in tens is that we have ten fingers. (Another word for 'finger' is 'digit'.) Our numeral system was brought to Europe from India, via the Arabs, in the Middle Ages; a considerable resistance to the 'infidel' symbols had to be overcome by Europeans accustomed to using Roman numerals. Eventually the ease with which calculations could be performed with the Indo-Arabic numerals won over the merchants and bankers. Roman numerals do not employ place value, and calculations are difficult to perform using these numerals. (Try adding XXIX and XLIV!)

We can help children towards an understanding of place value by exercises like the following:

(a) We give children a collection of objects, and ask them to count the objects by arranging them in tens as far as they can. The activity is like equal grouping where a remainder is involved (see page 101). Children can record the activity in pictures and symbols.

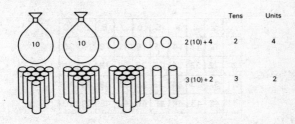

Whenever possible, we can exploit the opportunity to count books, pencils or paintbrushes, arranging them in tens and counting, 'Ten, twenty, thirty, thirty-one, thirty-two,' and so on. A teacher I know engineers an occasional 'accidental' dropping of her tin of buttons, asking the children to check that the correct number have been picked up by counting them in tens.

(b) Coins of value 10p can be introduced. Shopping games can involve buying and selling, using 10p and 1p coins, and prices can range from 10p to 50p. Children can complete worksheets on finding the value of a collection of coins.

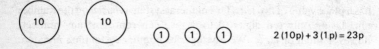

$$2(10p) + 3(1p) = 23p$$

Children can play the 'Fifty Pence Game', using a die and a collection of 10p and 1p coins. The game is similar to the 'Tenpence Game', described on page 98. At any stage of the game, children can exchange ten 1p coins for a 10p coin. The winner is the first child to collect five 10p coins.

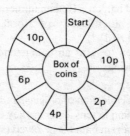

(c) Children can extend their '30 arrays' to include the numerals up to 50.

1	2	3	4	5	6	7	8	9	10
11	12	13	14	15	16	17	18	19	20
21	22	23	24	25	26	27	28	29	30
31	32	33	34	35	36	37	38	39	40
41	42	43	44	45	46	47	48	49	50

They can play a die game on the new 50 array, using counters that are moved a number of squares corresponding to the numeral thrown. A few 'bonus' squares can be coloured (say two in each row except for the last row); counters landing on those squares can be moved on ten squares. Children will soon see that moving on ten squares can be done by a 'short cut', moving down one square to the next row of the array. The new 50 array can then be used for reference while doing mental arithmetic, such as: What is 10 and 4? 20 and 4? 30 and 4? What is 10 + 10? 20 + 10? 30 + 10? What is 13 + 10? 23 + 10? 33 + 10? Which is more, 29 or 32? Find page 36 of a book, using the number array if it helps. What is the next page? The page before? What number is 2 more than 12? 2 more than 22? 2 more than 32? What must we add to 6 to get 10? To 16 to get 20? To 26 to get 30? Count along the array, line by line, in twos. Count along the array, line by line, in fives. A pleasing pattern is seen; children might like to colour every fifth numeral on their array to show the pattern.

Abler children might try some harder addition, such as 6 + 7 (add 4 to make 10, then 3 more to make 13), 16 + 7 (add 4 to make 20, then 3 more to make 23), 26 + 7, 36 + 7.

(d) Children can play 'Spot the Number'. They must locate the 'secret number' first by its tens digit, then by its units digit, referring to their 50 arrays while making their guesses. We give an example.

'My secret number is more than 30.'
'Is it more than 40?' 'No.'
'Is it 40?' 'No.' (This establishes the tens digit as '3'.)
'Is it more than 35?' 'Yes.'
'Is it more than 38?' 'Yes.'
This reveals the secret number.

(e) Children can make a calendar for the current month. What dates of the month are Tuesdays? What is special about the numbers of these dates? What days are on the seventh, the fourteenth, the twenty-first and twenty-eighth of the month? Why are these dates all on the same day of the week?

(f) Mental arithmetic can be consolidated in written exercises, some presented in pattern form, some not. Here are examples of a few exercises that children might be asked to copy and complete, with the help of their arrays. (They will need many more such exercises.)

4 + 3 =	6 + 10 =	6 + 11 =	10 − 4 =
14 + 3 =	12 + 10 =	16 + 11 =	20 − 4 =
24 + 3 =	26 + 10 =	26 + 11 =	30 − 4 =
34 + 3 =	33 + 10 =	36 + 11 =	40 − 4 =
45 + 3 =	18 + 10 =	22 + 11 =	50 − 5 =

(g) Lastly, we can play 'Number Spiders' using a number between 20 and 50 for the body. Here is a record of a possible game.

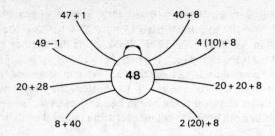

When children have gained considerable familiarity with numbers and numerals up to fifty by activities similar to those that we have described, we can extend their acquaintance with numbers and numerals up to ninety-nine in a similar fashion, and we can take the opportunity to use these new numbers and numerals in measuring, as we shall see in Chapter 13.

Equipment Needed for the Activities in This Chapter

Unifix cubes.
Counters, plastic bags labelled '10', tie bands.
Sticks and tie bands.
Numeral cards labelled 1 to 9 and larger ones labelled 10, 20, 30.
Coins of value 10p and 1p.
Large 50 array for class display.
Calendars.
Die for the 'Forty Game' and the 'Fifty Pence Game'.
Track for the 'Fifty Pence Game'.

Suggestions for the Reader

1. Put yourself in the position of a child learning to understand our number system and notation. Pretend that the counting numbers are 'one, two, three, four, umpty, umpty-one, umpty-two, umpty-three, umpty-four, dumpty, dumpty-one, dumpty-two, dumpty-three, dumpty-four, thrumpty', and so on. The numerals representing these strange numbers are written in a number array below.

1	2	3	4	10	(umpty)
11	12	13	14	20	(dumpty)
21	22	23	24	30	(thrumpty)
31	32	33	34		

Read the number array aloud. Check that you have umpty fingers on each hand, and that you have dumpty fingers altogether. How many legs has a fly? An octopus? Is 13 (umpty-three) an even number? Colour in the even numbers on the array above, and read them aloud.

Set yourself some additions such as umpty and four more, 21 + 3, 14 + 4, 23 + 3. Watch your mind at work! Which were easy, which hard? Did the number array help you? Do you think that your mental work was similar to that of a child learning to understand tens and units?

2. Write out a 50 array in Roman numerals. Observe where it has pattern and where it lacks pattern. Write out the table of nines in (a) Indo-Arabic and (b) Roman numerals. Which exhibits more pattern?

3. Ask some six- or seven-year-olds to tell you the numbers that are (a) twenty and four more, (b) thirty and six more. Note whether they have to 'count on' to find out, or whether they can be said to know that twenty-four *means* twenty and four more, and so on.

4. Show the same six- or seven-year-olds several 10p coins and ask them how much money you have put out. Then show a mixture of 10p and 1p coins and ask the same question. Make notes on their response.

5. In Chapter 10, we built up the table of twos by 'discovering' it with real objects. Why is it not necessary to build up the table of tens in this way?

12   *More about Shape*

New Maths – it's so simple, only a child can do it.

– *Tom Lehrer*

In Chapter 6, we met activities to help children learn to recognize and name some common solid and plane shapes. In this chapter we shall meet activities that will lead children to discover some properties of the shapes with which they have become familiar.

1. Right Angles

What is a right angle? The word 'right' is this connotation means 'upright'; a right angle is formed when a horizontal line meets a vertical (or upright) line. As we have seen from the work of Piaget (see Chapter 8), children may have a clear concept of a right angle before they have fully conceptualized 'horizontal' and 'vertical'. (The chimney in the child's drawing below has lines that are at *right angles* to the roof of the house, but it has no horizontal or vertical lines.)

When we introduce children to the term 'right angle', we need not base the term on the terms 'horizontal' and 'vertical'. The reason why right angles are 'all around us' is that they have the very useful property that two such angles, when juxtaposed, form a straight line. Take a sheet of paper and fold it. The fold is a straight line. Fold that fold on to itself, and you have made a right angle. When you open the paper out, you see for yourself that (a) two right angles together form a straight line, and (b) four right angles together 'fill the surface round a point'.

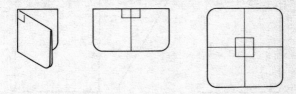

Through the activity described above, children can make a right angle for themselves. Each child can check that his own right angle matches his neighbour's right angle by superimposing the two angles. (The two pieces of paper will not necessarily match for shape or length; but the *corners* formed by the right angles *do* match.) The newly formed right angles can be used to identify other right angles; examples include the corners of cuboids, prisms, squares, rectangles, windows, tables and books. Children can observe that two adjacent right angles form a straight line (a) by partly opening out their folded paper angles, and (b) by observing adjacent right angles around them, for example in two adjacent bricks on a wall. They can observe that four adjacent right angles 'fill the surface round a point' by (a) fully opening out their folded paper and (b) observing four adjacent window panes or floor tiles.

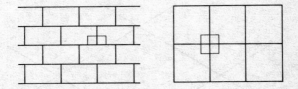

Children can use their folded right angles to draw right angles in various orientations. They can draw a shape whose corners are all right angles. They will find that they have drawn a rectangle. The word *rectangle* is derived from Latin *rectus* (straight, or upright) and *angulus* (angle).

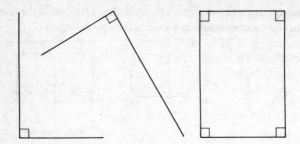

2. 'Parallel', 'Vertical' and 'Horizontal' Lines

As we noticed in Chapter 8, children show by their drawings that they have a concept of 'parallel' long before they are usually taught the word. Two lines are parallel to each other if they remain the same distance apart throughout their length. Examples around us are lines on writing paper, lines on brickwork, opposite pavements of roads and railway lines. Children can be asked to pick out parallel edges of solid or plane shapes and to identify parallel lines around them in a room. They can draw parallel lines by drawing along the top and bottom edges of a ruler. If they then place the ruler in a new orientation on the paper and draw two more parallel lines to meet the first pair, they will make a rhombus (or diamond).

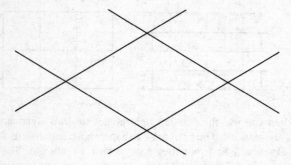

Vertical Lines

Vertical lines are upright lines. When we stand upright, our body makes an approximation of a vertical line; when we set up a toy soldier or a skittle, it is liable to fall over if it does not approximate to a vertical line. Children can be shown how a *plumb-line* always hangs vertically. (A plumb-line can easily be made by attaching a lump of plasticine to the end of a string.) Children can use plumb-lines to check that walls and windows have vertical edges. They can be invited to find other vertical lines around them and to notice that all vertical lines are parallel to one another.

Horizontal Lines

Horizontal lines are lines that are at right angles to vertical lines. Children can be invited to look for horizontal lines in a room, such as window ledges, table edges or lines on the floor, and to notice that not all horizontal lines are parallel to one another. They can be shown how the bubble in a spirit-level indicates whether the instrument is horizontal or not. They can observe the water level in a transparent jar and discover that it is always horizontal, whether the jar is tilted or not. (Strictly speaking, the water surface forms a horizontal plane rather than a line. Able children may enjoy drawing the distinction between horizontal lines and horizontal planes.)

3. Line Symmetry

Fold a sheet of paper in half and cut out a shape that includes part of your fold. Your cut-out shape will be symmetrical. The fold line divides the shape into two congruent halves, and the fold line is called an *axis of symmetry* of the shape.

Children develop a concept of symmetry at an early age. It is shown clearly in their drawings. For instance, the 'units' chosen by children to represent human features or limbs vary considerably, but each child's drawing of a human exhibits symmetry.

The folding and cutting activity just described can serve to introduce children to the terms 'symmetrical' and 'axis of symmetry'. Both the cut-out shape and its silhouette will be symmetrical. The symmetry can be highlighted by placing a mirror along the fold (at right angles to the plane of the paper); the mirror reflection completes the original shape.

Children's cut-out shapes and their silhouettes can be displayed on the wall. It is a good idea to display some shapes so that their axes of symmetry are vertical, and some so that their axes of symmetry are horizontal. (Symmetry about a horizontal axis is not as immediately discernible as symmetry about a vertical axis.) Children can collect objects, drawings or photographs that exhibit symmetry – such as leaves, butterflies, flowers, wallpaper patterns. My own children used to delight in some of the neat poses adopted by our cat: 'He's so symmetrical today!'

Children can draw round card templates of geometric plane shapes (such as those illustrated on pages 56 and 57) and test, by folding, whether they have axes of symmetry. When an experimental fold is found to be an axis of symmetry, it can be coloured in to identify it as such.

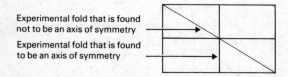

Experimental fold that is found
not to be an axis of symmetry →

Experimental fold that is found
to be an axis of symmetry →

Symmetry and Fractions

The act of folding demonstrates that an axis of symmetry shares (or divides) a plane shape into two congruent halves. Children can discover that a plane shape with two axes of symmetry is divided into four congruent quarters by those axes, and that the axes themselves are always at right angles to each other. We can point out to them that the three axes of symmetry that they discover for an equilateral triangle divide the triangle into six congruent parts, which are called *sixths* of the triangle, and that the four axes of symmetry that they discover for a square divide the square into eight congruent parts, which are called *eighths* of the square. Abler children will notice that there is no end to the number of axes of symmetry that can be found for a circle.

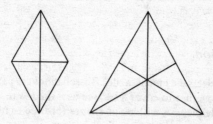

Congruence and Orientation

An axis of symmetry divides a plane shape into two congruent halves. These halves do not look alike in all ways. A 'left' feature of one half is matched by a 'right' feature of the other. They are reflections of each other.

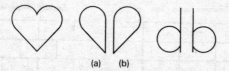

(a)   (b)

Children might show some reluctance in admitting that the parts (a) and (b) are congruent. After all, the letters **d** and **b** are reflections of each other, and children have been carefully taught to perceive these as different. In mathematics, we ask children to look for different similarities from those in reading. Change in orientation of a geometric shape does not change its name; change in orientation of a letter does. Even in mathematics, orientation can influence our perception irrelevantly. Many people will call shape (c) overleaf a *rhombus*, and shape (d), a *diamond*. Shape (c) can be rotated to appear identical to shape (d), and we do not actually need two names for the shapes, any more than we need two names for the shapes (e) and (f). But for reading purposes, we certainly need two names for the shapes (g) and (h).

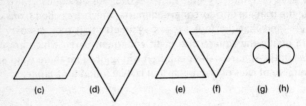

(c)   (d)   (e)   (f)   (g)   (h)

4. Tessellation

The Latin word *tessella* means 'a tile'. Tessellations are patterns of plane shapes fitted together to cover a surface as if they were tiles. Children who have made pictures with plane shapes (or tried to build one plane

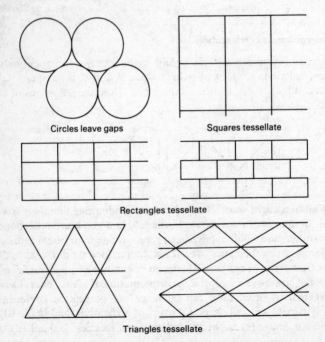

Circles leave gaps   Squares tessellate

Rectangles tessellate

Triangles tessellate

shape using others, as illustrated on page 58), will have discovered something about the way that plane shapes may or may not fit together. Now, each child can be given a set of congruent shapes such as circles, squares, rectangles or triangles of various shapes (the illustrations on pages 56 and 57 give a possible selection), and asked to explore whether that particular set can be arranged like a set of tiles to cover a surface without leaving gaps.

Children will discover that any set of congruent rectangles and any set of congruent triangles will tessellate, but congruent circles will not. When a child has arranged a set of shapes in a tessellating pattern, he can draw round the shapes to record his pattern. He can study this pattern to look for pairs of right angles making a straight line, groups of four right angles 'filling the surface round a point', and parallel lines.

Tessellations and Fractions

Children might be asked to draw an appropriate number of shapes in their tessellation so that they can colour the overall shape in quarters. The colouring might well suggest to bright children other shapes that will tessellate, such as the '**L**' shapes or the 'half hexagons' below.

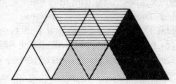

Free Tessellations

Imaginative children or adults might like to create a 'free' tessellation from an existing one by replacing its lines in some regular way. The free tessellations below are based on tessellating rectangles and equilateral triangles.

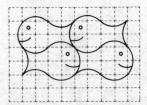
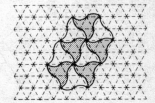

5. *Frameworks of Plane Shapes*

Building the framework of a plane shape focuses attention on the relation between the shape itself and the lengths of its edges. We need to prepare a number of narrow strips of card of several different lengths, say 14 cm, 18 cm and 22 cm, and pierce holes 1 cm from the ends of each strip. The holes must be large enough to allow a two-pronged paper fastener to be pushed through, to join pairs of strips when making frameworks. The effective lengths of the strips when they form parts of frameworks will then be 12 cm, 16 cm and 20 cm. (Instead of the home-made strips, commercially made Geostrips could be used.)

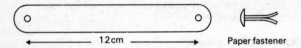

|←————————————— 12cm —————————————→| **Paper fastener**

Using the strips of effective length 12 cm only, children can be invited to make some closed frameworks. Having matched the strips and noted that they all have equal length, the children will realize that they will make shapes whose sides are equal in length. Such shapes are called *equilateral* shapes. Children may build equilateral triangles, equilateral four-sided figures such as squares or rhombuses (or diamonds), equilateral five-sided figures (or pentagons) and equilateral six-sided figures (or hexagons). They will notice that only the triangles are rigid. The other shapes can be pushed to form a variety of equilateral shapes.

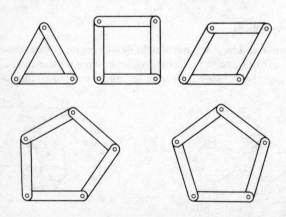

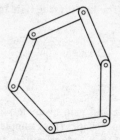
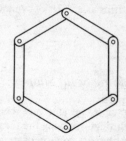

Using strips of two different lengths, children may build triangles with two equal sides (isosceles triangles), four-sided figures that are rectangles, parallelograms or kites, and a variety of five- or six-sided figures. Of these figures, only the triangles will be rigid.

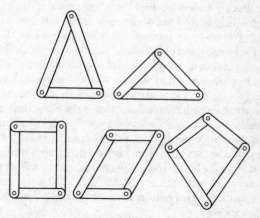

Using strips of three different lengths greatly extends the range of possible shapes that can be made. Using the lengths that we have suggested, one possible shape is a right-angled triangle. We can suggest that the children make some symmetrical shapes by using one of the

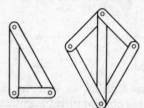
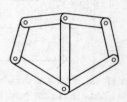

longest strips as an axis of symmetry. (The kite is made rigid by such a strip.)

6. Building Solid Shapes

In Chapter 6, we saw how children could gain awareness of plane shapes through studying the faces of solid shapes (for example, a cube has faces that are congruent squares). This awareness can be deepened by the activity of building solid shapes from card.

We show children a small box, and tell them that we are going to make another box just like it (or congruent to it). We put the box on a table and label its faces as they appear to the children: 'Top', 'Bottom', 'Front', 'Back', 'Left side, 'Right side'. We put the box bottom downwards on a sheet of card and draw round the bottom face in contact with the card. We label the rectangle that we have drawn 'Bottom', and replace the box to stand on the rectangle. Next, we rotate the box slowly towards the children, keeping the front edge in contact with the card, until the face labelled 'Front' is in contact with the card. We draw round the front face on the card, and then rotate the box so that its bottom face is in contact again with the rectangle that we labelled 'Bottom'. We label the second rectangle that we have drawn 'Front'. We continue rotating the box about its other bottom edges, drawing round new faces and labelling them as they are drawn, until we have drawn the four faces that are adjacent to the bottom face of the box. Children will see that we have drawn every face of the box except the top face. This face can be brought in contact with the card only by rotating the box twice, about one edge and then another.

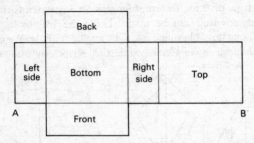

When all six faces are drawn and labelled, we study the drawing, which is called a *net* of the box. It contains many right angles, and each one corresponds to a certain right angle on the box itself. We note long straight lines, such as AB, which is straight because of the three pairs of right angles along it. We notice parallel lines in the net, some of which correspond to parallel lines in the box itself. Lastly, we cut out the net and fold it up, sticking appropriate edges together with adhesive tape, to form another box that is congruent to the original box. After this demonstration, children can be invited to work out for themselves how to make nets of other solids with which they are familiar, such as pyramids, prisms, cubes and cuboids. If children draw their nets in pencil, their drawings can be corrected if necessary before being cut out, thus avoiding waste of precious card.

Many of the shapes that we have suggested making in this chapter can be used again in the activities for measuring length that we shall describe in the next chapter.

Equipment Needed for the Activities of This Chapter

Sets of congruent circles, squares, rectangles and triangles.
Paper for folding and cutting; scissors.
Card strips (or Geostrips); paper fasteners.
Solid shapes; thin card for building solid shapes.
A spirit-level and a plumb-line.

Suggestions for the Reader

1. (Right angles) Test some six- and seven-year-old children to see whether they have the concept of a right angle. (You might ask them to observe the corners of windows, books, sheets of paper, and decide whether they are alike in any way.) Make notes on the words used by the children.

2. (Parallel) Test the same children to see whether (a) they have the concept of 'parallel', (b) they have the words to describe the concept.

3. (Horizontal) In Chapter 8, we referred to Piaget's claim that children in the intuitive period of development do not have a concept of 'horizontal'. His claim was based on the observation that children draw the water level in a tilted vessel as illustrated on page 74. Select some children of seven and administer Piaget's test, as described here, and follow it with some 'teaching'.

Prepare four sheets of pictures of the jar for each child, as shown.

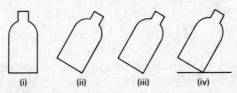

(i)   (ii)   (iii)   (iv)

(a) Show the children the jar in orientation (i), half full of water. On picture (i), ask them to show where the water is in the jar by drawing a line where the top of the water is.

(b) Ask them to draw a line on picture (ii) where they *think* the top of the water will be when the jar is tilted as in (ii). (Do *not* tilt the jar for them.)

(c) Tilt the jar, as in (iii), and ask the children to draw a line on picture (iii) where they *observe* the top of the water to be. This is the *end* of Piaget's test.

(d) Tilt the jar, as in (iv), and ask the children to notice that the top of the water is parallel to the table top on which the jar is resting. (The table top is drawn in the picture.) Now ask the children to draw a line on picture (iv) where they observe the top of the water to be.

4. (Symmetry) Show some six- or seven-year-old children a plane shape with one axis of symmetry drawn in (such as a 'heart' shape). Ask them to say how the two parts of the shape are (a) the same, (b) different.

5. (Symmetry) Consider all capital letters, and make lists of (a) those that are symmetrical about a vertical axis (such as 'A'), (b) those that are symmetrical about a horizontal axis (such as 'B').

Make up a word from some of the letters in list (a), and write the word like a 'Down' clue in a crossword. Look at your word in a mirror. Can you explain what you notice?

Make up a word from some of the letters in list (b), and write the word like an 'Across' clue in a crossword. Turn your word upside down and look at it in a mirror. Can you explain what you notice?

H
A   CHOICE
T

6. (Tessellation) A *regular* plane shape is one with equal sides and equal angles. You will find a regular pentagon and a regular hexagon illustrated on pages 120 and 121. Test for yourself whether congruent regular pentagons will tessellate, whether congruent regular hexagons will tessellate, and whether congruent regular octagons will tessellate.

13 Measurement

Twenty grains are 1 scruple; 3 scruples are 1 dram; 8 drams
are 1 ounce; 12 ounces are 1 pound.

– Apothecaries' weight chart

The measurements used in this country are not those which
would have been chosen had they been made all at one
time, and by a people well acquainted with arithmetic and
the sciences.

– Professor A. De Morgan, 1830

In Chapter 6, we discussed early experience in measuring length using
physical units of length, and in Chapter 7 we discussed similar experiences involving capacity, weight and time. In this chapter we shall
consider how children can progress towards using simple conventional
instruments for measuring in standard units.

1. Length

Look at a conventional ruler. It is marked with calibrations and numerals. One of the numerals is probably '0'. When you use the ruler to
measure a length, you must align the calibration that is nearest to the
numeral '0' with one end of the object to be measured, identify the
calibration nearest to the other end of the object, and then associate this
calibration with an appropriate numeral, which may or may not be
written on the ruler. Such an activity, you may feel, bears little or no
resemblance to that of measuring length with physical units. Children
need many intermediate experiences between using physical units and
using a conventional ruler.

One of the conventional standard units of length is the *centimetre*. A
centimetre is rather a short length. We cannot give children a collection
of sticks that are 1 centimetre long; but we can construct a primitive ruler
from card, 10 centimetres long, with ten coloured strips on it, each 1
centimetre wide. Two such rulers can be juxtaposed in various ways to
demonstrate that each coloured strip has the same width. We can tell
children that this width is called a *centimetre*.

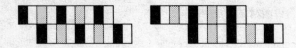

A primitive ruler has no numerals marked on it. It can be used to measure the length of an object that is shorter than 10 centimetres, by aligning the edge of the ruler with the edge of the object and counting the number of coloured strip edges that lie alongside the object.

The crayon is 8 centimetres long

Children might use primitive rulers to measure the lengths of some of the straight lines in the symmetrical shapes that they have made (see page 117), noting that lines that 'balance' on either side of the axis of symmetry have the same length. They might measure the length of some of the lines in their tessellation drawings (see page 118), picking out lines that have the same length; they can be reminded that the shapes used to make the tessellations were *congruent*, so we would expect certain lines in the tessellation patterns to have the same length. They might measure the length, width and height of some of the solids that they have built (see page 122). The primitive rulers can be used 'in series' to measure lengths that are longer than 10 centimetres. In measuring the length of a pencil, as illustrated below, children should count 'Ten (for the whole of the first card), eleven, twelve, thirteen, fourteen, fifteen'. The activity will deepen their concept of place value, by linking the new centimetre measuring with tens and units.

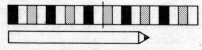

The pencil is 15 centimetres long

Relevance to number operations can be demonstrated by putting the crayon and the pencil in a line and measuring its length (illustrating that $8 + 15 = 23$), and by comparing the lengths of the crayon and the pencil (illustrating that $15 = 8 + 7$).

The simplest kind of conventional ruler to introduce to children is perhaps one that is a metre long, calibrated in centimetres and numbered in tens. Children can place their card rulers alongside this ruler and see that the calibrations on the ruler match the edges of the coloured strips. The metre ruler can then be used to measure lengths up to 50 centimetres (and more, when children have learnt to read and use numbers and numerals above 50). Measuring the length of a child's arm, as illustrated, will involve counting, 'Ten, twenty, thirty, forty, forty-one, forty-two, forty-three.'

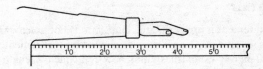

Estimation

Children should be encouraged to estimate lengths of objects before measuring them, because then they will concern themselves with the significance of the numbers that they obtain. A child who accidentally uses a metre ruler upside-down, for instance, in measuring the height of a cupboard that is 37 centimetres tall, might read the numeral 60 and count on, 'Sixty-one, sixty-two, sixty-three.' If he has previously estimated its height to be 40 centimetres, he will probably query his measurement and find his mistake.

Recording

In recording measurements, children might be allowed to abbreviate the word 'centimetres' in the customary way to 'cm'. Children might record both their estimates and measurements and work out the difference between these two quantities, as shown below.

	Estimate	Measurement	Difference
Tim's arm	40 cm	43 cm	3 cm
Mary's arm	50 cm	45 cm	5 cm
Shiva's arm	50 cm	48 cm	2 cm

Children often show reluctance to write down an estimate, because they feel that it is likely to be 'wrong'. I have often seen children fill in the column headed 'Estimate' *after* measuring; they write either a measurement exactly the same as their measurement, or one that differs from it by one or two cm. We must persuade children that the reason for estimating a measurement is to provide a check on the reasonableness of their results, rather than to see how well they can guess. Their mathematics will involve *more* estimation as they progress, not less. (When using a calculator, for instance, it is important to be able to form an estimate of what a calculation will be, so that an error of pressing a wrong button will not go undetected.)

'Bits Left Over'

All measurement is approximate. Tim's arm is not *exactly* 43 cm long, nor is it exactly 43·2 cm long. A measuring instrument, however accurate, merely establishes limits between which a length lies. One instrument will tell us that a length is between 43 and 44 cm while another may tell us that it is between 43·2 and 43·3 cm. Children who notice that the end of an object does not coincide exactly with a calibration on the ruler should be commended, but still encouraged to record the length as the nearest whole number of centimetres. The problem of 'exact measurement' will recur in all their measuring, of capacity, weight, time, area, volume and so on. They will learn only gradually that measuring is not an exact process.

Centimetres and Metres

The word 'centimetre' means 'a hundredth of a metre'. This is *not* a useful fact to tell children at this stage. They need to think of a centimetre as a unit in its own right.

Use of Standard Rulers

After considerable experience with primitive rulers and metre rulers as described above, children can be introduced to the smaller standard 30 cm rulers that are calibrated and numbered in cm. Because *one* is the first counting number, some children will feel that the calibration labelled '1' should be aligned with the end of an object to be measured. If the new 30 cm rulers are compared with the primitive rulers before being used, children will more easily see the significance of the calibration labelled '0'.

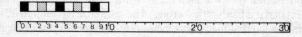

2. Weight

If centimetres are inconveniently small lengths, grams are even more inconveniently small weights. (A 1p coin weighs about 3 grams.) The people who decided on these units of measurement certainly did not have in mind the conceptual development of young children! Balance scales that are sensitive to differences in weight as small as 1 gram are *too* sensitive for children to use with ease. At the other extreme, a kilogram is an inconveniently heavy weight. A child cannot lift more than about 10 kilograms, and balance scales that children normally use will not support more than a few kilograms. So what are we to do?

The remedy seems to be to continue to use the plasticine balls that weigh 100 grams each, as described on page 68, giving these units no new name. (Their real name is 'hectogram', and a hectogram weighs about 3½ ounces.) At this stage, we can also provide some kilogram weights, and let children discover that each of these new weights balances ten balls. (Only later will children call these new weights 'kilograms'. At present, they should be thought of as the weight of ten balls.) Using balls and the new 'ten ball' weights, children can weigh ordinary objects such as books, groceries, pebbles and so on. By linking their weighing with tens and units, the weighing activities will deepen their concept of place value.

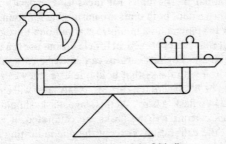

Our jug of pebbles weighs 21 balls

Children will find out such facts as:

One bag of sugar weighs 10 balls	Reinforcing their
Two bags of sugar weigh 20 balls	concept of
Three bags of sugar weigh 30 balls	'sets of ten',

and

A jugful of cornflakes weighs 4 balls ⎫ Reinforcing the concept
A jugful of sand weighs 14 balls ⎬ that weight is not
A jugful of pebbles weighs 21 balls ⎭ related to size.

Relevance to number operations can be shown by putting a bag of sugar on the pan with the jugful of pebbles, and finding that the total weight is 31 balls (illustrating that $10 + 21 = 31$), or by comparing the jugful of pebbles in one pan with a bag of sugar in the other, and noting that one 'ten ball' weight and one ball must be added to the pan containing the sugar to achieve a balance (illustrating that $21 = 10 + 11$).

It is desirable to plan weighing activities so that the number operations that we wish to illustrate are within the children's grasp, and so that, at least in the early stages, balance can be achieved using a whole number of balls. (Later, it is quite valuable to find that an object is heavier than, say, 11 balls, but lighter than 12 balls.) After extensive experience of weighing with balls and 'ten ball' weights, children should be tested for their understanding of weight conservation. The test is described on page 68.

3. Capacity

The conventional metric units for measuring capacity are *litres* and *millilitres*. Once again, both units are unsuitable for young children. (A litre is about 1¾ pints, and a millilitre is about one-third of a teaspoonful.) The unit that is most practical for classroom use is a tenth of a litre (or 100 millilitres). Yoghurt cartons can easily be cut to this size. If we provide children with flasks that hold one litre, they can discover that each flask can be filled with ten cartons. (Only later will children call the quantity held by a flask 'a litre'. At this stage, flasks should be thought of as holding *ten* cartons.) If the flasks are calibrated, it is advisable to obliterate all the calibrations (except the one indicating the litre measure), by sticking a ribbon of paper over them.

Children can now measure out amounts of water (or sand) in 'cartons'. To measure the amount of water that a saucepan will hold, children will fill the saucepan with water and empty it into flasks. Suppose that the saucepan fills one flask and part of another. The partly filled flask can then be poured into cartons. If it fills six cartons, children should say that the saucepan holds *sixteen* cartons of water. The measurement can be checked by pouring the contents of the flask and the six cartons back to fill the saucepan. An activity of this nature will deepen children's place value, by linking their capacity measurement with tens and units.

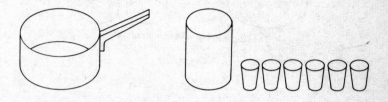

Capacity measurement can be linked with number operations. Suppose that we have found that a jug will hold seven cartons of water. We should find then that the saucepan and the jug together will fill twenty-three cartons (illustrating that $16 + 7 = 23$). When we compare the capacities of the saucepan and the jug, we should find that the saucepan will fill the jug and nine cartons more (illustrating that $16 = 7 + 9$).

Children can complete this section of work on measuring capacity by marking calibrations on the litre flasks to correspond to cartons. If a paper ribbon has already been stuck on the flasks to obliterate the ready-made calibrations, this paper can be used for making the new calibrations. Children start by pouring one carton of water into a flask and marking the water level reached on the ribbon; they write '1' beside the calibration that they have made. A second carton of water poured into the flask raises the water level. The new water level is marked and labelled '2'. (The significance of this mark can be reinforced by pouring the water back from the flask into two cartons.) Children continue calibrating and labelling the strip on the flask until the label '10' coincides with the calibration on the flask indicating 'one litre'. If there is a bad discrepancy between the '10 carton' mark and this calibration, the children's marks could be erased, and they could try again, this time filling the flask to the '10 carton' level and pouring out one carton of water at a time, making their calibrations from top to bottom of the flask.

After extensive experience of measuring capacity with cartons and flasks, children should be tested for their understanding of conservation of liquid. The test is described on page 66. Those who show that they understand conservation can be allowed, if they wish, to continue their capacity-measuring activities using the flasks that they have calibrated, as illustrated overleaf.

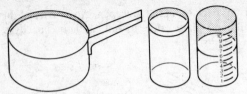

The saucepan holds 16 cartons of water

4. Area

Area measures an amount of surface. Like all measurement, area measurement should begin with matching activities and progress to ordering activities. Two congruent 'flat' shapes will fit exactly over each other, and we say that they cover the same amount of surface, or *have the same area* (see diagram (a)). If one 'flat' shape when placed over a second lies completely 'inside' it, we say that it covers a smaller amount of surface than the second shape, or *has a smaller area* than the second shape (see diagram (b)). We would not at this early stage confront children with shapes that overlap such that it is not obvious which has the greater area (see diagram (c)).

(a)   (b)   (c)

We normally measure the area of a shape by the number of congruent squares that it covers. Thus two shapes that are not congruent may well have the same area. In the early stages of measuring area, children may have some difficulty with this concept. They need experience in building many different shapes that have the same area. For this purpose, we can return to the tessellation patterns that children have made (see page 118). A child who has made a tessellation using twelve congruent squares should be invited to take another twelve squares and build several different shapes with those squares. Similarly, children who have made a tessellation using twelve triangles should be asked to build some different shapes with the same twelve triangles.

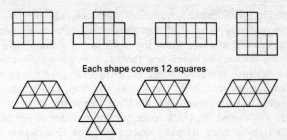

Each shape covers 12 squares

Each shape covers 12 triangles

Children can also be helped towards understanding conservation of area by playing with a simple 'Tangram'. This is a set of shapes that can form a square, as illustrated. Children can build a variety of shapes using the Tangram pieces. All the resulting shapes have the same area.

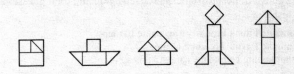

Children's introduction to area might be rounded off by their drawing some free shapes on squared paper and then arranging their shapes in order of area. They can investigate their own shapes first, and then one another's. Inventive children will want to include some half-squares in their drawings, and some may even include quarter-squares.

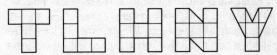

Arrange these letters in order of area

5. Time

In Chapter 7, we described how a metronome or a pendulum might be used to illustrate the regular rhythm through which time intervals are measured. By setting the metronome at 60, or fixing the length of the pendulum at 1 metre, those time intervals become seconds. We might now introduce children to a *stop clock* that measures seconds. A stop clock has a second hand which rotates a small amount each second; it completes one revolution round the clock in one minute. The instrument is much easier to understand than a conventional clock that tells the time, because the second hand rotates fast enough for its movement to be easily noticeable. Most stop clocks also have a minute hand; this hand should initially be ignored. Children can watch the second hand jump its way round the clock, counting the number of jumps that it makes on its journey. Having agreed that the time taken for this revolution is sixty seconds, children can be told that this interval of time is also called a *minute*. A stop clock is usually labelled 5, 10, 15 and so on. Children can count up to sixty in fives as they point round the stop clock. Children can then makes guesses as to what they can do in a minute: how many times they think they can jump, how many times they think they can write their name, how many breaths they will take, and so on. Having guessed, the stop clock is started again and their guesses are put to the test.

In one minute I think I can write my name 10 times.
In one minute I wrote my name 13 times.
In another minute I wrote my name 15 times.

We can use the stop clock to measure the time it takes to perform various activities. We show the children the calibrations on the clock and compare them with the calibrations on a metre ruler; some are labelled with numerals and some are not. We count round the calibrations in fives to see where the second hand will point after the clock has been going for fifteen seconds: 'Five, ten, fifteen.' We count round to see where the hand will point after twenty-three seconds: 'Five, ten, fifteen, twenty, twenty-one, twenty-two, twenty-three.' Now we are ready to time John doing up his shoe-laces. We start the clock when John starts, and stop it when he has finished, when the second hand is in the position as illustrated. We count round the clock until we reach the second hand: 'Five, ten, fifteen, sixteen, seventeen, eighteen.' John took eighteen seconds to do up his shoes.

Activities that take longer than a minute can also be timed. If the second hand moves right round the clock while an activity takes place, that activity has taken one minute. We can now call attention to the minute hand of the clock. This hand will be pointing to the first calibration on the clock, confirming that one minute has passed while the clock was ticking. If the second hand moves twice round the clock while an activity takes place, that activity has taken two minutes. The minute hand will be pointing to the second calibration on the clock, confirming that two minutes have passed while the clock was ticking. Now we can time activities that take several minutes. Suppose we start the clock when children begin to clear up after art work, and stop it when they have finished. If the minute hand points to the fourth calibration on the clock, and the second hand to the thirty-fifth calibration, children should be able to deduce that they have taken four minutes thirty-five seconds to clear up.

These activities are all good preparation for understanding the workings of a conventional clock.

6. *Telling the Time*

Children can be taught to 'read' the time from a conventional clock long before they understand how this reading is connected with the passing of time. We teach them the 'o'clock' times first; the big hand points up to '12' at such times, and the little hand points to the numeral that tells us what o'clock it is. Children will link certain o'clock times with certain recurring activities in their day, such as, 'I get up at 8 o'clock in the morning; I go to bed at 8 o'clock at night; we have lunch at 12 o'clock; we have tea at 5 o'clock.'

If children play with old clocks whose hands are in working order, they will notice that their two hands move round at different rates; they may notice that one revolution of the big hand causes the little hand to move from one numeral on the clock to the next. We can use these observations to help children understand the action of the hands of a conventional clock. When the conventional clock records the time as '2 o'clock', we can start the stop clock. After one minute, we observe what has happened to the big hand of the conventional clock. It has moved through one tiny interval, just as the minute hand of the stop clock has. It tells us that one minute has passed. The time is now *one minute past two*. Both clocks continue to tick away, and by the time we have guessed where the big hand will be after another minute has passed, we observe that it has indeed moved through another tiny interval to the next calibration on the clock. It is two minutes past two.

We can now call the big hand the *minute* hand of the clock. We might continue our predictions and observations until the clock tells us that the time is four minutes past two. At that moment, we might, if we have one, start a 'pinger' clock, setting it for two minutes, and predict what time the clock will 'say' when the pinger rings. While waiting for the pinger to ring, we could count the calibrations all the way round the clock, in ones and in fives. There are sixty. Whereas the second hand of a stop clock takes sixty seconds to rotate right round, the minute hand of a conventional clock takes sixty minutes to rotate round.

It is very much easier for children to learn to tell the time by reading minutes *past* the hour than minutes *to* the hour. 'Forty minutes past two' is much easier to read and conceptualize than 'Twenty minutes to three'. The latter requires the foreknowledge that after another twenty minutes the time will be 'Three o'clock'; in effect, you mentally arrange the clock at 'Three o'clock' and move it backwards twenty minutes. There is no need to teach children to say 'Twenty minutes to three', because all timetables and digital clocks will record this time as 2.40, as children will have to learn later.

In Chapter 15 we shall return to the subject of telling the time, and suggest how to introduce children to the concept of hours.

Equipment Needed for the Activities in This Chapter

Card strips, 10 cm long, calibrated in cm, but not labelled.
Metre rulers, calibrated in cm and labelled at 10 cm intervals.
Thirty-cm rulers, calibrated and labelled in cm.
Yoghurt cartons cut to the size of a tenth of a litre.
Litre flasks, with all calibrations except the litre one deleted.
Paper marked in squares; paper marked in equilateral triangles.
Card shapes of squares and equilateral triangles, for tessellating.
A stop clock in working order.
Old clocks whose hands are in working order.
A conventional clock that keeps reliable time.
A 'pinger' clock.

Suggestions for the Reader

1. (Length) Watch some seven-year-olds using rulers to measure length. Find out (a) whether they can estimate a length reasonably, (b) whether they align their rulers correctly when measuring a length, (c) whether they count centimetres or read numerals directly from the ruler to determine a length, and (d) whether they notice 'bits left over', and what they do about them.

2. (Weight) Watch some seven-year-olds weighing. Do they use standard metric weights? If so, which ones? Can they estimate the weight of an object? Do they know of any relation between the different weights that they use? (For instance, do ten of one weight balance one of another weight?) Do they have problems when an object is found to be heavier, say, than ten units and lighter than eleven units?

3. (Capacity) Watch the same seven-year-olds measuring capacity. Are they using containers whose relative capacity they know? (For instance, do they use a jug that holds as much as ten cups?) Are they using such knowledge in their measuring? (For instance, if a saucepan holds as much as two jugs, do they know that it must hold as much as twenty cups?)

4. (Area) Test some seven-year-olds to see if they understand *conservation of area*. Take six congruent squares, and arrange them in various shapes. Draw the shapes made, and ask children which is the largest shape, and why. Make notes on the words that children use.

5. (Time duration) Try to estimate the duration of a minute. Use a clock or watch with a second hand to test your estimate. Then, watch the second hand record a minute while you count how many breaths you take. Lastly, try again at estimating the duration of a minute. Has your estimation improved?

6. (Telling the time) Put yourself in the position of a child learning to tell the time. Pretend that you have a clock whose hands move *anticlockwise*. For such a clock, the numerals would have to be marked in anticlockwise order. Read the following times on your clock. Which are easy, and which hard?

14 *Operations Involving Numbers up to One Hundred*

By and by comes Mr Cooper . . . of whom I intend to
learn Mathematiques; . . . After an hour's being with him
at Arithmetique, my first attempt being to learn the
Multiplicacion table, then we parted till tomorrow.

> Samuel Pepys
> Diary entry for 4 July 1662
> (Pepys was at this time the equivalent of
> Secretary of the Navy)

In this chapter we shall consider how we can help children to become proficient at performing additions, subtractions, multiplications and divisions involving whole numbers up to one hundred. Let us begin by considering a typical everyday problem. Suppose that we are purchasing two articles whose prices are 29p and 25p. In the shop we shall mentally calculate the total price in one of several ways. We might argue: 'Twenty-nine and twenty is forty-nine; forty-nine and five is fifty-four; so the total price is 54p.' Or, we might argue: 'Thirty and twenty-five is fifty-five; twenty-nine is one less than thirty, so the total price is 1p less than 55p.' Compare these mental strategies with the strategy involved in the 'standard technique' that we learnt at school for writing in symbols the calculation '29 + 25'. The technique involves the following argument:

Nine and five is fourteen; write '4' in
the units column of the 'answer space'
and '1' in the tens column (but not in
the 'answer space').
Then add the tens: two and two and one
is five; so write '5' in the tens column.

$$
\begin{array}{r}
29\ + \\
25 \\
\hline
54 \\
\hline
1
\end{array}
$$

The written calculation enforces a particular thinking strategy. It is not a bad strategy, but it is certainly not the only useful one. If we want to give children the experience of choosing their own strategy for calculations, we must encourage them to perform calculations mentally and physically as well as writing them down using a standard technique.

The normal method of teaching children to perform a written calculation such as '29 + 25' is to provide them with structural apparatus which serves as pictures (P) of the numbers represented by the symbols. We need to bear in mind that concentrating on the 'P, s' aspects of a problem may divert children's attention from its original 'E, L' aspects. I once watched a seven-year-old tackle the problem, 'There are twenty-nine children in Class A and twenty-five in Class B. If both classes go on a coach trip, how many children will be on the coach?' The child, Denise, knew that she was expected to solve the problem using structural apparatus, in the way that she had been taught to use it. She got out two 'tens' and nine 'units' to represent the 'twenty-nine', and two 'tens' and five 'units' to represent the 'twenty-five'. She carefully counted out ten of the 'units' and exchanged them for a 'ten', as illustrated below. Then she counted the total number of 'tens' and 'units' present, and recorded her answer as shown below.

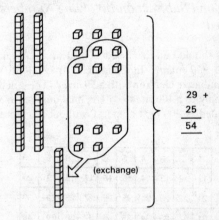

Denise was just about to proceed to her next problem, when I interrupted her. I asked her what she had been asked to do in her problem. Although she was anxious to progress to the next problem, she politely explained to me that she had been required to get out two 'tens' and nine 'units' to correspond to the 'twenty-nine', two 'tens' and five 'units' to correspond to the 'twenty-five', and to manipulate the apparatus and record her result as she had done. I then asked her the question 'How many children will be on the coach?' Denise read the question, closed her eyes, muttered, 'Twenty-nine and twenty-five,' and pondered long and hard. Then she looked at me questioningly. 'Fifty-four?' she asked. 'Yes!' I said. 'And what have you written down here?' With some surprise, she looked at her work. 'Fifty-four.'

Denise's practical activity, so correctly performed, had been quite unrelated in her mind to the original problem. When faced again with that problem, she had found it easier to solve it mentally than to link it with her practical activity. (Her exercise book was full of 'ticks' for her answers to similar problems.) Her written method of solution was concerned with the 'P, S' aspects of the problem, whereas her mental solution was concerned with its 'E, L' aspects. When we ask children to perform calculations, we should encourage them to concentrate on its 'E, L' aspects first. Its 'P, S' aspects should be seen as aids to solve it, rather than as a separate, unrelated problem. We should concentrate on mental calculations before written ones.

1. Addition and Subtraction Involving Numbers up to One Hundred

Addition. This should be introduced as oral work. A valuable aid for such work is a *100 square*. In Chapter 11 (page 108), we described activities to familiarize children with a *50 array*. These activities can be extended to apply to a 100 square. (The final number in a 100 square, 100, can be added as the 'next numeral' without reference to the place value of its digits.)

1	2	3	4	5	6	7	8	9	10
11	12	13	14	15	16	17	18	19	20
21	22	23	24	25	26	27	28	29	30
31	32	33	34	35	36	37	38	39	40
41	42	43	44	45	46	47	48	49	50
51	52	53	54	55	56	57	58	59	60
61	62	63	64	65	66	67	68	69	70
71	72	73	74	75	76	77	78	79	80
81	82	83	84	85	86	87	88	89	90
91	92	93	94	95	96	97	98	99	100

Oral work can be carried out with reference both to a 100 square and to structural apparatus. Consider the problem '42 + 10'. Reference to a 100 square invites the solution by counting ten squares beyond the one labelled '42', or by moving down the 'short cut' from '42' to '52'. Reference to structural apparatus reminds us that 42 means four tens and two units, and that adding 10 gives us five tens and two units. Problems that suitably follow '42 + 10' include '42 + 20', '42 + 30' and so on, '42 + 11', '42 + 12', and so on, '42 + 21', '42 + 22' and so on. Reference to a 100 square to solve '42 + 22' invites the sequential argument: 'Forty-two and twenty is sixty-two; sixty-two and two is sixty-four.' Reference to structural apparatus invites the argument: 'Forty and twenty is sixty; two and two is four; so the answer is sixty-four.' Children should be invited to choose and explain their own methods of calculation.

Subtraction. By now, the two problems '42 = 32 + □' and '42 − 32 = □' should be seen by children as equivalent. Reference to a 100 square gives the answer by seeing that the 'route' from '32' to '42' involves the 'short cut' for adding ten to a number. Reference to structural apparatus invites the solution by taking away three tens and two units from four tens and two units, as illustrated below.

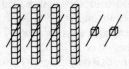

'Harder addition.' This involves cases where the units of the numbers to be added total more than ten, for example in the problem '37 + 25'. Reference to a 100 square invites the sequential argument, 'Thirty-seven and twenty is fifty-seven; fifty-seven and five is sixty-two.' (The latter step might be split into, 'Fifty-seven and three is sixty, and another two is sixty-two.') Reference to structural apparatus encourages adding the tens and units separately: 'Thirty and twenty is fifty, seven and five is twelve; fifty and twelve is sixty-two.'

When using structural apparatus for 'harder addition', children are usually encouraged to exchange ten of the unit pieces for one 'ten' piece, as was illustrated on page 139. Certainly, children who have difficulty in performing such an addition mentally should be told to manipulate the apparatus in this way.

'Harder subtraction.' This involves cases where the units to be subtracted are more than the units present in the original number, for example in the problem '52 − 36 = □', or '52 = 36 + □'. Reference to a

100 square invites the sequential argument, 'Thirty-six and ten is forty-six; fifty-two is six more than forty-six; so fifty-two is sixteen more than thirty-six.' (This is not an easy argument.) Reference to structural apparatus necessitates splitting (or 'decomposing', as it is often called) a 'ten' piece into ten unit pieces in order to take away six units. The process is illustrated below.

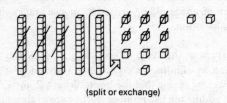

(split or exchange)

Written Recording

After many oral sessions of this nature, children can progress to recording their calculations in symbols. Now they must arrange the numbers involved in tens and units *columns*. This is new, and may be difficult for them. They should be allowed to use 100 squares or structural apparatus for aids if they choose. Those who choose structural apparatus must remember to consider the units of each example before the tens. This involves working from *right to left*, contradicting the rule of left to right which they have learnt in all their previous reading and writing. This may cause further problems. (The Arabs, from whom we derived our numeral system, read and write from right to left, so it was natural for them to invent a system that involves working from right to left in calculations.) Children who use structural apparatus as an aid may find it helpful to put additional numerals in their calculations as shown below.

$$
\begin{array}{r}
37 \\
25 \\
\hline
62 \\
\scriptstyle 1
\end{array} +
\qquad\qquad
\begin{array}{r}
\scriptstyle 4\ 1 \\
5\!\!\!/2 \\
36 \\
\hline
16
\end{array} -
$$

Children should be encouraged to invent stories to correspond to their calculations, such as, 'There were fifty-two flowers in the garden; thirty-six were picked, so there were sixteen flowers left.' Reference to the children's new measuring skills should not be ignored. Their new skills of addition and subtraction could well be taught alongside their measurement work.

2. Building and Learning Multiplication Tables

We saw in Chapter 10 how the table of twos could be built up and used, and in Chapter 11 how children might learn to count in fives. Now we can initiate a systematic approach to multiplication tables and a drive towards committing them to memory. The order in which we choose to present tables is probably linked to the relative appearance of pattern in them. The table of fives, for instance, exhibits an obvious pattern, while the table of sevens has a pattern which is scarcely discernible.

When British measurements were closely allied to the number twelve, (for example, twelve pence in a shilling, twelve inches in a foot), it was felt important for children to learn tables up to the table of twelves. European children, however, do not have to learn tables beyond the table of tens; and now British children need not do so.

The table of fives. Children who have counted along a fifty array in fives will find little difficulty in writing for themselves the table of fives. This table is exceptional in that there is some purpose in continuing it up to 12×5, because of its link with telling the time.

$1 \times 5 = 5$	$5 \times 5 = 25$	$9 \times 5 = 45$
$2 \times 5 = 10$	$6 \times 5 = 30$	$10 \times 5 = 50$
$3 \times 5 = 15$	$7 \times 5 = 35$	$11 \times 5 = 55$
$4 \times 5 = 20$	$8 \times 5 = 40$	$12 \times 5 = 60$

Having written the table, children should read it aloud. They should look for pattern in as many ways as possible – in the tens digits and in the units digits. They may notice that an even number times five is the same as *half* that number times ten; for example, $6 \times 5 = 3 \times 10$. They should try to repeat the table without reading it, and give each other 'spot' quizzes, such as 'Seven fives', 'Four fives', and so on. The table can be linked to their newly acquired skill of telling the time; when the minute hand points to '1', it is *five* past; when it points to '2', it is *ten* past, and so on. Coins of value 5p can be introduced. The table can be referred to in order to solve problems such as, 'If I have six 5p coins, how much money do I have?', or 'If lollipops cost 5p each, how many can I buy with 40p?'

The table of threes. Perhaps the next table to introduce to children is the table of threes. Children can count along a fifty array (or a 100 square) in threes. They will have pleasure in colouring every third numeral along the array and witnessing the pattern formed. They will have little difficulty in writing for themselves the table of threes up to 10×3.

1	2	**3**	4	5	**6**	7	8	**9**	10
11	**12**	13	14	**15**	16	17	**18**	19	20
21	22	23	**24**	25	26	**27**	28	29	**30**
31	32	**33**	34	35	**36**	37	38	**39**	40
41	**42**	43	44	**45**	46	47	**48**	49	50

$1 \times 3 = 3$	$6 \times 3 = 18$
$2 \times 3 = 6$	$7 \times 3 = 21$
$3 \times 3 = 9$	$8 \times 3 = 24$
$4 \times 3 = 12$	$9 \times 3 = 27$
$5 \times 3 = 15$	$10 \times 3 = 30$

Having written the table, children should read it aloud, and then look for pattern in as many ways as possible. Some children will notice that the digits of the right-hand numbers of the table add to 3, 6, 9, 3, 6, 9 and so on. They should try to repeat the table without reading it, and give each other 'spot' quizzes on the table. The table can be referred to in order to solve problems, such as, 'How many wheels are there on five tricycles?', or, 'How many triangles could we build with twelve sticks?'

Games to Assist the Learning of Tables

When children have built up and begun to learn any particular table, they can play several games that will help their learning. A set of twenty cards is needed for each table. We illustrate six of the cards to be made for games involving the table of threes. (The remaining cards cover all the other facts of the table.)

3	1×3	6	2×3	9	3×3
Ɛ	Ɛ×ⵑ	9	Ɛ×ⵖ	6	Ɛ×Ɛ

'*Pelmanism.*' The twenty cards are spread out, face down, on a table. Children take it in turns to overturn two cards. If the two cards denote the same number (for example, 7×3 and 21), they are taken by the child to score a 'pair'. If not, they are turned back. The winner is the child with the most pairs at the end of the game.

'*Snap.*' The cards are dealt out as in a normal game of 'Snap'. Two cards denoting the same number can be 'snapped'. The game of 'Snap' is improved if forty cards are used, twenty from each of two tables. If, for instance, the cards for the tables of threes and sixes are used, any pair from the cards '12', '4×3' and '2×6' can be snapped.

'*Tables Rummy*' (for two or three players). Each child is dealt five cards. The rest of the cards are put face down in a pile, and the top card is overturned and revealed beside the pile. Children take it in turns to take either the revealed card or the top unrevealed card from the pile, make as many pairs as they can from their hands and display them, and finally discard a card on top of the revealed card. The winner is the first child to get rid of all his cards. Like 'Snap', this game is improved if two sets of tables cards are used.

'*Number Spiders*.' After several tables have been learnt, a number can be written on the blackboard for the body of the spider. Children volunteer number combinations for the 'legs' that involve some knowledge of tables. Here is an example.

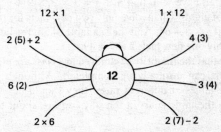

The learning of tables is a long process, which will be spread over the period of a year or more. The order in which tables are presented to children will probably be chosen on the basis of the amount of pattern that is discernible, and the consequent ease of learning. Each table has some pattern to be discovered in the digits of its 'right hand' numbers, and each can be demonstrated as a pattern on a 100 square. As each table is completed, it can be included on a *table chart*, which can be used for reference. We give an example of how a table chart might appear before all the tables have been completed.

1	2	3	4	5	6	7	8	9	10
2	4	6	8	10	12	14	16	18	20
3	6	9	12	15	18	21	24	27	30
4	8	12	16	20	24	28	32	36	40
5	10	15	20	25	30	35	40	45	50
6	12	18	24	30	36	42	48	54	60
7									
8									
9	18	27	36	45	54	63	72	81	90
10	20	30	40	50	60	70	80	90	100

The chart can be used as a check when the tables games are being played. To check, for instance, that $5 \times 3 = 15$, we locate '5' in the top row and run our finger down the column until it is in the row that begins with '3'. We notice that '15' also appears as the result for 3×5. The chart in fact is symmetrical about the diagonal that reads '1, 4, 9' and so on, reminding us that multiplication is *commutative*. The commutative property of multiplication is readily accepted by children, especially if it is illustrated by pictures. The diagram below can be seen as eight sets of three or as three sets of eight, illustrating that $8 \times 3 = 3 \times 8$.

```
0 0 0 0 0 0 0 0
0 0 0 0 0 0 0 0
0 0 0 0 0 0 0 0
```

When children have seen that $8 \times 3 = 3 \times 8$, $8 \times 4 = 4 \times 8$ and so on, the table of eights will involve only two new facts for them to learn: $7 \times 8 = 56$ and $8 \times 8 = 64$. And the last table of all, the table of sevens, will involve only one new fact: $7 \times 7 = 49$.

By the time that the majority of children in a class are eight years old, the table chart can normally be completed. Although children will memorize the tables at different rates, they should be able to understand and use the table chart in the ways we are about to describe in section 3.

3. Squares, Multiples, Factors and Primes

The completed table chart can be used as a starting-point in introducing children to the terms listed in the title of this section. Using the chart will, incidentally, help children to memorize the tables.

Square Numbers

The numbers in the diagonal of the table chart, 1, 4, 9, 16 and so on, can be seen to arise from the multiplications 1×1, 2×2, 3×3 and so on. We

```
o      o o      o o o      o o o o
       o o      o o o      o o o o
                o o o      o o o o
                           o o o o
```

Some square numbers

can tell children that such numbers are called *square* numbers, because they can be represented by objects arranged in squares.

At this point, children can be introduced to an interesting pattern, by the following exercise.

Complete these additions:

$$1 + 3 =$$
$$1 + 3 + 5 =$$
$$1 + 3 + 5 + 7 =$$
$$1 + 3 + 5 + 7 + 9 =$$

Write down the number sentence that might come next.
Write down the number sentence that might come after that one.
What kind of numbers are your answers?

The reader will notice the reappearance of the pattern that first appeared in this book on page 14.

Multiples

Because $24 = 8 \times 3$, we say that 24 is a *multiple* of 3. In fact, all the numbers in the third row of the table chart are multiples of 3. Children can do 'detective work' on multiples, using the table chart to help them: 'Find a multiple of 3 that is also a multiple of 5. How many numbers can you find that are multiples of 3 and 4? Is every multiple of 4 also a multiple of 2? Why? Is every multiple of 10 also a multiple of 5? And of 2?'

Referring still to the table chart, we can play 'Spot the Number'. Children may ask whether the secret number is a multiple of other numbers. Here is an example of how a game might proceed:

'My secret number is a multiple of 5, and it is less than 50.'
'Is it a multiple of 2?'   'No.'
'Is it a multiple of 3?'   'No.'
'Is it a multiple of 7?'   'Yes.'
This is sufficient to reveal the secret number.

Factors

Because $24 = 8 \times 3$, we say that 24 is a multiple of 3 and that 3 is a *factor* of 24. *All* the numbers in the third row of the table chart have 3 as a factor. Children can do 'detective work' on factors, using the table chart to help them: 'Find a number that is a factor of 24. How many numbers can you find that are factors of 24 and factors of 16? Can you find a number that is a factor of 27 and a factor of 3? (Possible answers are '3' or '1'.) Can you find a number that is a factor of 9 and a factor of 16?' (The only such number is 1.)

We can again play 'Spot the Number', this time allowing only questions about factors. Here is an example:

> 'My secret number is a factor of 24, and it is not 1.'
> 'Is it a factor of 8?'   'No.'
> 'Is it a factor of 9?'   'Yes.'
> This is sufficient to reveal the secret number.

Prime Numbers

Prime numbers have no factors other than themselves and 1. The table chart shows that the numbers 2, 5 and 7 are prime, because they are each found only in the first row and column of the chart. Children can be invited to find numbers that are absent from the chart. They might pick 11, 13 or 17, which are prime. However, absence from the chart does not guarantee that a number is prime. The number 55, for instance, does not appear on the chart, but it is not prime. Most children should not venture far at this stage in their search for prime numbers, although it might be a very suitable challenge for gifted children to do so.

4. Using Multiplication Tables

In section 2, we mentioned the importance of using tables to solve problems. In such problems, we need to refer to objects that occur naturally in sets of two, sets of three and so on. We give some examples:

Sets of two: shoes, gloves, wings, bicycle wheels, half pennies in pence.
Sets of three: triangle sides, tricycle wheels, clover leaves.
Sets of four: table legs, car wheels, animals' legs, sections of Kit-Kat.
Sets of five: fingers, legs of starfish, pentagon sides, pence in 5p pieces.
Sets of six: eggs in boxes, hexagon sides, faces of cubes, legs of insects.
Sets of seven: sides of 50p and 20p pieces, days in weeks, shirt buttons.
Sets of eight: spiders' legs, octagon sides, segments in chocolate bars.
Sets of nine: shirt buttons, squares on faces of Rubik cubes.
Sets of ten: fingers, pence in 10p pieces.

Problems might include: 'How many half pence are worth the same as 8p?' 'How many wheels are there on four tricycles?' 'How many boxes are needed for thirty eggs?' 'How many weeks are there in twenty-eight days?'

5. Multiplication and Division beyond the Tables

Children who have mastered a table, such as the table of fives, can be challenged to find out a multiplication that involves more than ten fives. Consider the problem, for instance, of finding the value of fourteen 5p coins. We know that ten 5p coins are worth 50p, and four 5p coins are worth 20p; we can deduce that fourteen 5p coins are worth 70p. The number sentence $14(5) = 10(5) + 4(5)$ illustrates the *distributive property of multiplication over addition*. These complicated-sounding words name a property that is readily accepted as obvious by children, especially if it is illustrated by a picture. The picture below can be used to illustrate that 14 fives are not only 10 fives and 4 fives, but also 9 fives and 5 fives, or 8 fives and 6 fives. Each of these *distributions* of 14 fives illustrates the distributive property.

Calculations that children are asked to perform at this stage should involve only multiplications whose answers are less than 100. Their calculations might be recorded in symbols in the following way.

Find 14×5 in two ways.

10 fives = 50	$8 \times 5 = 40$
4 fives = 20	$6 \times 5 = 30$
14 fives = 70	$14 \times 5 = 70$

Problems involving equal grouping can also involve multiplication facts beyond the tables. Consider the problem of finding how many sets of four cards can be made from fifty-two cards. Knowing that ten fours are 40 tells us that forty of the cards can be made into ten sets of four. Twelve cards remain, and they can be made into three sets of four cards, because three fours are 12. Calculations like this might be limited to oral work. But the calculation above could be recorded in symbols in the following way:

$$
\begin{array}{r}
52 \\
-40 \\
\hline
12 \\
-12 \\
\hline
0
\end{array}
\qquad
\begin{array}{l}
40 = 10 \text{ fours} \\[2ex]
12 = \ \ 3 \text{ fours} \\
\hline
52 = 13 \text{ fours}
\end{array}
$$

The recording above may look rather elaborate. But it is very much easier for children to understand than the conventional way of recording that they will learn later:

$$
4 \overline{)52}^{\,13}
$$

Equipment Needed for the Activities in This Chapter

Structural apparatus for tens and units.
Plenty of 100 squares, written on duplicated sheets, or bought commercially.
Squared paper for making table charts.

Suggestions for the Reader

1. (Addition and subtraction) Ask some seven-and-a-half-year-olds to try to perform the following calculations mentally: (a) 32 + 46; (b) 29 + 25; (c) 53 − 21; (d) 53 − 27. Ask those who succeed to explain how they worked out the answers. Then ask the children to perform each calculation by writing it in symbols as they have been taught. Can they explain their written calculations?

2. (Tables) Ask the same children which tables they have learnt. Give them some spot quizzes and some problems involving the tables that they have learnt. Then ask them to work out a multiplication beyond the tables that they have learnt, such as 13 × 5. Ask those who succeed to explain how they performed the calculation.

3. (Tables) Pretend that you know all the tables except the table of sevens. Think out *three* ways in which you might work out 7 × 7, using the tables that you know. Identify each time you use the commutative property of multiplication and each time you use the distributive property.

4. (Tables) From the table chart displayed on page 145, it might appear that there are 100 table facts to be memorized by children. If, however, children know the commutative property of multiplication, the number of facts to be memorized is considerably reduced. Bearing in mind that the table of ones is obvious and that the table of tens merely reminds us of the meanings of the numbers 20, 30 and so on, count the total number of table facts that actually have to be committed to memory.

5. (Square numbers) The number 9 can be represented by objects arranged in a square, as illustrated below. The square is partitioned to illustrate one of the incomplete number sentences on page 147. Extend the picture to four by four and five by five squares and use the extended picture to explain the number pattern obtained on page 147.

6. (Multiples, factors and primes) On a 100 square, cross out all the multiples of 2 except 2. Cross out all the multiples of 3 except 3. Cross out all the multiples of 5 except 5, and all the multiples of 7 except 7. What sort of numbers remain? Can you explain what you have found?

15 *Fractions – First Steps*

What can you say to draw a third more opulent than your
sisters?

– Shakespeare (King Lear)

Fractions are a well-identified area of difficulty for many children and
even for some adults. There seem to be two main obstacles to understanding fractions. The first is that fractions cannot be thought of as
separate, independent entities. They have meaning only in relation to
the *whole* to which they apply. To recognize a fraction of something, you
need a concept of the *whole* something. It is relatively easy to imagine
the whole apple of which you have a quarter; but it is not easy to imagine
the whole kilogram of which you have a quarter, or the whole hour of
which a quarter has passed.

The second obstacle to understanding is the complicated notation by
which fractions are symbolized. The numeral at the bottom of a fraction
(the denominator) has an entirely different function from the numeral at
the top (the numerator). The denominator of the fraction $\frac{2}{3}$ tells us that
the 'whole' has been divided into three equal shares. The numerator
tells us that two of those shares are under consideration. The word
denominator means 'the thing that names'. The denominator of the
fraction $\frac{2}{3}$ gives the fraction its name: 'third'. The word *numerator* means
'the thing that numbers'. The numerator of the fraction $\frac{2}{3}$ tells us the
number of thirds to be considered. The *numerator–denominator* notation for fractions also makes it possible to denote the *same* fraction in
infinitely many ways; for example $\frac{2}{3}$ is the same as $\frac{4}{6}$, $\frac{10}{15}$, $\frac{14}{21}$ and so on.
This idea takes a long time to sink in, and can prove another obstacle to
understanding.

To overcome the first obstacle, we should always in the early stages
refer to the *whole* to which any fraction applies. We should not talk
about a *quarter*, but about a quarter *of an apple*, a quarter of *a metre*, or a
quarter of *twelve*, and so on. To overcome the second obstacle, we
should avoid using the notation for fractions until children's concepts
are well formed. An exception can be made for the symbol $\frac{1}{2}$, which is
widely used on coins, stamps and shoes. Children can learn to read it as
'a half' without having any particular explanation of why the symbol is

made up of a '1' and a '2'. In this chapter we shall describe activities suitable for developing the concepts of fractions, leaving the discussion of notation until Chapter 18.

1. *Fraction Names and Equal Sharing*

In Chapter 10, we saw how equal sharing can lead naturally to fraction concepts. When we share a number of biscuits equally between four people, each person gets a quarter of the biscuits. We can also use fraction names to describe equal shares of shapes, such as are obtained in work on symmetry and tessellation (see pages 116 and 119). Children need systematic practice in expressing equal sharing in terms of fraction names, either as oral or as written work. We give some examples:

When we share biscuits equally between four people, each person gets | a quarter | of the biscuits.

When we share a chocolate bar equally between six people, each person gets | a sixth | of the chocolate.

When we share a square into eight equal parts, each part is | an eighth | of the square.

Find *a fifth* of 20 sweets.

$20 = 5 \times 4$
So a fifth of 20 sweets is 4 sweets.

Find *a third* of 12 centimetres.

$12 = 3 \times 4$.
So a third of 12 cm is 4 cm.

2. *Fractions and Shapes*

We have already shown how symmetry can lead to fraction concepts. An axis of symmetry divides a shape into two halves. If a shape has exactly two axes of symmetry, those axes divide the shape into four quarters. If it has exactly three axes, they divide the shape into six sixths. Children can be invited to colour their symmetrical shapes with several colours, and describe their colouring in terms of fractions of the whole shape. We give an example.

2 eighths of the square are red
2 eighths of the square are blue
4 eighths of the square are white
There are 8 eighths altogether

Notice that in this instance we have used *numerals* to denote the number of eighths of the square in each case. These numerals are the numerators of the fractions concerned. Numerators of fractions are counting numbers. Two eighths and two more eighths are four eighths. Later, children will write $\frac{2}{8} + \frac{2}{8} = \frac{4}{8}$. The numerators, 2 and 2, add to 4; but the denominators must *not* be added when we add the fractions. Denominators are *not* counting numbers.

In activities involving tessellation, or area, we again have the opportunity for colouring parts of the whole shape and describing the colouring in terms of fractions of the whole shape. We give an example.

3 ninths of the triangle are red
6 ninths of the triangle are white
There are 9 ninths altogether

Colouring fractions of shapes might give children their first notions that the same fraction can be named in more than one way. The child who coloured the square, for instance, may well see that one quarter of the square is red, and one half of the square is white. The child who coloured the triangle might have written 'one third of the triangle is red', because he sees that 3 is a third of 9.

3. Fractions and Length

A simple way to link fractions with length is to take a paper ribbon and fold it end to end. The fold clearly divides the ribbon into halves. If we fold the folded paper again end to end, we have divided it into quarters; and if we repeat the process once more, we have divided the ribbon into eighths.

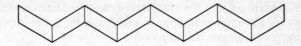

If the ribbon was originally 16 cm long, we have a ready-made link with manageable number work; a half of 16 cm is 8 cm, a quarter of 16 cm is 4 cm and an eighth of 16 cm is 2 cm.

Children can use number work to find other fractions of lengths, as the following examples illustrate:

Find 1 sixth of 12 cm.
   $12 = 6 \times 2$.
So 1 sixth of 12 cm is 2 cm.

Find 2 fifths of 10 cm.
   $10 = 5 \times 2$.
So 1 fifth of 10 cm is 2 cm.
So 2 fifths of 10 cm are 4 cm.

Metres. In Chapter 13, we described how a metre ruler could be used by children to measure lengths in centimetres. At that stage, the ruler was thought of by the children as measuring 100 cm. The word 'metre' was not necessarily used in their measuring. Now we can tell children that the ruler is 1 metre long. Children might use several metre rulers to measure some lengths in metres. They might discover, for instance, that the door is about 2 metres tall, or that the classroom is 6 metres wide and 8 metres long.

We now have an opportunity to introduce *tenths* of a metre. Using the 10 cm card strips that were made for length measurement (see page 126) children can discover that ten of them match the metre ruler for length, so that each must be a tenth of a metre long. They can now measure the lengths of some objects in tenths of a metre, using the strips. They may find, for instance, that four strips match the width of a cupboard, so the cupboard is four tenths of a metre wide. Some commercially made metre rulers are marked on the reverse side with coloured portions that are a tenth of a metre long. These are useful for measuring in tenths of a metre. With such a ruler, children can measure heights of tables and chairs. (It would be rather awkward to use the strips for measuring heights.)

Mixed fractions. Teachers are normally wary of introducing mixed fractions at an early stage of work on fractions. But if children find that an object is as long as 1 metre and 2 tenths of a metre, they should not find it difficult to say so. They *would* have difficulty in understanding the symbols $1\frac{2}{10}$ metres as recording the length; it is the notation that we must postpone for them, not the concept.

4. Fractions and Capacity

In Chapter 13 (page 130) we introduced cartons and flasks that will hold ten cartons. We can now tell children that each flask holds a *litre* of water. Since ten of the cartons fill a flask, they can deduce that a carton must hold a *tenth* of a litre of water. Children can now record their capacity measurements in tenths of a litre; a container that will fill three cartons must hold three tenths of a litre. Children who have calibrated the flasks in 'cartons' will see that the flasks are calibrated in tenths of a litre. They can use their calibrated flasks to measure capacity in tenths of litres. (They might be encouraged to estimate capacities before measuring them.)

Children can obtain half a litre by sharing a litre of water equally (by eye) between two congruent containers. They can check that each half litre will fill five cartons, or fill a calibrated flask up to the five tenths calibration.

I think the saucepan holds about two litres of water

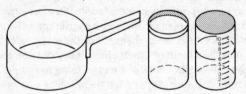

The saucepan holds 1 and 6 tenths litres of water

There is half a litre of water in each bottle

5. *Fractions and Weight*

In Chapter 13 we described how children could continue to use plasticine balls as units of weight, together with kilogram weights, each of which balances ten balls. We can now tell children that the large weights are called *kilograms*. Since ten balls balance a kilogram weight, they can deduce that each ball weighs a *tenth* of a kilogram. Children can now be asked to estimate and record their weight measurements in tenths of a kilogram. They might be allowed to abbreviate the word 'kilogram' in the customary way to 'kg'. We give an example of how their work might be recorded.

	Estimate	*Weight*	*Difference*
Jug of cornflakes	8 tenths kg	4 tenths kg	4 tenths kg
Jug of pebbles	2 kg	2 and 2 tenths kg	2 tenths kg

Children should estimate weights by holding objects in their hands. Their estimates will probably be quite far out initially, but they will improve with experience. Estimating weight is not as easy as estimating length. Children could obtain half of a kg by weighing out a kg of sand, then dividing that sand carefully between the two balance pans until they balance. They could check that each half kg of sand balances five tenths of a kg.

6. *Fractions and Time*

Half Minutes

In Chapter 13 we described how children can use a stop clock to measure time in seconds. The second hand takes sixty seconds to move right round the clock, and children were told that this time is called a *minute*. We can now introduce children to *half* a minute. We start the clock and let it run for thirty seconds, stopping it when the second hand points to 30. We give children some duplicated sheets of pictures of a stop-clock face. We ask them to draw on one picture lines to represent the two positions of the hand before and after the thirty-second interval, and to colour the part of the clock face which the hand has covered during its journey, as illustrated below. We point out to them that they have coloured exactly *half* of the clock face, showing that the hand has moved *half-way* round the clock.

How many more seconds must pass before the hand again points to 60? By counting the intervals between 30 and 60 on the picture of the clock face, children can find that the answer is thirty. Because 30 + 30 = 60, or 2 × 30 = 60, we can say that thirty is a half of sixty; so thirty seconds are *half a minute*.

Now we can generalize the idea that the hand moves half-way round the clock in half a minute. We start the clock and stop it when the second hand points to 10. We ask the children to draw a line on one of their clock-face pictures to represent its position. We ask them to guess where the hand will point after the clock has gone on for another half a minute. Bright children may work out the answer by counting thirty beyond ten, or by imagining the clock face divided into halves by a line through the numeral 10. Other children may merely make a random guess. We must let the clock tick on for another thirty seconds and then stop it. The second hand points to 40. Children can now draw the position of the hand on their picture, and colour the part of the clock face which the hand has covered during its journey, as illustrated below. Their picture illustrates that the hand has again moved half-way round the clock. They can check that after another thirty seconds the hand will again point to 10.

This activity is good preparation for predicting time intervals of half an hour from a conventional clock face. It is easier for children to understand the movement of a stop clock than a conventional clock, because the second hand can be seen moving, and because predictions can be checked in a suitably short time. The activity can be followed by exercises in drawing further pictures to help predict where the hand will point half a minute after pointing to various numerals, such as 20, 25, 35 and so on. When children have completed a sheet of exercises, they should be allowed to check one of their answers by using the stop clock.

Quarter Minutes

Quarter minutes can be introduced in a similar way to half minutes. We start the clock and let it run for fifteen seconds. The drawing of the two positions of the hand and the colouring will illustrate that the hand has moved a quarter of the way round the clock. Because $15 + 15 + 15 + 15 = 60$, or $4 \times 15 = 60$, we can say that fifteen is a *quarter* of sixty; so fifteen seconds are a quarter of a minute. Exercises in drawing pictures will help to consolidate children's concept of a quarter of a minute, and will prepare the ground for their future understanding of quarter hours.

Hours and Half Hours

In Chapter 13 we described how children can learn to tell the time in forms such as 'Two o'clock', 'Ten minutes past two', 'Forty minutes past two' and so on. They have learnt that the minute hand of a conventional clock records the number of minutes that pass, and that sixty minutes after two o'clock the minute hand will again point to the numeral 12. We can now introduce children to the concept of an *hour*. We have not yet deliberately focused attention on the movement of the little hand of the clock. We can now ask children to watch this hand as we move the minute hand manually from two o'clock to three o'clock. They will notice that the little hand has moved from the numeral 2 to the numeral 3. We tell children that the little hand is called an *hour* hand; it tells us that one hour has passed between the times two o'clock and three o'clock. What will it tell us after another hour has passed after three o'clock? Where will it point two hours after three o'clock? How many minutes last as long as an hour? Sixty minutes seems a very long time to children – probably too long to be related to any activity that they do. They are more likely to be able to form a concept of the duration of half an hour, when that is introduced.

To introduce children to half an hour, we can put the clock back to saying two o'clock, and ask children to predict where the minute hand will point when it is half-way round the clock. It will point to the numeral 6, and it will take thirty minutes to reach this position, because thirty is a half of sixty. We ask them to predict where the hour hand will point when the minute hand has gone half-way round the clock. It will point half-way between the numerals 2 and 3, because it will be half-way on its journey between these numerals. We slowly move the minute hand manually until it points to the numeral 6, and check that the hour hand has moved as was predicted. Both hands are half-way on their journey between recording two o'clock and three o'clock, and we say that *half an hour* has passed since two o'clock. The time recorded on the clock can be read either as *thirty minutes past two*, as they have already learnt, or as *half past two* (meaning *half an hour* past two). We can relate the duration of half an hour to the duration of a meal, or a favourite TV programme, such as *Blue Peter*.

Some mental calculations are now appropriate to relate the new concepts of an hour and half an hour to telling the time. If the time is three o'clock, what time will it be after half an hour? After one hour? After two hours? After an hour and a half? If it is half past four, what time will it be after half an hour? After one hour? After one hour and a half? If it is ten past five, what time will it be after half an hour? An hour? Each prediction should be checked by moving the hands of the clock manually through the appropriate number of minutes. Children can time some class activity, such as a lesson or a craft session, that is expected to last half an hour.

Quarter Hours

After introducing half hours, we can introduce quarter hours in a similar way, moving the minute hand a quarter of its way round the clock. The duration of a quarter of an hour can be linked to the time taken for some familiar activities, such as walking to school, having a bath, or watching *Jackanory* on TV. Children should have practice in predicting what the time will be a quarter of an hour after certain times. They should be allowed to move the hands of clocks themselves in order to check the predictions that they make.

Musical Notation

Musical rhythm is not usually considered as part of a mathematics syllabus. However, there are more mathematical concepts to be found here than in the order and duration of calendar months, which are normally considered as part of children's mathematical education.

The duration of a musical note is specified by its name: crotchet, quaver, semiquaver and so on. A quaver lasts half as long as a crotchet, and a semiquaver lasts half as long as a quaver. The symbols for these durations are as follows:

a crotchet

two quavers (lasting as long as one crotchet)

four semiquavers (lasting as long as one crotchet)

A piece of music has an underlying *metre*, or steady 'beat' of time. A piece whose metre is $\frac{4}{4}$ will have four crotchet 'beats' in each bar. This means that the notes in each bar must last as long as four crotchets would. If you set a metronome or a stop clock to tick seconds, you can pretend that these are the crotchets of a tune in $\frac{4}{4}$ metre, and tap the following rhythms. (Children might learn to play them on percussion instruments.)

metre
first rhythm
second rhythm

Do you agree that time concepts and fraction concepts are very much involved in musical rhythms?

7. Measurement and Cookery

In cookery, many measurement skills are called into play: one must measure weight, capacity, length, time, and even temperature. We have not yet considered how to teach children to understand temperature, but all the other measuring skills mentioned can be brought into play when children are invited to make rock buns to the following recipe:

Measure out:
2 tenths kg self-raising flour
1 tenth kg sugar
1 tenth kg margarine
1 tenth kg currants
1 tenth litre milk

Rub the margarine and flour together, using fingers. With a spoon, stir in the sugar and currants. Then add milk gradually, stirring it in, until a soft dough is formed. (The whole of the milk may not be needed.) Share the dough into twelve rough shapes, about 2 cm high, and place the shapes on a baking sheet which has been greased. The cakes should be baked in a hot oven (230°C or 450°F) for a quarter of an hour.

Equipment Needed for the Activities in This Chapter

Counters, objects and 'sharing boxes' as mentioned in Chapter 10.
Cut-out shapes with axes of symmetry.
Tessellation patterns.
Paper ribbons for folding into various fractions of their length.
Rulers.
Metre rulers calibrated in tenths of a metre.
Litre flasks calibrated in tenths (by children).
Cartons that hold a tenth of a litre.
Bottles or other containers.
Kilogram weights.
Weights of one tenth of a kg (e.g. plasticine balls).
A stop clock.
Duplicated sheets of pictures of stop-clock faces.
A conventional clock in working order.
Other clocks whose hands are in working order.
Simple musical scores, preferably for percussion instruments.
Cooking ingredients and an oven.

Suggestions for the Reader

1. (Fractions and equal sharing) Test some eight-year-olds on their concepts of fractions as equal shares of numbers. Ask them what fraction of a bag of sweets will be had by each child if it is shared between (a) two children, (b) four children, (c) six children, (d) eight children.

2. (Fractions and shape) Test the same children on their concepts of fractions as equal shares of shapes. Prepare some symmetrical shapes, and ask the children to fold appropriate ones into (a) halves, (b) quarters, (c) eighths, (d) sixths. Test their fraction concepts similarly with tessellation patterns.

3. (Fractions and length) Prepare some paper ribbons that are 12 cm and 20 cm long. Ask the children to measure each ribbon, and to predict, for the appropriate ribbon: (a) how long a half of the ribbon will be, (b) how long a quarter of the ribbon will be, (c) how long a third of the ribbon will be, and (d) how long a fifth of the ribbon will be.

4. (Fractions and capacity) Find out which physical units of capacity are familiar to the children. Ask them how they might obtain an amount that is *half* that of the physical unit. Test also their ability to estimate capacities in terms of the physical units that they are using.

5. (Fractions and weight) Find out what physical units of weight are familiar to the children. Ask them how they might obtain a weight that is *half* the weight of one of those physical units. Test also their ability to estimate weights in terms of the physical units that they are using.

6. (Fractions and time) Set a clock at *half past two* and ask the children to tell you what time the clock says. Ask them why we call that time *half past* two. Ask them what time it will say after (a) half an hour, (b) an hour. Ask them to think of something they do that lasts about half an hour.

16 Graphs

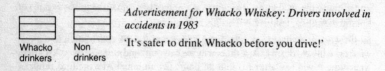

A graph is a drawing showing the relation between two or more
numerical quantities. In Chapters 3 and 4, we described how children
can make and read very simple block graphs depicting the relation
between two quantities, such as the numbers of boys and girls at a table.
Many of the illustrations that have appeared so far in this book could be
considered as block graphs. We shall describe how children's experience
of graphs can develop from this early pictorial representation.

1. Block Graphs

From the age of five, children can usefully make block graphs to
illustrate their discoveries in many areas, such as nature findings,
scientific observations, class surveys, measuring, traffic surveys and so
on. The number of categories, limited to two for their earliest graphs,
can gradually be increased as occasion demands. The total number of
statistics graphed, limited to fewer than ten for their early graphs, can be
increased as children's number familiarity increases. The 'Pets' graph
that follows here involves six categories and thirty-six statistics
altogether. In gathering the information for this graph, children will
need to make a 'tally' of the relevant pets belonging to children in the
class. They can be taught to make their tallies in fives, the fifth tally being
a line that crosses the four previous tallies. The tallies can then be
counted in fives when the graph is being constructed.

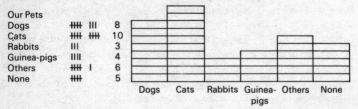

Our Pets		
Dogs	ﬀﬀﬀ III	8
Cats	ﬀﬀﬀ ﬀﬀﬀ	10
Rabbits	III	3
Guinea-pigs	IIII	4
Others	ﬀﬀﬀ I	6
None	ﬀﬀﬀ	5

The graph can be made with matchboxes, picture cards, or coloured rectangles on squared paper. Each column should be built from the bottom upwards. When the graph is completed, children should discuss the information that it portrays. How many dogs are owned by children in the class? Which is the most common pet? How many children have no pets? How many more dogs are owned than rabbits? How many pets are owned by the class altogether? Why are there more rectangles in the graph than there are children in the class? (This indicates that some children have more than one pet.) These questions will be of interest to the children, provided that the graph was originally motivated by a general interest in pets.

Other subjects that might motivate block graphs include the following:

Our favourite TV programmes (categories *Top Cat*, *Blue Peter* etc).
Our birthday months (categories *January*, *February* etc.).
The weather on days in May (categories *sunny*, *rainy*, *cloudy*, *mixed*).
Vehicles passing school at break time (categories *lorries*, *cars* etc.).
Vowels on a page of a book (categories *a*, *e*, *i*, *o*, *u*).
Measurements.

We give an example of a graph of measurements: 'My Weighing'.

Object	Weight
Jug of cornflakes	4 balls
Jug of sand	14 balls
Jug of pebbles	21 balls
Jug of water	9 balls

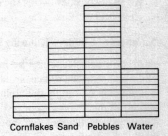

Cornflakes Sand Pebbles Water

Block Graphs Whose Shape is Significant

For the block graphs mentioned so far, the order in which the categories are placed is irrelevant. For the 'Pets' graph, for instance, it is of no significance that the category 'Rabbits' is listed before 'Guinea-pigs'. However, for some block graphs there is a definite logical order in which to place the categories. Suppose, for example, we wish to make a graph depicting the numbers of children in each of our families, and we find the following information:

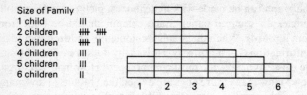

Size of Family	
1 child	III
2 children	‖‖ ‖‖
3 children	‖‖ II
4 children	III
5 children	III
6 children	II

The logical order in which to place the categories is *1 child, 2 children, 3 children* and so on. For such a graph, the resulting shape is significant, and attention can be drawn to it. (This one has a peak at *2 children* and it tails off to the right of this column; most 'Family size' graphs will have an overall shape somewhat similar to this one.) Eight-year-old children can make other block graphs whose overall shape can be interpreted. Examples include:

Shoe sizes of children.
Multiplication tables known by children.
Heights of children (to nearest 5 cm).
Numbers of goals scored in a set of football matches.
Scores from tossing two dice simultaneously.

We shall consider two of these examples in detail.

Numbers of Children Knowing Multiplication Tables

A graph of this type can be made at any time during a period when children are trying to master table learning. The criterion for 'knowing' a table may be simply the ability to recite it, or it may be the ability to score full marks on a 'spot test'. In either case, the number of children knowing a particular table should increase over a short period of time, such as a school term. Children might make one graph at the beginning of a term, and another at the end, to record their general progress. The order of the categories (tables) for the graph will be the order in which the tables are presented for learning by the teacher. We give hypothetical examples.

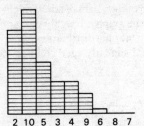

Tables that we know (September)

2 10 5 3 4 9 6 8 7

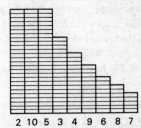

Tables that we know (December)

2 10 5 3 4 9 6 8 7

These graphs are bound to have a shape somewhat similar to a 'Family size' graph. They will taper off to the right, provided that the order of table learning is almost the same for each child. Perusal of the two graphs will indicate to children that the tables of two, ten and five are easier to learn than the subsequent tables, and that progress has been made during the term. Each child's achievement has contributed to the graphs, but the absence of names means that no child is exhibited as a slow learner. The graph records class achievement rather than individual achievement.

Shoe Sizes of Children

Most children of eight know their shoe size. However, since shoe size is related to length of foot, it is easy to find out the size taken by an individual whose shoes are not marked with a size. Children can contribute to a tally of shoe sizes that might appear similar to the following.

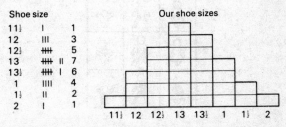

Shoe size		
11½	I	1
12	III	3
12½	₥	5
13	₥ II	7
13½	₥ I	6
1	IIII	4
1½	II	2
2	I	1

Our shoe sizes

11½ 12 12½ 13 13½ 1 1½ 2

Children could discuss the shape of this graph, noting that it is somewhat symmetrical in shape, looking like a hill with its peak near the middle. It shows that most children take a shoe size near the middle of the range of sizes, and that the further away from the middle a certain size is, the fewer children take that size. They can discuss whether the graph of shoe sizes of another class of children could be expected to have a similar shape, and whether the graph of shoe sizes of adults might have a similar shape. (In fact, the shape of the graph is roughly similar to the graph that is called in statistical terms a 'normal distribution'. Graphs of the heights, weights or IQs of a class of similarly aged children can be expected to have roughly this shape.)

2. Regions on a Grid

A grid is a network of squares arranged in columns and rows. The drawings of number arrays, such as the 50 array and the 100 square, have been presented in grids, and children's work with the arrays has drawn their attention to their columns and rows. We now wish to focus attention on grids themselves, and to teach children to assign 'addresses' to the squares of a grid, as we do when we are reading a map. Besides being a suitable preparation for map reading, this work is valuable preparation for later graphical work using coordinates. Maps vary in the systems used to label their regions in squares. Some label rows and columns by letters, some by numbers. Some label rows from top to bottom, some from bottom to top. With graphical work in mind, we shall choose a system of labelling that labels rows from bottom to top, and to distinguish clearly the column labels from the row labels, we shall label columns by letters and rows by numerals. The grid below is labelled in this way.

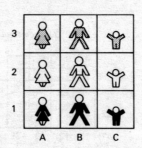

We might introduce the labelling by presenting children with a collection of pictures arranged in the grid, as shown. They have been sorted for two criteria, family role and colour. We can ask children to point to all the mothers. They are all in the column labelled A. We similarly identify the other columns by the fathers or babies that are in them.

Next, we look at the rows. All the Grey family are in the row labelled 1. The White family are in row 2, and the Black family are in row 3. Now we remove six of the pictures, leaving just one picture in each row and column. We might leave the three pictures illustrated below. We invite children to replace the pictures that have been removed. Where must we put Mrs White? She must go in column A, which contains the mothers, and in row 2, which contains the whites. Her home 'address' is A2. As each picture is replaced in its home square, we give that square its address, saying the letter of its column followed by the numeral of its row. (This is the conventional order used when giving the address of a region.)

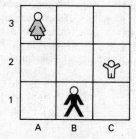

After all the pictures have been replaced in their home squares and these squares have been named as A2, B2, B3 and so on, the game can be replayed, giving the pictures different home squares. This game might be followed by a game of 'Blackboard Noughts and Crosses'. In this game, children must name the squares in which they wish their symbols to be drawn, and the teacher (or another child) draws them.

The games can be followed by written work using duplicated sheets of grids. We give some examples.

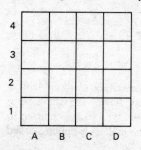

Colour column A of your grid red.
Colour row 2 of your grid yellow.
Write down the colours of these squares:
A4, B2, C3, A2.

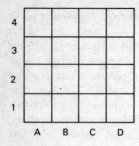

Play this game with a friend. This grid is a map of the sea. You have six ships. Draw your ships on six squares of your grid so that they cover a rectangle.

Your friend must try to find your ships without looking at your grid. Let him or her name a square of your grid. You mark that square, and tell him or her if one of your ships has been found. How many squares must your friend name before finding all your ships?

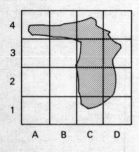

'*Secret Island.*' This is a map of Secret Island. Answer this question, and tell John and Tim what to do:

'Help! I am stuck in B2. Will you rescue me by car or by boat?'

John is in C1. He wants to walk to B4. Tell him what squares to go through on his walk.

Tim is also in C1. He wants to take his boat to B4. Tell him what squares to go through with his boat.

A game using a larger grid is 'Make the Picture'. For this, we need a drawing that is simple and that can be reproduced mainly by filling in squares. (A knitting pattern can provide an idea for such a picture.) Children are instructed to fill in certain squares. We give an example.

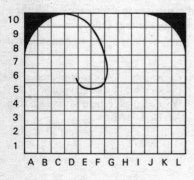

Use a pencil to shade squares, A1, B1, B2, B3, B4, B7, C1, C2, C3, C4, F1, F2, G1, G2, H1, H2, I1, I2, J1, J2.

Another activity that proves popular with children is making coded messages. We arrange the letters of the alphabet in a grid similar to the following. Children can send each other coded messages such as this: C4 A4 G3 D1 A2 G2 C4 A2 F3 E4 F2 A2 F3 D1 B2 A4 D2 F2 D1 G1

4	a	b	c	d	e	f	g
3	h	i	j	k	l	m	n
2	o	p	q	r	s	t	u
1	v	w	x	y	z	.	?
	A	B	C	D	E	F	G

You may have noticed that the only activities that we have *not* so far suggested in connection with regions on a grid are those involving graphs! It can actually be quite useful to draw a block graph with reference to a grid whose columns and rows are labelled. The vertical numbering of the columns provides an easy way of locating the height for any particular category. (For instance, the making of the graph of 'Tables That We Know', shown on page 167, is simplified by labelling the rows by the numerals 1 to 26.) But the main purpose of this work on grids is to lay the foundations for future graphical work.

Equipment Needed for the Activities in This Chapter

Matchboxes, cotton reels or squares of sticky paper for making block graphs.
Squared paper and rulers for drawing block graphs.
A large three-by-three grid, and nine pictures to put in its squares.
Duplicated sheets of four-by-four grids for various activities.
Duplicated sheets for 'Secret Island' and 'Make the Picture'.

Suggestions for the Reader

1. (Block graphs). 'Many of the illustrations that have appeared so far in this book could be considered as block graphs' (page 164). Find some such illustrations.

2. (The shape of a block graph) Find your height to the nearest 5 cm. (If it is between $157\frac{1}{2}$ and 162 cm, record it as 160 cm; if it is between $162\frac{1}{2}$ cm and 167 cm, record it as 165 cm.) Find the heights of about twenty other adults of the same sex as yourself, recording each height to the nearest 5 cm. Make a block graph of the heights that you have found. Is the shape of your graph somewhat similar to a 'normal distribution'?

3. (Statistics of dice throwing) Make two dice from cubes, labelling the six faces of each cube with the numerals 1, 1, 2, 2, 3, 3. If you play a game using these two dice instead of one normal one labelled 1, 2, 3, 4, 5, 6, you will never score '1', but you can score any number from 2 to 6. Would you expect to score '6' more often with these two dice than with a normal die? Throw the two dice together thirty-six times and make a block graph of the thirty-six scores that you obtain. (Your categories will be the scores '2', '3', '4', '5' and '6'.)

4. (Regions on a grid) Study some maps, and note how they give references to regions.

5. (Regions on a grid) Present some seven- and eight-year-olds with some varied grids of squares, six by five, seven by four, eight by three and so on. Ask them to tell you the number of squares in each grid. (Note whether they count the squares one by one or whether they merely count the numbers of columns and rows.) Label the columns and rows of one of your grids and test the children's ability to locate particular squares in it by reference to the labels that you have written.

17 Numbers beyond One Hundred

It is from the Indians that there has come to us the
ingenious method of expressing all numbers by ten
characters by giving them a place value; an idea fine and
important, which appears so simple, that for this very
reason we do not sufficiently recognize its merit.

– Laplace, 1796

We have remarked before that our number system is *based* on the
number ten, and that each digit of a numeral has a value according to its
place in the numeral (called its *place value*). Children obtain their first
concepts of place value from the words and symbols used to describe
numbers between eleven and ninety-nine, as well as from the structural
apparatus that they use to represent these numbers. The number
sixty-five, for instance, means six tens and five more, while the numeral
65 indicates a value of six tens for the '6' and five units for the '5'. When
we introduce children to numbers in the hundreds, their ideas of place
value must be extended. In the numeral 222, just as the second 2 has ten
times the value of the third 2, the first 2 has ten times the value of the
second 2. It is important that children should link the word 'hundred'
with ten tens.

1. Numbers between One Hundred and Two Hundred

To introduce these numbers, we can use the structural apparatus with
which children are already familiar, such as bags of ten counters and
bundles of ten sticks. The interlocking cubes used earlier might be
replaced now by smaller apparatus consisting of centimetre cubes

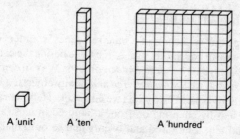

A 'unit'   A 'ten'   A 'hundred'

(called 'units'), rods that are 10 cm long, that match ten cubes (called 'tens'), and square-shaped blocks that match one hundred unit cubes or ten 'tens' (called 'hundreds'). If commercial apparatus is not to hand, equally suitable apparatus can be made by cutting card into centimetre squares, strips that are 10 cm by 1 cm, and squares that are 10 cm by 10 cm.

For the introductory work, we use apparatus that represents sets of ten. For each apparatus, we put out ten sets of ten, and count them in tens: 'Ten, twenty, thirty' and so on.

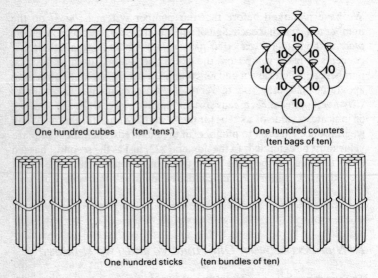

One hundred cubes   (ten 'tens')

One hundred counters
(ten bags of ten)

One hundred sticks   (ten bundles of ten)

At this stage, children can be shown that the ten 'ten' pieces match one 'hundred' piece. In future, a hundred can be represented with this apparatus by either ten 'tens' or one 'hundred'.

Sets of Ten beyond One Hundred

Having made our collection of a hundred cubes, counters or sticks, in sets of ten, we can add another set of ten to lie beside the collection. We now have displayed *a hundred and ten* objects. We can continue to add sets of ten, so that we have *a hundred and twenty* objects, *a hundred and thirty* objects and so on. Each time we add a set of ten, we can count the objects present by counting on from a hundred in tens: a hundred, a hundred and ten, a hundred and twenty and so on. Finally, when we have added ten sets of ten objects, we see that we have added a hundred to our original collection, so that we have *two hundred* objects before us.

After this oral work with apparatus (the E and L stages of learning), children can be introduced to the symbols that denote the numbers that we have considered. For this, we can use numeral cards similar to those described in Chapter 11 (page 106), together with wider cards labelled '100'. Appropriate cards are selected to represent the separate parts of the apparatus put out, and then the cards are superimposed to reveal the appropriate numeral for the whole collection, as illustrated below.

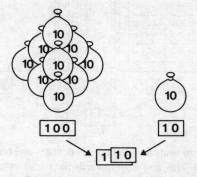

Although we cannot at this stage expect children to understand these numerals in terms of place value, nevertheless we can expect them to see that they are connected with the numerals with which they have been familiar: 120 is '20' with a '1' in front of it to denote the 'hundred'; 120 is also twelve tens. At this stage, children should have practice in writing the new numerals as the results of simple calculations, such as the following. (Apparatus should be available for children who wish to use it.)

Twelve tens are . . .	$120 + 20 =$
Eighteen tens are . . .	$140 + 50 =$
$100 + 30 =$	$120 - 20 =$
$100 + 80 =$	$150 - 30 =$

The Numerals 111 to 199

We can next introduce children to numbers and numerals between 111 and 199. (The numerals 101 to 109 are the hardest to understand; they will be discussed later in this section.) We put out a set of a hundred objects and some sets of ten (two, perhaps). To these we add a few single objects (three, perhaps). We count the objects: 'A hundred, a hundred and ten, a hundred and twenty, a hundred and twenty-one, a hundred and twenty-two, a hundred and twenty-three.' We label the separate parts of the apparatus with appropriate numeral cards, and then superimpose the cards to reveal the appropriate numeral for the whole collection, as illustrated below.

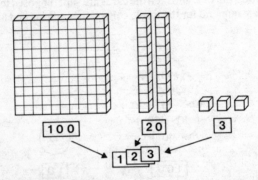

We tell children that the numeral 123 denotes one hundred, two tens and three units. This is a step towards their understanding the place value of digits in three-figure numbers. At this stage, children need practice in writing numerals between 111 and 199 as the results of simple calculations such as the following. (Apparatus should be available to help children who wish to use it.)

$100 + 20 + 3 =$	$24 + 50 =$	$78 - 5 =$
$100 + 50 + 9 =$	$124 + 50 =$	$178 - 5 =$
$24 + 5 =$	$24 + 52 =$	$78 - 50 =$
$124 + 5 =$	$124 + 52 =$	$178 - 50 =$

The Numerals 101 to 109

The numerals 101 to 109 are harder to understand than the other numerals between 100 and 199, because they involve the symbol '0' as a *placeholder*. If we did not write '0' in the numeral 102, the digit '1' would not be assigned the value of a hundred. The '0' serves to hold the '1' in its place. Apparatus and numeral cards will help children to learn to read and write the numerals 101 to 109, as the following picture illustrates. We can tell children that the numeral 102 denotes one hundred, *no* tens and two units.

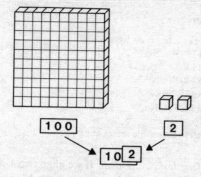

When children have met all the numerals between 100 and 199, they can make a chart of these numerals on squared paper, as shown below. The actual making of the chart is a useful exercise, because writing the numerals in order reminds children of that order. Children can compare the chart with a 100 square and notice the similar patterns in both. They can use the chart to help with simple mental arithmetic, such as calculating 134 + 4, 134 + 10, 134 + 20. They can pursue some 'tables' patterns beyond 100, seeing for example that the patterns of twos, fives and tens continue by repeating the patterns they made on a 100 square (see page 144). They can use the chart to help them locate a certain page of a book or a certain hymn number, to put a set of scores in order (for example 109, 150, 135, 172), and to play 'Spot the Number'. An example of this game follows the chart.

101	102	103	104	105	106	107	108	109	110
111	112	113	114	115	116	117	118	119	120
121	122	123	124	125	126	127	128	129	130
131	132	133	134	135	136	137	138	139	140
141	142	143	144	145	146	147	148	149	150
151	152	153	154	155	156	157	158	159	160
161	162	163	164	165	166	167	168	169	170
171	172	173	174	175	176	177	178	179	180
181	182	183	184	185	186	187	188	189	190
191	192	193	194	195	196	197	198	199	

'Spot the Number'

'My secret number is between 100 and 199.'
'Is it more than 150?'   'No.'
'Is it more than 130?'   'Yes.'
'Is it more than 140?'   'No.'
'Is it more than 135?'   'No.'
'Is it more than 132?'   'No.'
'Is it 131?'   'No.'
This is enough to reveal the secret number.

Application to length measurement. If we align two 1-metre rulers, we have a length of 200 cm. Children can arrange 10 cm strips alongside these rulers, checking that ten strips match 100 cm, twelve strips match 120 cm and so on. This reinforces, in terms of length, facts such as 'twelve tens are 120'.

Children can be introduced to tape measures. They can stretch a tape measure alongside the two 1-metre rulers to see how the calibrations match. A tape measure can be attached to a wall in a vertical position to measure heights. One child can measure the height of another child by placing a ruler horizontally across the top of his head to meet the tape measure on the wall. In Chapter 16 (page 166), we mentioned that children could make a block graph of their heights recorded to the nearest 5 cm. If the height categories are 115 cm, 120 cm, 125 cm and so on, a height of 118 cm will be recorded in the 120 cm category, and so will a height of 122 cm.

Other uses of tape measures will be discussed in Chapter 19.

2. Addition and Subtraction Involving Numbers to 199

We have already given examples of 'simple' additions and subtractions in section 1. Here we shall be concerned with additions and subtractions 'across 100', such as 70 + 40, 46 + 83, 120 − 50, 127 − 35. We shall deal with various types in order of difficulty.

Adding or Subtracting Sets of Ten

To perform an addition such as 70 + 40, one might argue, 'Seven and four is eleven; so seven tens and four tens are eleven tens; eleven tens are a hundred and ten.' Some children will need apparatus to help them, putting out seven 'tens' and four 'tens' and seeing the total as eleven 'tens'. The calculation might be recorded in the written form:

$$7 + 4 = 11, \text{ so } 70 + 40 = 110.$$

To perform a subtraction such as $120 - 50$, one might argue, 'Twelve take away five is seven; so twelve tens take away five tens are seven tens; seven tens are seventy.' Children should be encouraged to perform such mental calculations, and also to record them in written form:

$$12 - 5 = 7, \text{ so } 120 - 50 = 70.$$

Addition of Tens and Units

To perform an addition such as $46 + 83$, one might argue, 'Forty and eighty is a hundred and twenty; six and three is nine; a hundred and twenty and nine is a hundred and twenty-nine.' Apparatus might help children perform such calculations, which they can perform orally and record in written form. For the written recording, it is useful to label the columns in which the digits are arranged by H, T, U (for hundreds, tens and units).

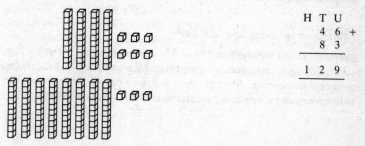

The calculation $49 + 83$ is harder than the above example. If one argues, 'Forty and eighty is a hundred and twenty; nine and three is twelve', one then has to add a hundred and twenty and twelve. Most children will need considerable experience with apparatus before being able to tackle such a calculation mentally. The exchange of ten units for a 'ten' can be recorded by writing '1' in the 'T' column below the area in which the other digits are recorded.

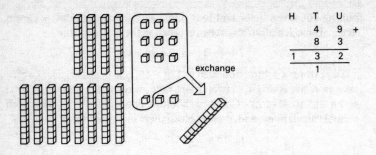

Children should be encouraged to make up stories to accompany their calculations, or, better still, to connect them with practical problems. Suppose, for instance, that they had discovered that the height of a chair seat was 49 cm and that the height of a box was 83 cm. They could predict that when the box was put on top of the chair seat, its top would be 132 cm above the floor. Their prediction could be checked, using the height measure on the wall.

Subtraction Involving Tens and Units

To perform the subtraction 127 − 35, one might argue, 'Twelve tens take away three tens is nine tens; seven take away five is two; so the answer is ninety-two.' Most children will need considerable experience with apparatus before being able to tackle such a calculation mentally.

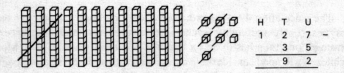

The calculation 127 − 38 is harder than the above example. If one argues, 'Twelve tens take away three tens is nine tens', one is then faced with 'Seven take away eight', which at this stage is meaningless. Recourse to apparatus reminds children that one of the 'tens' must be exchanged for ten 'units' before eight 'units' can be subtracted. The use of apparatus and a possible written recording is shown below.

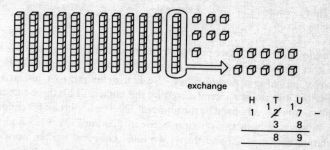

exchange

$$
\begin{array}{ccc}
H & T & U \\
1 & {}^1\!\!\not{2}\,{}^1 & 7 \\
 & 3 & 8 \\
\hline
 & 8 & 9 \\
\end{array}
$$

−

A story that might accompany the above calculation is, 'There were 127 eggs in the incubator; 38 eggs hatched into chickens today, so there are 89 eggs left to hatch.'

The work described in this section has not leant heavily on the concept of place value. The emphasis has been on linking 100 with ten tens, 120 with twelve tens and so on. We have suggested recording children's calculations in columns labelled H T U, but the column labelled H has never contained a numeral other than '1'. The full significance of place value for numerals up to 999 will be revealed when numbers beyond 199 are introduced.

3. Numbers up to 999

Once children are familiar with numbers and numerals up to 199, it is relatively easy to extend their knowledge to numbers up to 999. For introducing such numbers, it is more convenient to use the apparatus that consists of 'unit' cubes, 'ten' pieces and 'hundred' pieces than the other apparatus included in section 1. We might introduce the numbers in stages.

Sets of a hundred. Here we introduce the numerals 200, 300 and so on. If we put out two 'hundreds', we see that we have the equivalent of *two hundred* cubes. We teach children that the numeral to represent this number is 200. At the same time, we should put out twenty 'tens' and see that they can be exchanged for two 'hundreds' showing that twenty tens are two hundred. We similarly introduce the numerals 300, 400 and so on up to 900.

Children can do simple oral and written calculations with these numbers, such as

Thirty tens are . . .	$200 + 300 =$	$400 - 100 =$
Fifty tens are . . .	$400 + 500 =$	$700 - 300 =$

Hundreds and tens. If we put out three 'hundreds' and two 'tens' we see that we have *three* sets of a hundred cubes and *twenty* more cubes, or *three hundred and twenty* cubes. We teach children that just as one hundred and twenty is symbolized by the numeral 120, three hundred and twenty is symbolized by the numeral 320. It is important for children to appreciate both the relation between 320 and $300 + 20$ and the relation between 320 and thirty-two tens..Oral and written exercises should emphasize such relations:

$300 + 20 =$	32 tens are
$600 + 40 =$	64 tens are

Hundreds, tens and units. Finally, we reach the stage where we focus on place value. We now use structural apparatus to represent any number up to 999. We ask children to put out structural apparatus in the form of a number of 'hundreds', a number of 'tens' and a number of 'units', to say the number represented and to write the numeral represented. At this stage, we might also introduce an *abacus*, an ancient tallying device consisting of three rods, on which beads are threaded to represent the hundreds, tens and units of a number. Examples are illustrated below.

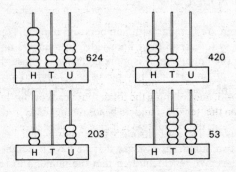

It is not practical to display *all* the numerals between 200 and 999 for children, because there are so many of them. Instead, we can display a few in sequence and ask children to continue each sequence:

316, 317, 318,   ,   , . . .
297, 298, 299,   ,   , . . .
499, 500, 501,   ,   , ...

We can ask children to find page 504 in a large book (such as a dictionary), to select the highest and lowest from a set of cricket scores (such as 302, 290, 288, 315). We can ask them to count up in twos from a number (such as 400), and to decide whether all the numbers that they say are even or odd. We can ask them to guess what kinds of collections will amount to numbers in the hundreds (the number of children in a school, the number of houses in a street, the number of pages in a book, the number of days in a year, the number of seats in a theatre and so on).

4. Addition and Subtraction Involving Numbers to 999

Most additions and subtractions of numbers up to 999 are difficult to perform mentally, because rather a lot of steps must be retained in the memory. Use of structural apparatus or an abacus should help children to develop a technique for performing such calculations, dealing first with the units, then the tens, then the hundreds. Consider the problem of 193 + 227. Using structural apparatus, it would be solved by putting out one 'hundred', nine 'tens' and three 'units'; then putting out two 'hundreds', two 'tens' and seven 'units'; then (a) exchanging ten 'units' for a 'ten', (b) exchanging ten 'tens' for a 'hundred', (c) counting the total: four 'hundreds', two 'tens' and no 'units'.

Using an abacus, the problem would be solved by threading one bead on the 'hundreds' rod, nine beads on the 'tens' rod, three beads on the 'units' rod, and then (a) adding seven beads to the 'units' rod and exchanging ten beads from this rod for one bead on the 'tens' rod, (b) adding two beads to the 'tens' rod and exchanging ten beads from this rod for one bead on the 'hundreds' rod, (c) adding two beads to the 'hundreds' rod, and counting the total: four beads on the 'hundreds' rod, two beads on the 'tens' rod and no beads on the 'units' rod.

In either case, the calculation is logically recorded in symbols by:

$$
\begin{array}{ccc}
\text{H} & \text{T} & \text{U} \\
1 & 9 & 3 \; + \\
2 & 2 & 7 \\
\hline
4 & 2 & 0 \\
\hline
1 & 1 &
\end{array}
$$

As always, children should be encouraged to invent stories to accompany their calculations, such as, 'Tim has 193 stamps in one stamp album and 227 stamps in another, so he has 420 stamps altogether.'

Subtraction is rather more complex than addition. Children should use structural apparatus as well as an abacus to help them develop a technique for a written calculation, dealing first with the units, then the tens, then the hundreds. Consider the problem of 324 − 176. Using structural apparatus, it would be solved by putting out three 'hundreds', two 'tens' and four 'units', and then: (a) exchanging one of the 'tens' for ten 'units', and removing six of them; (b) exchanging one of the 'hundreds' for ten 'tens', and removing seven of them; (c) removing one 'hundred', and counting the remainder: one 'hundred', four 'tens' and eight 'units'.

The problem can also be solved using an abacus. Whichever apparatus is used, the solution is logically recorded in symbols by:

$$
\begin{array}{ccc}
H & T & U \\
2 & {}^{1}1 & \\
\cancel{3} & \cancel{2} & {}^{1}4 \\
1 & 7 & 6 \\
\hline
1 & 4 & 8 \\
\end{array} \quad -
$$

As always, children should be encouraged to invent stories to accompany their calculations, such as, 'Our school has 324 children, and the Infant School has 176 children; so our school has 148 more children than the Infant School.'

An added complication arises when the tens digit of the first numeral of a subtraction problem is *zero*. In such a case, a 'hundred' has to be exchanged for ten 'tens' before a 'ten' can be exchanged for ten 'units'. Children who have begun to be 'weaned' from using apparatus might find it helpful to consider the three hundred as thirty tens, which are reduced to twenty-nine tens when one of them is theoretically exchanged for ten units.

$$
\begin{array}{ccc}
H & T & U \\
2 & 9 & \\
\cancel{3} & \cancel{0} & {}^{1}1 \\
1 & 7 & 6 \\
\hline
1 & 2 & 5 \\
\end{array} \quad -
$$

(A possible story: In darts, you need to score 301. If you have scored 176, you need to score 125 more.)

5. *Multiplication beyond the Tables*

In Chapter 14 (page 149) we saw how children can be taught to perform multiplication beyond the multiplication tables they have learnt, by using the distributive property. At that stage, calculations involved only multiplications whose results were less than 100. Now, no such restrictions are necessary, and a problem such as 26×4 can be approached. The conventional way to solve 26×4 is to split the problem into $20 \times 4 + 6 \times 4$. So far, we have met no means of solving such a problem as 20×4. Clearly, this type of problem must be tackled before progressing to a problem such as 26×4.

Multiplying Any Number up to 10 by 20, 30, etc., up to 90

Consider the problem of finding out how many nails you will get if you buy four packets of nails, when there are twenty nails in each packet. The problem is solved by calculating 4×20, and the calculation can be performed by the following argument:

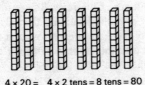

$4 \times 20 = \quad 4 \times 2 \text{ tens} = 8 \text{ tens} = 80$

The argument involves a 'hidden' property of multiplication, which is exposed when it is written in the form:

$$4 \times (2 \times 10) = (4 \times 2) \times 10.$$

This property is called the *associative property* of multiplication. Children will have no difficulty in accepting this property as obvious, provided it is presented to them in concrete form as illustrated above. Having seen that $4 \times 20 = 80$, children who are familiar with the commutative property of multiplication (see page 146) will readily deduce that $20 \times 4 = 80$.

Children will now need plenty of practice with such calculations as 4×20, 20×4, 3×60, 60×3 and so on before proceeding to a calculation such as 26×4.

Multiplying Any Number up to 10 by a Number up to 100

A problem such as 26 × 4 can now be tackled in a manner similar to the calculations described in Chapter 14 (page 149). Children's written recording should initially take the form suggested in Chapter 14 (if that is the recording with which they are familiar), but when they have developed some competence with their calculations, they should be encouraged to progress to the shorter, more conventional form:

```
           H T U                    H T U
20 × 4 =     8 0    leading to        2 6 ×
 6 × 4 =     2 4                          4
           ------                     ------
26 × 4 =   1 0 4                      1 0 4
                                     ------
                                        2
```

As always, stories should accompany children's calculations. A story for 26 × 4 might be, 'Twenty-six cars will have a hundred and four wheels', and a story for 3 × 60 might be, 'In three hours there are a hundred and eighty minutes'. Children will show their recognition of the *commutative* property of multiplication if they also invent stories such as, 'If there are twenty-six seats in each row of a theatre, in four rows there are a hundred and four seats', or 'Sixty tricycles will have a hundred and eighty wheels'.

6. Division

In Chapter 14 (page 149) we discussed equal grouping problems which involved multiplication facts beyond the tables, such as how many sets of four can be made from fifty-two cards. We now consider equal sharing and equal grouping of numbers up to 999. Most children find division harder to perform and to understand than multiplication. It is advisable to introduce division problems in stages of difficulty. Because a division problem is normally solved by dealing first with the hundreds digit, then the tens digit and finally the units digit, our first stage will involve division of hundreds only.

Equal Sharing and Equal Grouping of Hundreds

Consider the two problems:

(a) Share 600 potatoes equally between three boxes; how many potatoes will go in each box? (Or, find *a third* of 600 potatoes.)
(b) How many sets of three can be made from 600 objects?

Given six sets of a hundred potatoes, it is extremely easy to imagine the process of sharing these sets equally between three boxes. A picture helps children to imagine the activity.

$600 = 3 \times 200$

200 potatoes go in each box

To solve the second problem by physically grouping 600 objects into sets of three would indeed be a mammoth task. But, having seen that $600 = 3 \times 200$, familiarity with the commutative property of multiplication enables us to deduce that $600 = 200 \times 3$. The second problem is solved indirectly, by considering the equal-sharing problem first.

Equal Sharing and Equal Grouping of Hundreds and Tens

Consider the two problems:

(a) Share 120 stamps equally between three people; how many will each person have? (Or, find *a third* of 120 stamps.)
(b) How many sets of three can be made from 120 objects?

As before, the equal-sharing problem is easier to imagine and perform than the equal-grouping one. Structural apparatus leads children nicely towards the conventional technique that they will eventually use. When they put out one 'hundred' and two 'tens', they will see that the 'hundred' cannot be shared as it is. It will have to be exchanged for ten 'tens'. They are then faced with twelve 'tens' to be shared equally between three people. The 'tens' can be arranged in three sets of four, showing that $120 = 3 \times 40$. So each person will have forty stamps. The second problem is solved indirectly, by considering the related problem of equal sharing. Because $120 = 3 \times 40$, we also know that $120 = 40 \times 3$. So 120 objects can be made into forty sets of three.

The problem of sharing 420 objects into three equal shares is a little more complex than the previous problems. When children have put out four 'hundreds' and two 'tens', they will see that three of the 'hundreds' can be shared out immediately, leaving one 'hundred' still to be shared. The rest of the problem is solved in the same way as (a) above. Because of the extra step involved, children might record the calculation in written form as follows:

```
H  T  U
4  2  0  –
3  0  0            300 = 3 × 100
_____
1  2  0  –
1  2  0            120 = 3 ×  40
_____
      0            420 = 3 × 140
```

Equal Sharing and Equal Grouping of Hundreds, Tens and Units

Consider the two problems:

(a) Share 144 pence equally between three charities; how much will be given to each charity? (Or, find *a third* of 144.)
(b) How many sets of three can be made from 144 objects?

When children put out one 'hundred', four 'tens' and four 'units' they will see that the 'hundred' must be exchanged for ten 'tens' before it can be shared out. There are then fourteen 'tens' which can be shared into three sets of four 'tens', with two 'tens' remaining. These two 'tens' must be exchanged for twenty 'units' before they can be shared out. There are now twenty-four 'units', which can be shared into three sets of eight.

The calculation involves several steps, which are recorded logically in written form by the following:

```
H  T  U
1  4  4  –
1  2  0            120 = 3 × 40
_____
   2  4  –
   2  4             24 = 3 ×  8
   _____
      0            144 = 3 × 48    We will give 48p to each charity.
```

As children become competent at the process, they can be shown a more conventional way of recording their work:

$$\begin{array}{r|ccc l}
 & H & T & U & \\
 & & 4 & 8 & \\
\cline{2-4}
3 & 1 & 4 & 4 & - \\
 & 1 & 2 & 0 & \\
\cline{2-4}
 & & 2 & 4 & - \\
 & & 2 & 4 & \\
\cline{2-4}
 & & & 0 &
\end{array}
\qquad \text{or} \qquad
\begin{array}{r}
48 \\
3\overline{)14^{2}4}
\end{array}$$

The second problem is solved by an identical calculation, followed by the statement, '144 = 48 × 3, so forty-eight sets of three can be made.'

7. *Numbers above One Thousand*

The work described in this chapter spans a considerable period of time in children's mathematical development. By the end of this period, children can be introduced to numbers in the thousands in a similar way to that described here for numbers in the hundreds. The apparatus of 'units', 'tens' and 'hundreds', illustrated on page 173), also contains 'thousand' pieces, each of which matches ten 'hundreds'.

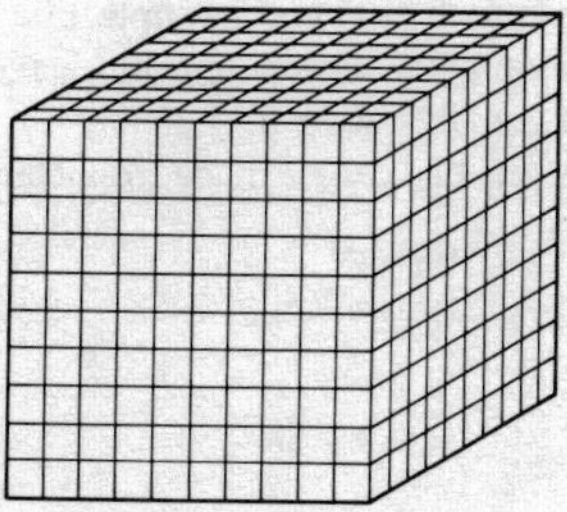

A 'thousand' piece

In Chapter 20 we shall meet (page 223) an alternative approach to numbers in the thousands, using calculators.

Equipment Needed for the Activities in This Chapter

Cm cubes, 10-cm rods and 'hundred' pieces to represent units, tens and hundreds
(or cm squares, strips of card 10 cm by 1 cm, and squares of card 10 cm by
10 cm).
Other structural apparatus for sets of ten.
An abacus.

Suggestions for the Reader

1. Test some eight-year-olds on their understanding of numbers and numerals in
the hundreds. For example, ask them which is the largest number in the set 317,
504, 299. Ask them to find pages 317, 504 and 299 in a book, and watch their
strategy.

2. For those children who show sufficient understanding of numbers and numerals, try some graded mental work:
(a) Test their understanding of hundreds by asking them what is 200 + 300,
    700 − 400 etc.
(b) Test their understanding of the link between tens and hundreds by asking
    them what are ten tens, fourteen tens, thirty tens, forty-five tens; what is
    60 + 40, 60 + 60, 100 − 50, 120 − 50, 450 + 30, 450 + 60, 450 − 30, 450 − 60;
    4 × 20, 5 × 30.
(c) Test their ability to calculate mentally with hundreds, tens and units by
    asking them what is 62 + 40, 62 + 43; 127 + 50, 127 + 52; 127 + 80, 127 + 85.

3. The calculation 26 × 4 requires the use of the associative property of
multiplication and the use of the distributive property. Explain why.

4. Ask some eight- or nine-year-olds to explain to you how they perform written
calculations 193 + 227, 324 − 176, and 26 × 4. Do they seem to understand the
processes that they perform?

5. How do the the same children tackle the problems of:
(a) sharing 600 objects equally between 3 people,
(b) sharing 120 objects equally between 3 people,
(c) sharing 144 objects equally between 3 people,
(d) deciding how many sets of 3 can be made from 600, 120 or 144 objects?

18 *Fractions – New Numbers from Old*

If any man thinks that in expounding the use of decimal
fractions I am boasting of my cleverness in devising them,
he shows without doubt that he has neither the judgement
nor the intelligence to distinguish simple things from
difficult . . . Just as the mariner who has found by chance
an unknown isle may declare all its riches to the king . . .
so may I speak freely of the great usefulness of this
invention, a usefulness greater than I think any of you
anticipates.

– Stevin of Bruges, 1634

In Chapter 15 we saw the advisability of giving children plenty of
practice with fractions before introducing them to the conventional
symbols used to denote fractions. We now turn to these symbols. There
are two common notations for fractions – the numerator–denominator
notation and the decimal notation. We shall consider ways of introducing children to both.

1. Numerator–Denominator Notation

When children are thoroughly familiar with fraction *names* (such as a
half, a *third*, a *quarter*) and with the meaning of those names in relation
to various *wholes* (for instance, a third of *a cake*), they are ready to be
introduced to symbols for fractions. We tell them that instead of writing
'one third', they can draw a line under a '1' and write '3' beneath that
line. They will need practice in translating fraction names to fraction
symbols. Initially they should consider only fractions whose numerators
are '1', so that attention is focused on the significance of the denominator. Children might be asked to complete a table like this one:

Number of equal shares of the whole	2	3	4	5	6
Name of each share	1 half	1 third	1 quarter		
Symbol for one share	$\frac{1}{2}$	$\frac{1}{3}$			

Children should now repeat exercises like those mentioned in section
1 of Chapter 15 (page 153), using the new notation. (For example, 'Find
$\frac{1}{5}$ of 20 sweets.')

We have not yet told children the whole story of the numerator–denominator notation. This notation gives us a fraction in terms of *two* numbers; one tells us its name and the other tells us how many shares we have. We tell children that '2 eighths' can be written as '$\frac{2}{8}$', '3 fifths' can be written as '$\frac{3}{5}$' and so on. They will need practice in translating between the familiar and the unfamiliar ways of writing fractions, and in using the new notation in exercises like those suggested throughout Chapter 15. For example, for the square illustrated on page 154, children will write '$\frac{2}{8}$ of the square are red, $\frac{4}{8}$ of the square are white', and so on.

2. Equivalence of Fractions

By now, children are bound to have come across many instances where the same fraction can be named in more than one way. (For example, we can equally well say '$\frac{2}{8}$ of the square are red' or '$\frac{1}{4}$ of the square is red'.) We can now ask children to do 'detective work' on a particular fraction to see how many other names they can find for it. This detective work needs to be structured. We might start with a paper strip folded into eighths, and invite children to find another way of naming *one half* of the strip. They will find that

$$\tfrac{1}{2} \text{ of the strip is } \tfrac{2}{4} \text{ of the strip and also } \tfrac{4}{8} \text{ of the strip.}$$

We should ask them to investigate similarly a square divided into eighths. They will find that

$$\tfrac{1}{2} \text{ of the square is } \tfrac{2}{4} \text{ of the square and also } \tfrac{4}{8} \text{ of the square.}$$

Lastly, they should investigate a number divided into eighths, finding for example that

$$\tfrac{1}{2} \text{ of 16 is } \tfrac{2}{4} \text{ of 16 and also } \tfrac{4}{8} \text{ of 16.}$$

Equivalence. We say that one half is *equivalent* to two quarters. When we write '$\frac{1}{2} = \frac{2}{4}$', we mean that one half is the *same number* as two quarters. The fact that a fraction is really a number takes time for children to digest. Nevertheless, we can invite them to record the general findings they have made above by writing

$$\tfrac{1}{2} = \tfrac{2}{4} = \tfrac{4}{8}.$$

Children can continue detective work on finding fractions equivalent to *one half* by exploring strips, shapes and numbers that can be divided into fifths, sixths or tenths. They will discover that *one half* is not equivalent to a whole number of fifths, but that it *is* equivalent to three sixths and also to five tenths. They will collect a number of fractions equivalent to one half, which we might call members of the *family of one half*:

$$\tfrac{1}{2} = \tfrac{2}{4} = \tfrac{4}{8} = \tfrac{3}{6} = \tfrac{5}{10}.$$

Pattern and prediction. In studying the above list, children may notice a pattern in the denominators and numerators of the fractions, in particular that the denominator of each fraction is two times the numerator. We can ask children to suggest other fractions that might belong to the family. They might suggest $\tfrac{6}{12}$; to test this prediction, they will need a shape or strip divided into twelfths.

All the materials used in detective work on the family of one half can be used again in looking for fractions that are equivalent to one whole (the family of *one*), one third, one quarter, two thirds and so on. This work is exciting and valuable for children, and on no account should we tell them the rule for cancelling a fraction to its lowest terms, thereby robbing them of the experience of discovery, which is essential for the understanding of mathematics.

3. Number Lines

A number line is a line that is calibrated and labelled like a ruler. The distance along the line between any two calibrations represents the difference between the numbers assigned to them. For instance, the distance between the calibrations labelled 2 and 5 is 3 units of length. Here are two examples of number lines.

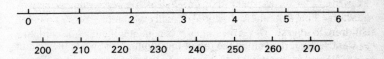

A number line is an excellent visual aid for representing fractions because it helps children to see how fractions are related to whole numbers. A calibration representing $\frac{1}{2}$ can be put midway between the calibrations for 0 and 1, and a calibration for $1\frac{1}{2}$ midway between 1 and 2. After some years of experience with number lines, children will realize that number is a *continuous quantity*. Between any two calibrations on a number line, however close, another calibration can theoretically be inserted; between any two numbers, however small the difference between them, there is another number.

A number line is not a useful visual aid for helping younger children to add and subtract whole numbers. I have seen many young children struggle to use a number line in this way, when a number strip (see page 46) would have been a far more simple and logical aid for them. The premature use of a number line confuses young children, because they consider number as a *discrete* rather than a *continuous* quantity. The value of a number line is in representing fractions, large numbers and, at a later stage, negative numbers.

We can provide children with duplicated copies of number lines; the first one might look like this.

We can ask children to notice that the first unlabelled calibration on this line is half-way between the calibrations for 0 and 1. We label this calibration '$\frac{1}{2}$'. The other unmarked calibrations can be discussed and labelled '$1\frac{1}{2}$', '$2\frac{1}{2}$' and '$3\frac{1}{2}$'. Children can now read along the number line while they count up to 'three' in halves, and they can use the line as an aid to finding other ways of writing fractions (3 halves, 4 halves and so on). On the same number line, children can be asked to make calibrations that are half-way between those for 0 and $\frac{1}{2}$, $\frac{1}{2}$ and 1 and so on. The calibrations now divide unit lengths into quarters. We label them *above* the number line, so that the line finally appears as follows.

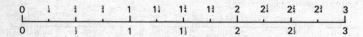

Children can read along the top of this number line while they count up to 'three' in quarters; and they can use the line as an aid to finding other ways of writing $\frac{2}{4}$ (2 quarters), $\frac{6}{4}$ (6 quarters) and so on. (For instance, $\frac{6}{4}$ can be written as $1\frac{2}{4}$, $1\frac{1}{2}$ or $\frac{3}{2}$.)

A new number line can be used to introduce calibrations for fifths and tenths, appearing initially as follows.

When the unmarked calibrations have been discussed and labelled '$\frac{1}{5}$', '$\frac{2}{5}$' and so on, children can read along this number line while counting up to 'two' in fifths; and they can use the number line as an aid to finding other ways of writing $\frac{5}{5}$ (5 fifths), $\frac{7}{5}$ (7 fifths) and so on. On the same number line, children can mark calibrations that are half-way between '0' and '$\frac{1}{5}$', half-way between '$\frac{1}{5}$' and '$\frac{2}{5}$' and so on. The calibrations now divide unit lengths into tenths, and they can be labelled above the line so that the final number line appears as follows.

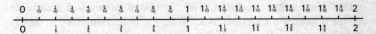

Children can read along the top of this number line while they count up to 'two' in tenths; and they can use the number line as an aid to finding other ways of writing $\frac{2}{10}$, $\frac{12}{10}$, and so on.

Work like this with number lines encourages children to consider fractions as numbers in their own right. It also prepares children for reading scales on instruments such as rulers, weighing machines and capacity measures; on such instruments, not all the calibrations are labelled.

Operations with Fractions

The Cockcroft Report states: 'It is difficult to find everyday situations which require fractions to be added or multiplied and there seems to be little justification for teaching the routines for adding, subtracting, multiplying or dividing fractions to the majority of children during the primary years' (Para. 300).

While agreeing with this statement, I would point out the advantages of challenging children to find out for themselves how to add (or subtract) suitably chosen fractions. Such exercises: (a) reinforce the fact that fractions are *numbers*; just as whole numbers can be added or subtracted, so can fractions; (b) require children to *use* the concept of equivalence. You cannot add $\frac{1}{5}$ and $\frac{3}{10}$ without knowing that $\frac{1}{5}$ is the same number as $\frac{2}{10}$. The argument might proceed as follows:

$$\tfrac{1}{5} + \tfrac{3}{10} = \tfrac{2}{10} + \tfrac{3}{10} \text{ (or 2 tenths and 3 tenths)}$$
$$= \tfrac{5}{10}$$

The answer to this calculation can be checked by locating '⅕' on an appropriate number line and moving a distance of ³⁄₁₀ beyond it.

4. Decimal Notation for Tenths

Initially, we should introduce children to decimal notation for *tenths* only; at a later stage children will realize the value of extending decimal notation to hundredths, thousandths and so on, and eventually they will learn that we can represent *any fraction we like* in decimal notation.

We might introduce the notation by referring to car distance meters, which interest most children. The right-hand numeral of a distance meter is usually a different colour from the other numerals, to signify that it records *tenths* of a mile (or kilometre). We can tell children that we can record tenths in the same way as a distance meter; but instead of writing the tenths in a different colour from the other numerals, we can put a *point* to separate the tenths from the units. We can write $3\frac{1}{10}$ as 3·1, and $1\frac{4}{10}$ as 1·4 (reading these numbers as 'three point one', 'one point four'). Two peculiarities of decimal notation should be pointed out to children. The number $\frac{6}{10}$, which is less than 1, is recorded in decimal notation as 0·6, and not as ·6, to make quite sure that the reader will notice the decimal point and not think it an irrelevant smudge. Also, a whole number is sometimes recorded using a decimal point. In a gymnastics competition, for instance, where scores are awarded in whole numbers and tenths, a score of 6 will be recorded as 6·0.

After some simple translations between fraction and decimal notation, children can be asked to label a number line calibrated in tenths with both notations that they have learnt.

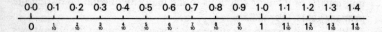

Children can read along the top of this number line while they count up in tenths. They can use the number line to help with such problems as, 'A distance meter reads 0·2; what will it read after another mile (or kilometre)? And after another 0·2 of a mile (or kilometre)?' 'Which is the larger number, 1·1 or 0·8?'

Children can consider problems such as, 'The competitors in a gymnastics competition score 4·8, 5·2, 4·6. Who wins?' and, 'Three athletes run 100 metres in 11·6 seconds, 11·2 seconds and 10·9 seconds. Who is the fastest runner?' They can repeat measurement of length in metres and tenths of a metre (see page 155), recording their results in decimal form (for example, 'The cupboard is 0·4 m wide'). They can repeat measurement of capacity in litres and tenths (see page 156) and measurement of weight in kg and tenths (see page 157), recording their results in decimal form.

Addition of Decimals

We can give children simple problems that lead to the addition of decimals. For instance, suppose that two cupboards standing next to each other have been found to have lengths of 0·4 m and 0·8 m. Children can measure the total length of the cupboards and find it to be 1·2 m. How could they have *calculated* this result? Setting out their written record as shown below, they will see that because $4 + 8 = 12$, the total is 12 tenths of a metre, which is the same as 1·2 m.

	metres		tenths
Small cupboard	0	·	4
Big cupboard	0	·	8
Total length	1	·	2

Children will soon see that the process of adding tenths can be performed by the same routine as that for adding whole numbers. They can progress to becoming 'judges' in a gymnastics competition, deciding the awards of first, second and third places.

	Tamara	Janet	Helga
Vault	5·7	5·3	4·8
Balance beam	5·2	5·8	5·3
Floor work	5·0	5·1	5·3
Total score	...	...	...

5. Decimal Notation for Hundredths

The Cockcroft Report states that very few eleven-year-olds are able to understand two places of decimals. 'Not until the age of *fifteen* are at least half the children in a year group able to read a scale to two decimal places, or to state that the 1 in the number 2·31 represents 1 hundredth' (Para. 341). Although this remark should warn us to exercise caution, it should not be taken as meaning that primary-level children are incapable of learning to understand two places of decimals. (In a local primary school I found that thirty-nine out of the fifty-two ten-year-olds could state correctly, without prompting, what the 1 means in the number 2·31.) Because so many of our measurements are recorded using two places of decimals, there is a case for introducing the notation to primary-level children who have had considerable experience with decimal notation for tenths. The sum of money of £2 and 25p is always recorded as £2.25; a length of 1 m 25 cm is often recorded as 1·25 m; when we watch athletics or certain panel games on television, we see recorded on the screen not only the seconds that pass, but also the tenths and hundredths of a second. We shall consider here activities that can help children understand the notation for two places of decimals in terms of shape and money.

Shape

We can consider as our unit shape a square which is divided into ten rows of ten squares. The long thin rectangles that are tenths of the square should be clearly marked, so that children have a visual demonstration that ten hundredths of the square are the same as one tenth of it.

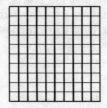

When children have identified the shapes that are to be called tenths and hundredths of the square, we can ask them how many hundredths of the square make a *tenth* of it, how many make two tenths of it, and so on. We can colour twenty-four hundredths of the square and ask children how many tenths of the square are coloured and how many additional hundredths. They know that we can record the two tenths as 0·2; we tell them that we can record the two tenths and four additional hundredths as 0·24.

We can now ask children to colour various fractions of similar squares and to record these fractions in decimal form, perhaps as follows:

	Tenths	Additional hundredths	Fraction of square
Black	2	4	0·24
White	7	6	0·76

Practice should include cases where the fraction of a square to be coloured is less than one tenth, for example 0·06.

Addition. On the square of which 0·24 is coloured black, we can ask children to colour the next three tenths of the square blue. What fraction of the square is now coloured? Children will quickly see that this fraction is 0·54; but they can be shown how an addition can be set out to give the result. They can compare this addition with 24 + 30.

	Units		Tenths	Hundredths		T	U
Black	0	·	2	4 +		2	4 +
Blue	0	·	3	0		3	0
Total	0	·	5	4		5	4

After this, they can be asked to colour six more hundredths of the square blue, so that 0·36 of the square is now blue. When this addition is set out in columns, the total number of hundredths is seen to be ten. We must remind children that since ten hundredths are the same as one tenth, they should record '1' in the tenths column. They can compare this addition with 24 + 36.

	Units		Tenths	Hundredths		T	U
Black	0	·	2	4 +		2	4 +
Blue	0	·	3	6		3	6
Total	0	·	6	0		6	0
			1			1	

Note. This work on addition of decimals is not intended to be comprehensive. It merely consolidates and uses the new notation that children are learning.

Money

We can introduce £1 coins (imitation or real) and draw children's attention to the fact that a 10p coin is worth a *tenth* of a pound, and a 1p coin is worth a *hundredth* of a pound. Children will enjoy counting out the value of a collection of coins. Initially no collection should contain more than nine 10p coins or nine 1p coins. Children can record their counting as follows:

£1 coins	10p coins	1p coins	Value
2	3	5	£2.35
3	6	0	£3.60
1	0	0	£1.00
0	0	6	£0.06

When a collection includes ten or more 1p coins, children will have to exchange ten of them for a 10p coin before recording the value. A similar exchange has to be made if a collection includes ten or more 10p coins. Children can progress to recording simple bills, using coins to help them if they wish.

Tractor	£2.35		2 3 5 +
Car	£1.06	Compare this with	1 0 6
Total	£3.41		3 4 1

Note. Children who can cope with bills and other money problems do not necessarily think of pence as hundredths of a pound. They need frequent reminders of facts such as, '35p is three tenths of a pound and five hundredths of a pound.' If we give them these reminders, we are helping them to come to terms with decimal notation in general.

Equipment Needed for the Activities in This Chapter

Drawings of plane shapes divided into congruent fractional parts.
Paper ribbons for folding into various fractions of their length.
Rulers and tape measures.
Litre flasks calibrated in tenths.
Weights of 1 kg and 0·1 kg.
Balance scales.
Duplicated sheets of number lines.
Duplicated sheets of squares divided into tenths and hundredths.
£1 coins, 10p coins and 1p coins, imitation or real.

Suggestions for the Reader

1. Test some nine-year-olds on their understanding of fraction notation. Show them a shape of which one fifth has clearly been coloured, and ask them to write down the fraction of the shape that is coloured, and the fraction of the shape that is uncoloured. Ask them if they can find the number that is $\frac{1}{10}$ of 100, and the number that is $\frac{3}{10}$ of 100.

2. Find out from some nine- and ten-year-olds whether they think of fractions as numbers in their own right. Can they tell you, for instance, whether $\frac{9}{10}$ is more than 2, or do they find the question meaningless? Can they tell you what $1\frac{2}{10}$ means, and whether this number is more than $\frac{12}{10}$?

3. Test the same children on their notions of *equivalence of fractions*. Ask them to tell you another fraction that is the same value as $\frac{1}{2}$. If they give a correct answer, ask them how they know it is correct. Can they tell you another fraction that has the same value as $\frac{1}{3}$? And as $\frac{2}{3}$?

4. Look up dictionary definitions of the words 'discrete' and 'continuous'. These words are used on page 194, where it also says that the author has seen many young children struggle in trying to use a number line as a visual aid for addition and subtraction of whole numbers. Can you suggest some problems that they might have had?

5. 'It is difficult to find everyday situations which require fractions to be added or multiplied . . .' (Cockcroft Report, Para. 300). Can you think of any?

6. Test some ten-year-olds on their understanding of one place of decimals. Ask them to tell you what 2·6, 3·0 and 0·9 mean. Ask them which is the largest of these numbers. Ask them to tell you the result of adding them. Ask them if they can think of a situation in real life when they would need to add these numbers.

7. Test some ten- and eleven-year-olds on their understanding of place value. Remind them that the digit '1' in the numeral 16 means *ten*. Ask them to tell you what the '1' means in the following numerals:

216, 301, 2103, 1203, 2·1, 2·31.

19   *Further Measurement*

The 20 pipe should be 5 digits plus $\frac{1}{24}$ in diameter, and have
a capacity of 16 quinariae plus $\frac{3}{12}$ plus $\frac{1}{24}$. The one built by
the water men measures 4 digits plus $\frac{1}{2}$ in diameter,
holding only 13 quinariae.

*– Frontinus, showing how the Romans were cheated
by the water men who built their aqueducts*
(The Aqueducts of Rome, 72 AD)

The activity of measurement often helps children to consolidate their
ideas about numbers. In this chapter we shall consider ways of using
children's number concepts in connection with a variety of problems of
measurement. For instance, calibrated instruments for measuring
length, weight and fluid volume provide a nice back-up to the work
described in Chapter 18 on number lines. In this chapter we shall discuss
such instruments, and also the measurement of area, angles and time.

1. Length

By now, we expect children to be competent at using rulers and tape
measures for measuring lengths of straight lines. We are going to see
how they can progress to finding the perimeters of shapes and how they
can be introduced to scale drawings and maps.

Perimeters of Shapes with Straight Edges

The perimeter of a flat shape is the total distance around it. We can
always find the perimeter of a shape by manoeuvring a tape measure
around it. But if the shape has straight edges, it is actually easier to
measure the lengths of those edges and add them. On page 203 there
are some examples that children might try.

Extra long tape measures can be used to measure distances of more
than 3 m. With such a tape measure, children can measure the length
and width of a room and calculate its perimeter. For instance, if the
room is 6·2 m long and 3·5 m wide, its perimeter is 19·4 m.

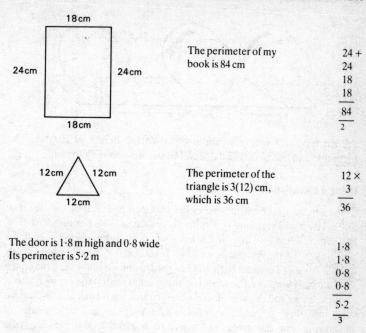

The perimeter of my
book is 84 cm

```
24 +
24
18
18
——
84
——
 2
```

The perimeter of the
triangle is 3(12) cm,
which is 36 cm

```
12 ×
 3
——
36
```

The door is 1·8 m high and 0·8 wide
Its perimeter is 5·2 m

```
1·8
1·8
0·8
0·8
——
5·2
——
 3
```

Perimeters of Curved Objects

It will be a new idea to children that we can measure *curved* lengths as
well as straight ones. If we wrap a tape measure round the top edge of a
cylindrical tin and read its calibration at the point where it meets its
'zero' calibration, we can find the perimeter of its circular face. (Martin,
aged ten, found this a 'brilliant idea'!) If we repeat the measurement
round the bottom edge of the tin, we should obtain the same measurement, because the circles that form the top and bottom faces of a
cylinder are congruent.

It is useful for children to pursue an alternative method of measuring
this perimeter. They might roll the tin over a large sheet of paper,
marking on the tin edge and on the paper the point at which they initially
meet, and also the point where the mark on the tin edge again meets the
paper. The distance between the two marks on the paper is the perimeter of the tin top.

A nice-follow-up to this exercise is to make a paper 'wrapper' for the
tin. Children draw a rectangle whose length is equal to the perimeter of

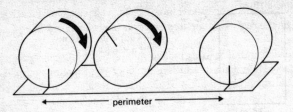

the tin top, and whose width is equal to the height of the tin. The rectangle can be cut out and decorated before adorning the tin.

Using a Click-wheel

The exercise described above helps children to see that the distance moved by a wheel in one revolution is the same as its perimeter. This is the principle underlying the *click-wheel*. A common click-wheel has a perimeter of 1 m. At one point of its revolution, a flexible prong on its handle comes in contact with a metal protrusion on the wheel, making a loud click. If we place the wheel on the ground so that the prong is about to click, as we roll the wheel along the ground, each click tells us that we have travelled a metre. A click-wheel provides a quick means of measuring long distances, and it will be a useful tool in making scale drawings (see 'Scale Drawings' below).

Drawing Circles

At this point, it is appropriate to introduce children to the idea that a circle has a *centre* and a *radius*. Make a card strip and punch a hole at one end of it. Children can pin one end of the strip to paper, put a pencil point through the hole at the other end, and draw. The shape that they draw will be a circle. The distance between the pin and the pencil is *constant*, and this distance is called the *radius* of the circle. The point where the pin was placed is called the *centre* of the circle. Using a card strip to draw a circle makes it obvious that all points on the edge are the same distance from the centre. Children can progress from drawing circles with card strips to using compasses to draw circles. They will enjoy making patterns of intersecting circles.

Scale Drawings

Children are intuitively acquainted with the idea of *scale*. A model car may be 6 cm long, whereas the actual car of which it is a model is 3 m long. What makes the model look like the real car is the fact that *every* length on the real car is the *same multiple* of the corresponding length on the model.

Children can begin to formalize their concept of scale by drawing a plan of a well-defined area such as the floor of a room or a netball court. They can draw their plan on paper that is marked in cm squares; such paper provides plenty of ready-made right angles and distances. Suppose that children have measured a netball court to be 30 m long and 20 m wide. It is not practical to make a drawing of the court as large as the actual court, but we could *represent* a length of 1 m on the court by a length of 1 cm on our drawing. Children can now work together to make the necessary measurements on the court in order to complete a drawing of it. They will need some help in drawing the semi-circular goal areas. If they measure the distance AB to be 10 m, the goal line can be drawn on the plan by drawing a semicircle centre O (the mid-point of AB) and radius 5 cm (to represent $\frac{1}{2}$ of AB).

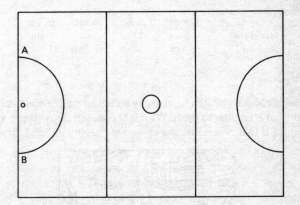

When the plan is complete, children might use it to help them find answers to questions such as 'What is the shortest distance from a third line to the goal circle?' and 'What is the shortest distance between the two goal circles?' Their answers can be checked by returning to the court and measuring these distance as well as is possible. Children might discuss whether their predictions from the plan are likely to be more accurate than the actual measurements that they make.

Another useful exercise on scale is to compare some dimensions of a car with those of a model of the car. To find the *scale* on which the model is based, we need to measure a specific length on the real car and the corresponding length on the model car. We might choose to measure the length of each from bumper to bumper. (This length can be found by holding a stick vertically at the centre of each bumper and marking the points where the sticks meet the ground or the paper; remove the car and measure the distance between the two marked points in each case.) It is important initially to choose a model that provides a scale that is easy to use. (When children have become confident at using calculators, this restriction can be relaxed, as is explained in more detail on page 230.) A suitable example would be a car 3 m long whose model is 6 cm long. This means that on the model, 6 cm represents 3 m, or 300 cm. So 1 cm on the model represents a sixth of 300 cm, or 50 cm. The car is fifty times as long as the model. Having expressed the scale in these terms, children can now measure certain lengths on the model and deduce the corresponding lengths on the real car. A child's record might read as follows. (The measurements in brackets show his predictions about the real car.)

	Length	Scale	Width	Height
Model car	6 cm	1 cm	3 cm	3 cm
Real car	3 m	½ m	(1·5 m)	(1·5 m)

Map Reading

We can introduce children to maps by means of a large-scale map of a locality that is familiar to them. We might concentrate at first on a small portion of it that represents the immediate neighbourhood. The map

here has a scale of 5 cm to 1 km. (If you feel that *miles* are more appropriate units to introduce to children, choose – or make – a map whose scale is 10 cm to 1 mile.) Children can place lengths of cotton along straight or curved distances on the map and then measure the lengths of cotton, to find out such real distances as: (a) the length of Hanley Park (0·4 km); (b) the distance from the station to the Electricity Works (1 km); (c) the distance from school, along College Road, to the station (0·4 km). (Example (a) was chosen because it involves measuring a straight length, which is relatively easy. Example (b) was chosen because it provides an example of a distance of 1 km; in order to conceptualize a distance of 1 km, children need to link this distance with one that is familiar to them.)

2. Area

In Chapter 13 (pages 132–3), we described how children can be introduced to the concept of area by counting the congruent squares (or triangles) covered by a plane shape. They were measuring area in *arbitrary physical units*. Although any shape that tessellates can be used as a unit for measuring area, the units used conventionally are squares, such as square centimetres. Children can now measure area using these units.

Area and Perimeter

It is a common fallacy to suppose that the area of a region is related to its perimeter. Perhaps one of the first exercises on finding areas in square centimetres should require children to find both the perimeter and the area of shapes drawn on paper marked in centimetre squares. We must tell children that each of these squares has an area of *1 square cm*.

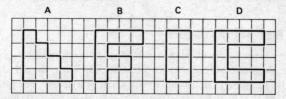

Find the area and the perimeter of the shapes A, B, C and D.
Which shape has the largest area?
Which shape has the largest perimeter?

Area of Rectangles

The next exercise is confined to rectangles, in order to invite children to discover the relation between the length, width and area of any rectangle. Some of the rectangles should be covered with squares and some not; children should be allowed to draw squares in the blank rectangles if they feel the need to do so.

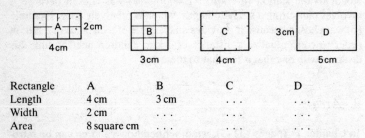

Rectangle	A	B	C	D
Length	4 cm	3 cm	. . .	. . .
Width	2 cm	. . .	. . .	. . .
Area	8 square cm	. . .	. . .	. . .

Having realized that the area of a rectangle can be found by multiplying the number of squares (real or imaginary) in a row by the number of rows, children can progress to calculating and comparing the areas of book pages, box tops and floors that are covered with congruent tiles. (The floor areas can be measured in *tiles* rather than square centimetres.) A typical exercise is shown.

Which is larger, our classroom or the cloakroom?

Our classroom is covered with 16 rows of tiles.
There are 12 tiles in each row.
The floor area is 16 × 12 tiles.
16 × 12 = (16 × 10) + (16 × 2)
= 160 + 32 = 192.
The floor area is 192 tiles.

The cloakroom floor is covered with 10 rows of tiles.
There are 18 tiles in each row.
The floor area is 10 × 18 tiles, or 180 tiles.
So our classroom is larger than the cloakroom.

Area of Right-angled Triangles

Children who have absorbed the work on area of rectangles can progress to some detective work on area of triangles. They should start by considering a triangle that is obviously a half of a square. For instance, the triangles that form halves of the square shown on page 209 must each have an area of 8 sq cm, since the square has an area of 16 sq cm. (We can check that the area of each triangle is 8 sq cm by counting the six whole squares and the four half squares that each covers.)

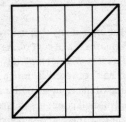

Next, we should consider triangles that are halves of rectangles. The triangles that form halves of the rectangle illustrated below must each have an area of 6 sq cm, since the rectangle has an area of 12 sq cm. (In this case, we cannot check by counting squares that the area of each triangle is exactly 6 sq cm.)

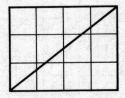

Exercises can follow on finding the area of right-angled triangles. Children should be given pictures of the triangles; they will probably want to extend the picture of a triangle into a rectangle and calculate the area of that rectangle before deciding the area of the triangle. They can proceed to draw a variety of shapes on squared paper and investigate their areas. One way of finding the area of the boat illustrated below is to divide the shape into a rectangle and four right-angled triangles.)

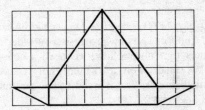

Area of Irregular Shapes

We can always *estimate* the area of any shape drawn on squared paper by counting the number of squares that it covers. A square that is more than half covered is counted as if it were completely covered, and a square that is half, or less than half, covered is not counted. If we apply this counting procedure to one of the right-angled triangles on page 209 that have an area of 6 sq cm, we shall count six squares and estimate its area to be 6 sq cm. But the fact that this estimate agrees with the mathematical result should not lead us to believe that such estimates always give us exact results.

The illustration below was obtained by drawing round the edge of a leaf. Each square cm that is to be counted is marked with a '1', and the number of squares marked in each row is recorded beside that row.

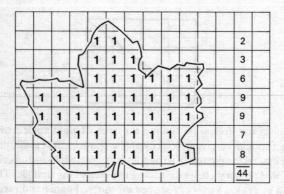

3. Angles

In Chapter 12 (page 112) we described how children can be introduced to *right angles*. Children can now progress to considering other angles. For the activities that now follow, we need a collection of angles cut from card. We can draw on card a number of circles of varying radii, divide them with diameters drawn as illustrated, and cut out the sectors formed.

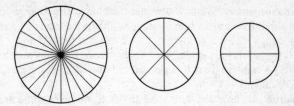

Matching. Children can pick out from the collection the angles that are right angles. They can superimpose two right angles (preferably from circles of different radii), to check that they match, and put them side by side to check that they make up a straight line. They can mark the right angles with the conventional symbol.

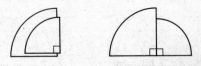

Sorting. Children can sort the whole collection of angles into three subsets of matching angles, and colour angles that match with the same colour. (We can now call our angles right angles, red angles and blue angles.)

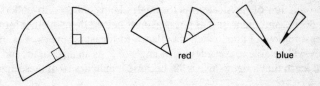

Ordering. Children can compare a red angle with a right angle. However we place a red angle on top of a right angle, some of the right angle's marking can still be seen, and we say that the right angle is *larger* than the red angle. A similar activity shows us that the red angle is larger than a blue angle. So the angles can be ordered for size.

Angle measurement. We now consider the blue angles as *angle units*. If we put three blue angles side by side, as illustrated below, we see that together they match a red angle. So we can call the red angle *3 angle units*. If we put six blue angles side by side, we see that they match a right angle. So a right angle is 6 angle units. Two red angles match a right angle, because 3 + 3 = 6.

Children can now use their card angles to measure some angles in shapes with which they are familiar. Each angle of an equilateral triangle, for instance, matches 4 angle units (or a red angle and a blue angle); each of the smaller angles of an isosceles right-angled triangle (illustrated on page 209) matches 3 angle units (or a red angle); each angle of a regular hexagon (illustrated on page 121) matches 8 angle units (or a right angle and two blue angles).

Measuring angles in degrees. Many children who appear to be able to use a conventional protractor to measure angles in degrees do not really understand the relevance of the numerals on the protractor. If they have no concept that angles can be added, these numerals will be seen by them as mere guides for making appropriate marks on paper. The introduction of physical units for angles helps children to understand angle measurement, just as physical units helped them in other forms of measurement. Later, when they learn to measure angles in degrees, they will be able to consider a tiny angle of 1° as an angle unit, and they will learn that a right angle is 90° because it matches 90 of these units.

4. Weight

In Chapter 13 we described how children can link their weighing activities with their concepts of tens and units, by weighing objects with plasticine balls and 'ten ball' weights; and in Chapter 15 teen we discussed weighing in kg and tenths of kg. In this section we are going to consider: (a) how children can be introduced to weighing in grams; and (b) how they can learn to use kitchen and bathroom scales.

Weighing in Grams

As mentioned in Chapter 13, a *gram* is a very tiny weight, and balance scales that are suitable for primary children are not sensitive to such a small weight. They are, however, sensitive to a weight as large as 10 grams; so we shall have to confine our weighing in grams to multiples of 10 grams. We need a number of commercially made weights of 10 grams. It is useful to have some weights of 1 gram, because children need to feel how light a 1 gram weight is. They have to be told that on sufficiently sensitive scales, ten of them will balance a 10-gram weight. (Children's scales will probably allow anything from 8 to 12 of them to balance a 10 gram weight.)

Having introduced the 10 g weights (and the shortened form 'g' to denote 'grams'), we can weigh some small objects, such as a ruler, a reading book, and one of our familiar plasticine balls. (A reading book will weigh about 80 g and a plasticine ball will weigh 100 g.) Objects that weigh less than 10 g need not be excluded; but they should be weighed in tens. If ten 2 p coins weigh 60 g, we know that each coin must weigh 6 g, because $60 = 10 \times 6$. (We can tell children that a bank clerk will check the value of a bag of copper coins by weighing it rather than by counting the coins.) To weigh objects heavier than 100 g, such as grocery items, children can use the plasticine balls as 100 g weights. Most grocery packages are labelled with their weight. A tin of soup, for instance, may be labelled 300 g. When we weigh it, we may find that it balances three plasticine balls and eight 10 g weights, indicating a weight of 380 g. This does not mean that the tin is incorrectly labelled, for the label is supposed to tell us the weight of the soup. The tin itself should weigh 80 g, because $380 = 300 + 80$. Children might enjoy having the tin opened and emptied so that they can check whether it does in fact weigh 80 g. (The contents, of course, can be consumed as a reward for scientific study.)

We see how number work is quite naturally involved in weight measurement. It can be extended by children calculating the total weight of some groceries that they have weighed, and checking the result by weighing, for example:

Cornflakes	350 g
Tin of soup	380 g
Shopping bag	80 g
Total weight	810 g

Kitchen and Bathroom Scales

Normal kitchen scales weigh quantities up to 3 kg, and bathroom scales weigh quantities up to about 125 kg. The weight of an object placed on such scales pushes a platform downwards, and this downwards movement causes a pointer to move round a calibrated scale (or, the calibrated scale itself moves). The scale looks like a number line. Children need to discover that pushing on the platform makes the pointer (or scale) move; the harder you push, the further the pointer (or scale) moves.

Next, children's attention must be drawn to the calibrations and labels on the scale. Kitchen scales should be studied first. They are usually calibrated at 50 g intervals and labelled at 100 g intervals. Children should practise pushing the pan until the pointer records 100 g. Then they should put one plasticine ball on the pan and note that the pointer records 100 g. A push is a force, and weight is also a force; the ball pushes on the pan as much as the child's hand did. Children can add balls to the pan, one at a time, and note the pointer recording 200 g, 300 g and so on. Then they should add some 10 g weights, in fives, and see that each set of five 10 g weights pushes the pointer to the next 50 g calibration. They can put a 1 kg weight in the pan and note that the pointer records 1 kg. They can put ten 100 g weights in the pan and note that the pointer again records 1 kg. Children can now use kitchen scales to weigh objects and groceries as described above under 'Weighing in Grams'. If bags of shopping are now allowed to have a total weight of more than 1 kg, in calculating these totals children will have to remember that ten 100 g weights are the same as 1 kg.

	kg	g
Soap powder		930
Tin of soup		380
Shopping bag		80
	1	390

Bathroom scales. Children need the experience of placing weights on bathroom scales so that they can discover the significance of the calibrations in terms of the weights that are familiar to them. They can then use the scales to weigh bags of shopping and heavier weights, such as themselves.

Again, we can bring in number work. If John weighs 42 kg and the bag of shopping weighs 2 kg, what will the scale register when John stands on the platform holding the bag? Although the bag does not touch the platform, the scales respond to the extra weight that they are supporting, and register a total weight of 44 kg, because $42 + 2 = 44$. Suppose that we would like to know the weight of a cat. The cat is not likely to sit obligingly on the platform while we read off his weight. But John can hold the cat in his arms while standing on the platform. If John and the cat together weigh 46 kg, we can deduce that the cat must weigh 4 kg, because $46 = 42 + 4$.

5. *Volume*

The volume of an object is the amount of space it takes up. If it is fluid, we can measure its volume by pouring it into containers of known capacity, as we have described earlier. If it is solid, we measure its volume in terms of the number of congruent cubes with which it could theoretically be built. A common physical unit of volume is a *cubic centimetre,* which is the volume of a centimetre cube. Children can use centimetre cubes to build solid shapes, and record the volume of each shape in cubic cm. It is important for children to realize that the volume of a solid is not dependent on its shape; a child who has built a tower using twenty-four cubes should be encouraged to build several more shapes with twenty-four cubes.

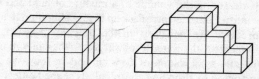

As well as using centimetre cubes, children can build with 'ten' rods and 'hundred' pieces (illustrated on page 173). A cuboid built with two layers of 'tens' with three 'tens' in each layer has a volume of 60 cubic cm; a stack of five 'hundreds' makes a cuboid whose volume is 500 cubic cm; a stack of ten 'hundreds' makes a cube whose volume is 1000 cubic cm.

Linking Volume and Capacity

We can make a 'bath' that will hold 10 cubic cm of water by forming a long 'sausage' of plasticine and gently pushing a 'ten' rod into the sausage until its top surface is level with the surface of the plasticine. On removing the rod, we have our bath. We can pour a dessertspoonful of water into it; if the dessertspoon is of standard size, the bath is just filled by the water, showing that a standard dessertspoon holds 10 cubic cm.

In Chapter 13, we described how children could measure capacity in terms of cartons cut to the size of $\frac{1}{10}$ litre. We can now find out how many cubic cm a carton will hold. We find that it holds ten dessertspoonfuls of water; so a carton will hold 100 cubic cm.

How many cubic cm make a litre? Children have already used litre flasks for measuring capacity, and they can be reminded that a litre flask holds ten cartons. Since each carton holds 100 cubic cm, a litre must be the same amount as *ten hundred*, or *a thousand*, cubic cm. Most household goods are sold in containers that are labelled with the amount of liquid in them. The amount is usually given in cubic cm (abbreviated to 'cc') or in millilitres (abbreviated to 'ml'). A millilitre is the same volume as 1 cubic cm. Thus we find shampoo labelled 150 ml, TCP labelled 100 ml and so on. Save the bottles when they are empty, so that children can fill them with water and check their capacity by pouring the water into cartons or calibrated litre flasks.

We can consolidate the newly found links between fluid and solid volume by measuring the volume of a mixture of fluid and solid. We pour water into a calibrated litre flask up to the calibration that indicates a volume of 500 cc. We then drop ten 'ten' rods into the water. Provided they are submerged, the water level will rise to the calibration '600 cc', because this is the total volume of the water and the rods. We can follow this demonstration by dropping an irregularly shaped object, such as a potato, into the water, and deducing its volume. (If the flask is calibrated only in tenths of a litre, we shall be reduced to estimating the volume of the potato to the nearest 50 cc.)

6. *Time*

In Chapter 13, we described how children can learn to tell the time from a conventional clock in terms of '20 minutes past 2', '40 minutes past 2' and so on. We shall now consider how to introduce children to digital clocks, timetables and time intervals.

Digital Clocks

The study of digital clocks is a good preparation for understanding timetables, because a digital clock displays the time in numerals in the same way that a timetable does. When the clock records '2.40', the time is 40 minutes past 2. Children should see a digital clock working alongside a conventional clock to help them understand what the numerals are telling them. The hardest times to read on a digital clock are those between the hour and 9 minutes past the hour. At 2 o'clock, the clock records '2.00'; at 5 past 2, it records '2.05'. The '0' in '2.05' is a placeholder, just as it is in the number 205 and the decimal number 2·05.

After some written practice in translating conventional clock times to digital recording, children are ready to consider timetables.

Timetables

We should teach children to read timetables alongside teaching them to understand time intervals. The best way to introduce children to time-tables is to help them make up one themselves, so that no number is recorded in the table until they have decided that it is appropriate. Children could make up a timetable for a bus service (real or imaginary) running between two places that are familiar to them. We shall suppose that the bus journey from, say, Waterloo to Euston takes 20 minutes, and that the first bus leaves at 7.10 in the morning. When will it arrive at Euston? Children can calculate the answer to this question in one of three ways:

(a) By using a clock and manipulating the hands, as was suggested in Chapter 15.

(b) By learning to arrange the numerals in columns and performing addition

$$\begin{array}{r} 7.10\ + \\ 20 \\ \hline 7.30 \end{array}$$

(c) by learning to use a *time line*:

7·00	7·10	7·20	7·30	7·40	7·50	8·00	8·10	8·20	8·30	8·40	8·50	9·00

To use this time line to find out when the 7.10 bus arrives at Euston, we must locate the point on the line that represents 7.10 and move along to the right a distance that represents 20 minutes. We can count in tens as we do this, arriving at the point that represents 7.30.

While method (a) is the best method for children who still need to become familiar with the movement of the hands of a conventional clock, at some stage it has to be discarded. While method (b) provides a link for children between adding numbers and adding times, it carries the onus of remembering that the columns are *not* arranged in base ten. (Try using this method to calculate 20 minutes beyond 7.55, for example.) Method (c) has the advantages of linking time with a number line and of preparing children for future graph work concerning time. Although, like (a), it has to be discarded at some stage, its graphical clarity might be retained in children's minds.

Whichever method we have used to calculate the time of arrival of the bus, we can now begin to make our timetable. Suppose that buses leave Waterloo at 10-minute intervals; we must calculate the times that buses leave Waterloo before calculating the times that they arrive at Euston; but there are several ways of completing the timetable.

| Waterloo | 7.10 | 7.20 | 7.30 | 7.40 | | |
| Euston | 7.30 | 7.40 | | | | |

Reading timetables. In our daily life, we have to adapt to timetables rather than make them up ourselves, and it is important for us to be able to understand them. Perhaps the first timetables that interest children are TV timetables. Children might be given a copy of such a timetable and invited to record the times given on a time line. This gives them a visual means of finding which is the longest programme, and indeed the duration of any one programme.

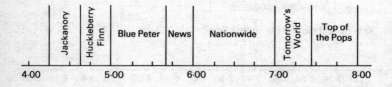

The disadvantage of using TV timetables is that they record some times in an unconventional manner: 6.00 is recorded as 6.0 and 6.05 as 6.5. I have been unable to get any explanation from TV editors as to why they persist in this idiosyncratic recording.

The 24-hour clock. To understand most bus and rail timetables, we need to be familiar with the 24-hour clock. The concept can be made understandable for children if we extend a time line to include more than 24 hours, and shade the 'night' hours as illustrated.

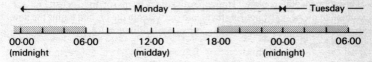

Equipment Needed for the Activities in This Chapter

Rulers and tape measures.
Cylindrical objects, such as tins.
A click-wheel.
Card strips and compasses for drawing circles.
Paper marked in cm squares.
A real car and a model of it.
A local map.
Angles cut from card.
Ten 10 g weights and several 1 g weights and 1 kg weights.
Ten plasticine balls weighing 100 g each, or ten 100 g weights.
Balance pans.
Grocery items for weighing.
Kitchen scales and bathroom scales.
Centimetre cubes, 'ten' rods and 'hundred' pieces.
A standard-size dessertspoon.
Cartons cut to the size of 0.1 litre.
Litre flasks calibrated in tenths of a litre.
A digital clock and a conventional clock.
A television timetable.
A bus or train timetable.

Suggestions for the Reader

1. (Perimeter and area) Draw a number of rectangles each with a perimeter of 24 cm. Find the area of each rectangle. Which has the largest area? If you had a piece of string 24 cm long, could you make it form the perimeter of a shape of even larger area than your largest rectangle? (Answers at the end of Chapter 20, page 236.)

2. (Scale) On page 127 there is a drawing of a child's arm. Find the scale to which it is drawn.

3. (Angles) Draw any triangle on paper and cut it out carefully. Tear off its three angles and arrange them side by side. What do you notice?

4. (Weight) Use kitchen scales to find out the weight of (a) twenty 1p coins, and (b) ten 2p coins. What do you notice?

5. (Volume) Fill a cup with water. Find the volume of the water by pouring it into a calibrated litre jug or flask. Note this volume. Pour water into the jug up to the calibration for 500 cc. Now fill the cup with kidney beans (or dried peas). Find the volume of the beans by pouring them into the water in the jug and noting the new water level. Why is the volume of a cup of water different from the volume of a cup of beans?

6. (Time) Test some ten- and eleven-year-olds on (a) their understanding of digital clocks, and (b) their understanding of a bus or train timetable.

20 Calculators and Computers

Computers, calculators, typewriters . . . food mixers, TV
sets and cars are all part of today's and tomorrow's world.
Students should be at home with such equipment.

> – *Fifteen-year-old schoolboy*

A computer lies obsolete in the corner,
Good only for last year's curriculum.

> – *From a poem by a thirteen-year-old boy*

Calculators and computers are features of our age. Pocket calculators
are cheaper than watches, and there can be few people who have not
used one or seen one in use. Most people are aware that invoices, bank
statements and circularized letters are produced by computers. For
these reasons, if for no other, calculators and computers cannot be
ignored in school. In this chapter we shall consider some of the ways in
which these machines can enrich and support children's learning of
mathematics. At the end I shall comment on some of the advantages and
disadvantages of using computers for this purpose in primary school.

1. Calculators and Confidence

Many adults feel an understandable unease about the wisdom of allowing children to use calculators to perform calculations. A child who uses
a calculator to find out the answer to 5×10 is losing an opportunity to
consolidate his understanding of place value. But the child who *knows*
that $5 \times 10 = 50$ and presses the keys $\boxed{5}$ $\boxed{X}$ $\boxed{1}$ $\boxed{0}$ $\boxed{=}$ on a
calculator is going to gain confidence in the machine. I would suggest
that no primary-level child should be encouraged to use a calculator to
perform a calculation before he or she has formed an idea of what the
answer might be. The child who presses the key $\boxed{6}$ in error for $\boxed{5}$
must not think for a moment that $5 \times 10 = 60$.

Free play to discover how a calculator works. As with all mathematical
apparatus, children should be allowed to play with a calculator before
using it for a definite purpose. Through such play, they will discover
some of its functions. We can check their discoveries by asking them,

'Can you make it say 12? Can you make it say 102? Can you make it tell you the answer to $3 + 5 = \square$? To $5 + 5 + 5 = \square$? To $3 \times 5 = \square$? What must you add to 99 to make it say 100? How can you get it to say 99 again? What must you add to 102 to make it say 172? How can you get it to say 102 again?'

Checking work. Perhaps the first *practical* use of calculators for children is to check their own calculations. For example, children who have completed an exercise on addition or subtraction of numbers in the hundreds might use a calculator to help them mark their own work. Answers that disagree with the calculator can be brought to the teacher for analysis.

The division sign ($\div$). In earlier chapters, I have suggested that children record division using a multiplication sign. For instance, the result of dividing 144 into three equal shares has been recorded as '$144 = 3 \times 48$' (see page 188). Postponing the use of the symbol '$\div$' for division forces children to record division using a multiplication symbol, so helping them to form the essential link between multiplication and division. However, a calculator has a key marked '$\div$'. Children can be invited to discover the function of this key. They can press the keys $\boxed{6}$ $\boxed{\div}$ $\boxed{3}$ $\boxed{=}$ and note that the calculator's answer suggests that 6 has been divided into three equal shares; they can press the keys $\boxed{1}$ $\boxed{0}$ $\boxed{0}$ $\boxed{\div}$ $\boxed{1}$ $\boxed{0}$ $\boxed{=}$ and note that the calculator's answer suggests that 100 has been divided into ten equal shares.

Children can now use a calculator to check their calculations involving multiplication or equal sharing. To check the calculation $7 \times 16 = 112$, for instance, they can press the keys $\boxed{1}$ $\boxed{1}$ $\boxed{2}$ $\boxed{\div}$ $\boxed{7}$ $\boxed{=}$; to check the calculation $144 = 3 \times 48$, they can press the keys $\boxed{1}$ $\boxed{4}$ $\boxed{4}$ $\boxed{\div}$ $\boxed{3}$ $\boxed{=}$.

Estimation. It is essential to be able to check that a result produced by a calculator is reasonable. For instance, if a calculator appears to tell us that $52 + 49 = 111$, we should suspect that an incorrect key has been pressed, because the answer should be *near* $50 + 50$.

As mentioned earlier in this book, children often show a reluctance to form estimates, because in general estimates give 'wrong answers'. It is only with maturity that children learn that estimates and conjectures form the basis of mathematical thinking. Perhaps calculators can provide one of the first opportunities to learn this important lesson. Children might be invited to estimate (by rounding numbers to easily manageable ones) the results of some calculations, and then perform these calculations using a calculator. Their work might be recorded as follows:

Calculation	Estimate	Calculator result
52 + 49	50 + 50 = 100	101
55 + 47	60 + 50 = 110	102
127 + 452	100 + 500 = 600	579
76 − 28	80 − 30 = 50	48
563 − 208	600 − 200 = 400	355
63 × 7	60 × 7 = 420	441
4·8 × 5·2	5 × 5 = 25	24·96

2. Numbers in the Thousands

In Chapter 17 (page 189) I suggested that children who have mastered the concept of place value in terms of numbers in the hundreds will have little difficulty in extending the concept to numbers in the thousands. However we teach children about numbers in the thousands, we have to *tell* them that a thousand means *ten hundreds*, and help them also to see that a thousand is one more than 999. Having done this, we could see what numerals the calculator produces for the results of 10 × 100 = □ and 999 + 1 = □. Children could then use calculators to help them to become familiar with numbers in the thousands.

Place value and addition. We might ask children to guess, and then check, using a calculator, the answers to addition problems like those below. Children who cannot predict correctly what the calculator will say should use structural material to help them (as described in Chapter 17).

1000 + 1 =	1000 + 100 + 20 =
1000 + 5 =	1000 + 100 + 20 + 4 =
1000 + 10 =	1000 + 1000 =
1000 + 10 + 5 =	2000 + 3000 =
1000 + 20 =	500 + 500 =
1000 + 100 =	300 + 700 =

When children have shown that they understand the additive principle behind place value, they need practice in ordering numbers in the thousands. They could be asked to decide who has won an election if the votes for the three candidates were: Fred Brown, 2008 votes; Mary Jones, 2018 votes; Hugh Smith, 1998 votes.

A calculator game that helps reinforce the relation between hundreds and thousands is 'Make 3000'. The game is for two children. They put 1000 on the calculator display. One child adds to this on the calculator *one* of the numbers 100, 200, 300, 400 or 500. The second child then adds to the new total one of those five numbers. The game continues until one child – the winner – makes the total 3000 appear on the calculator.

Multiplying by hundreds. Children who know that 1000 means *ten hundreds* could be asked to guess and then to check, using a calculator, the answers to multiplication problems like those below. In calculating 11×100, the argument should be, 'eleven hundreds is ten hundreds and one hundred, which is one thousand and one hundred', and *not*, 'Write down 11 and add two noughts.' The first of these arguments is logical; the second is merely an application of a rule that works. If, in the course of their work, children discover this rule for themselves and test it in further examples, the rule becomes part of their own logical thinking rather than a 'trick' to be remembered.

$$11 \times 100 = \qquad\qquad 20 \times 200 =$$
$$16 \times 100 = \qquad\qquad 30 \times 200 =$$
$$20 \times 100 = \qquad\qquad 40 \times 200 =$$
$$40 \times 100 = \qquad\qquad 20 \times 300 =$$

Multiplying tens by tens. Children who know facts such as 'Ten fifties are five hundred' and 'Ten forties are four hundred' might be asked to guess and then to check, using a calculator, the answers to problems like those below. In calculating 20×50, the argument should be 'twenty fifties are ten fifties and ten more fifties, which is five hundreds and five more hundreds, which is ten hundreds, or one thousand', and *not*, '$2 \times 5 = 10$, so write down 10 and add two noughts'. In the course of their work, children might well discover this rule for themselves and test its validity.

$$20 \times 50 = \qquad\qquad 20 \times 40 =$$
$$30 \times 50 = \qquad\qquad 30 \times 40 =$$
$$40 \times 50 = \qquad\qquad 40 \times 40 =$$

Calculations in the thousands. Children can now progress to estimating, (by rounding numbers) the results of calculations involving numbers in the thousands, and then perform these calculations using a calculator. Their work might be recorded as follows:

Calculation	Estimate	Calculator result
1048 + 1804	1000 + 2000 = 3000	2852
5207 − 1782	5000 − 2000 = 3000	3425
5 × 1123	5 × 1000 = 5000	5615
56 × 105	60 × 100 = 6000	5880
47 × 53	50 × 50 = 2500	2491

Some children might be concerned that the calculator's answer to the third problem above is nearer to 6000 than the 5000 of their estimate. They can allay their concern by (a) revising this estimate to 5 × 1100 = 5500, or (b) using the calculator to calculate 5615 ÷ 5.

I have deliberately avoided mentioning the conventional routines for calculating in the thousands. Because of the wide accessibility of calculators, it is really not necessary to teach children such routines, although it is very necessary to teach them to form estimates. However, able children could be encouraged to think of ways of performing such calculations. For instance, an able child might calculate 47 × 53 as follows:

$$
\begin{array}{ll}
40 \times 50 = 2000 & \\
\underline{7 \times 50 = 350} & \quad 47 \times \\
47 \times 50 = 2350 & \quad \underline{3} \\
\underline{47 \times 3 = 141} \longleftarrow 141 & \\
47 \times 53 = 2491 &
\end{array}
$$

3. Fractions and Decimals

Most calculators express all fractions in decimal form. Children who know that a tenth of 60 is 6 (or 60 ÷ 10 = 6), should be able to guess that a tenth of 61 (or 61 ÷ 10) must be a little more than 6. The calculator tells them that 61 ÷ 10 = 6·1. They can be invited to estimate the results of other division calculations and then perform these calculations using a calculator. Their work might be recorded as follows:

Calculation	Estimate	Calculator result
61 ÷ 10	60 ÷ 10 = 6	6·1
41 ÷ 4	40 ÷ 4 = 10	10·25
33 ÷ 8	32 ÷ 8 = 4	4·125
30 ÷ 7	28 ÷ 7 = 4	4·2857142
10 ÷ 3	9 ÷ 3 = 3	3·3333333

Children will wonder what the digit '5' means in the number 4·125 shown on the calculator. They can be told that just as the '1' means 1 tenth and the '2' means 2 hundredths, the '5' means 5 thousandths, because 10 thousandths are the same as 1 hundredth. They will be intrigued to discover from the calculator results for the last examples that decimal notation can be continued further, each decimal place representing a tinier subdivision than the previous (by a tenth).

When children have completed division calculations like these, they should be invited to check them by appropriate multiplication calculations. For instance, a calculator tells us that $6·1 \times 10 = 61$, confirming the first calculation above. But it tells us that $3·3333333 \times 3 = 9·9999999$, showing us that the answer it gave for $10 \div 3$ was not exact.

At this stage, we can introduce divisions in which the dividend is less than the divisor – for example $4 \div 10$. At first we should limit the divisor to 10 or a factor of 10. We should ask children to record the divisions in fraction form and then estimate the result in decimal form. Their work might be recorded as follows.

Calculation	Fraction	Estimate in decimals	Calculator result
$1 \div 10$	$\frac{1}{10}$	$\frac{1}{10} = 0·1$	0·1
$4 \div 10$	$\frac{4}{10}$	$\frac{4}{10} = 0·4$	0·4
$1 \div 2$	$\frac{1}{2}$	$\frac{5}{10} = 0·5$	0·5
$1 \div 5$	$\frac{1}{5}$	$\frac{2}{10} = 0·2$	0·2
$2 \div 5$	$\frac{2}{5}$	$\frac{4}{10} = 0·4$	0·4
$1 \div 4$	$\frac{1}{4}$	$\frac{2}{10} = 0·2$	0·25
$1 \div 9$	$\frac{1}{9}$	$\frac{1}{10} = 0·1$	0·1111111
$3 \div 9$	$\frac{3}{9}$	$\frac{3}{10} = 0·3$	0·3333333

4. Number Patterns

Mathematics has been described as 'the study of patterns'. As we have seen, the study of number patterns can lead children to mathematical investigation. Eventually it can lead them on to algebra. Conjectures concerning patterns can be made as a result of simple mental calculations and then tested using a calculator. The idea is exciting to many children.

Table patterns. Perhaps the most important number patterns that we need to impress on primary-level children are those formed by the multiplication tables. The table of fives, for instance, exhibits a pattern of 5, 0, 5, 0 and so on for the final digit of every multiple. Children might predict the final digit of any number obtained on the calculator by multiplying by 5, for instance 632 × 5 or 623 × 5.

The table of eights exhibits a pattern of 8, 6, 4, 2, 0, 8, 6 and so on for the final digit of every multiple. Children might predict the final digit of multiplications such as 63 × 8, 145 × 8 and so on. They can extend their predictions to the final digit of multiplications such as 153 × 18, 145 × 28 and so on.

Divisibility tests. On examining their table of threes, children may have noticed that when we add the digits of a multiple of three we obtain 3, 6 or 9. Does this 'rule' hold for multiples of three beyond the table? We can find out from a calculator that 42, 126 and 1101 are divisible by three; and their digits add to 6, 9 and 3. But 39, 78 and 99 are also multiples of three, and their digits add to 12, 15 and 18. It looks as if we must extend the rule to say that multiples of three have digits that add to a multiple of three.

What about numbers that are not multiples of three? The calculator tells us that 46, 173 and 3185, for instance, are not multiples of three. Their digits do not add to multiples of three. Our rule can perhaps be extended to give us a test for finding whether a number is divisible by three: if its digits add to a multiple of three, then it is itself a multiple of three; if they do not, then it is not a multiple of three.

A number that is divisible by six must be an even number as well as being divisible by three. Children can apply both tests to decide whether given numbers are divisible by six, using a calculator to check their decisions.

Other number patterns. Children who meet many number patterns are being given a foundation on which their later understanding of algebra can be based. An algebraic identity, such as $(n + 1)^2 = n^2 + 2n + 1$, is a generalization of a number pattern. The letter n can be represented by *any* number, and the equality will hold. Number patterns that appear to be true for any number can lead children towards the sophisticated concept of a *variable* (in this case, n). At this stage, however, we are concerned not with algebra, but with number patterns. Each pattern that children investigate should be detectable from a few simple examples. Children can then make a prediction concerning large numbers and check their prediction using a calculator. For instance, children who have noticed that the first two odd numbers add to 4, the first three odd numbers add to 9 and so on might predict that the first ten odd numbers add to 100. Later, when they learn algebra, they will express this pattern in the form 'The first n odd numbers add to n^2'.

Children might study the pattern formed by the following multiplications:

$2 \times 2 = 4$	$3 \times 3 = 9$	$4 \times 4 = 16$
$1 \times 3 = 3$	$2 \times 4 = 8$	$3 \times 5 = 15$

When they have continued this pattern a little further, they might make a prediction such as, '$20 \times 20 = 400$, so 19×21 must be 399.' Later, when they learn algebra, they will express this pattern in the form $(n - 1)(n + 1) = n^2 - 1$.

Negative numbers. Children may discover quite spontaneously that a calculator seems to give a result for a subtraction that 'can't be done'. The calculation $5 - 8$, for instance, is reported by a calculator to have an answer of 3 accompanied by a subtraction sign. Different calculators display this answer in different ways; we shall record it as -3, and call it 'negative three'. (The 'minus' sign attached to the 3 does not signify an operation like 'take away'. It is actually part of the number itself.)

What can the number -3 mean? Let us see what the calculator gives as the answer to $0 - 1$. It tells us that $0 - 1 = -1$; so -1 must be the number that is 1 less than 0. Similarly, $0 - 2 = -2$; so -2 is the number that is 2 less than 0. And -3 is the number that is 3 less than 0. We can tell children that these new numbers are called *negative numbers*, and that they were invented to describe quantities that are less than 0, such as temperatures below zero, or times before 'zero hour'.

Children can now predict and check on a calculator the result of calculations such as those below. Stories should be produced to accompany some of these calculations, such as 'The temperature was 2 degrees above zero and then it fell 4 degrees, so it was then -2 degrees.'

$1 - 1$	$2 - 1$	$3 - 1$
$1 - 2$	$2 - 2$	$3 - 2$
$1 - 3$	$2 - 3$	$3 - 3$
$1 - 4$	$2 - 4$	$3 - 4$

After this gentle introduction to negative numbers, children could label some points on a number line to represent negative numbers, and use the line to help them calculate $4 - 6$, $0 - 5$, $-3 + 5$, $-2 + 7$ and so on. They could solve problems such as, 'The temperature was -3

degrees but it has gone up 5 degrees. What is the temperature now?', or
'How old were you fourteen years ago?' (A child of ten might enjoy
answering this by saying, 'Negative four'.)

```
 ┴────┴────┴────┴────┴────┴────┴────┴────┴────┴────┴────┴────┴────┴────┴────┴
-7   -6   -5   -4   -3   -2   -1    0    1    2    3    4    5    6    7    8
```

5. The Memory Key of a Calculator

The memory key of a calculator provides a valuable link between
calculators and computers. Children should think of the *memory* of a
calculator as a hidden store where numbers can be added. By pressing
the key $\boxed{\text{M+}}$ the number displayed on the calculator is added to the
number already in the memory store, and this sum becomes the new
contents of the memory store. The key $\boxed{\text{RM}}$ (meaning 'reveal memory') shows what is hidden in the memory store. Children can experi-
ment by pressing the keys $\boxed{1}$ $\boxed{\text{M+}}$ $\boxed{\text{RM}}$ in sequence for as long as
they like. They will notice that the $\boxed{\text{RM}}$ key reveals the numbers 1, 2, 3,
4 and so on. They might then try to predict what the $\boxed{\text{RM}}$ key will
reveal for the following sequential 'programs':

```
2  M+  RM  2  M+  RM  2  M+  RM . . .     (2, 4, 6 . . .)
6  M+  RM  6  M+  RM  6  M+  RM . . .     (6, 12, 18 . . .)
1  M+  RM  2  M+  RM  2  M+  RM . . .     (1, 3, 5 . . .)
1  M+  RM  3  M+  RM  5  M+  RM . . .     (1, 4, 9 . . .)
```

Children might then try to devise and write 'programs' similar to the
above so that the $[\text{RM}]$ key will reveal the table of sevens or the
progressive totals of a set of numbers.

Averages. Suppose we wish to find out the total number of children in
the families of a group of sixteen children. We will feed in turn the
number of children in each family into the calculator memory. Assum-
ing that there are no siblings in the group, there are sixteen relevant
numbers. The $\boxed{\text{RM}}$ key will reveal the total number of children in the
sixteen families. Suppose this total is thirty-two. Let us pretend for a
moment that all these thirty-two children were shared equally between
the sixteen families so that each family had the same number of children.
To find out how many children would be in each family, we would have
to divide thirty-two by sixteen. The answer to $32 \div 16$ is 2, and we say
that 2 is the *average* number of children per family. If the total number of
children in the sixteen families had been forty, the average number of

children per family would have turned out to be 2·5. Children will be intrigued to see that an average need not be a whole number, although you cannot have a fraction of a child in a family. Children can follow this by using calculators to find the average age, average height and average weight of the children in a group.

6. *Using Calculators in Investigations*

Sometimes an investigation or project may lead to the need for a complicated calculation. In Chapter 19 we described (page 206) an investigation into scale based on comparing the dimensions of a car with those of a model of the car. For the example we chose, it was relatively easy to see that the scale of the model was 1 to 50. Suppose, however, that the real car had been 310 cm long and the model was 6·5 cm long. To find the scale, we would need to divide 310 by 6·5. The calculator can tell us that the scale of this model is 1 to 47·692307. This number can be stored in the memory of the calculator and multiplied by appropriate numbers to make predictions about various dimensions of the real car.

7. *Computers*

A computer is a grand calculator with a host of memory stores. We shall consider computers that consist of a keyboard linked with a television screen. We can store the number 2 in the memory store called A by typing 'LET A = 2. To reveal the contents of store A, we type 'PRINT A'. The numeral 2 will then appear on the screen. The sentences 'LET A = 2' and 'PRINT A' are examples of BASIC, the 'language' commonly used to instruct a computer (BASIC stands for 'Beginners' All-Purpose Symbolic Instruction Code'). Using BASIC, we could follow these two instructions by typing 'LET A = A + 3'. This strange-looking instruction has the effect of replacing the number in store A: (2), by this number plus 3: (2 + 3). If we now type 'PRINT A', the numeral 5 will appear on the screen.

Children could experiment with the keys LET and PRINT, to help them see how a computer behaves, before trying to predict what a computer will display in response to some simple programs. A program (so spelt) is a sequence of typed instructions. If we label the instructions with numerals they will appear on the screen in the order of the numerals.

(We usually label the instructions by 10, 20, 30 etc., so that a forgotten instruction can be numbered with an appropriate intermediate numeral and inserted in its correct place without altering the other instructions.) When the key RUN is pressed, the machine will obey the sequence of instructions. Children can pretend to be the computer for some simple programs, and fill in boxes that represent the successive contents of the hidden store A as well as fill in what they expect to appear on the screen. Then they can type out the program and run it to check their predictions.

```
10 LET A = 2
20 PRINT A
30 LET A = A + 3
40 PRINT A
50 LET A = A + 3
60 PRINT A
```

A: 2, 5, 8

Screen: 2, 5, 8

```
10 LET A = 2
20 PRINT A
30 LET A = A + 3
40 GOTO 20
```

A: 2, 5, 8

Screen: 2, 5, 8

The second program includes an instruction GOTO (or GO TO) 20, which tells the computer to return to the instruction labelled 20. The instructions then form a 'loop', which will be followed as long as there is space on the screen for numbers to be printed. Children will be fascinated by the seemingly endless sequence of numbers appearing on the screen. When children have appreciated the power of the key GOTO, they can try to design programs themselves to give multiplication tables, odd numbers, square numbers and so on. Here are some examples. (The symbol * is used in computing to represent multiplication.)

```
10 LET A = 7          10 LET A = 1          10 LET A = 1
20 PRINT A            20 PRINT A            20 PRINT A * A
30 LET A = A + 7      30 LET A = A + 2      30 LET A = A + 1
40 GOTO 20            40 GOTO 20            40 GOTO 20
```

The first of the above programs is designed to print out the table of sevens. A rather more elegant way to present this program is:

```
10 PRINT 'NUMBER', 'TIMES 7'
20 LET A = 1
30 PRINT A, A * 7
40 LET A = A + 1
50 PAUSE 100
60 GOTO 30
```

The effect of line 10 is to display the words 'NUMBER' and 'TIMES 7' on the screen at a well-spaced interval. Line 30 causes the computer to print the numbers 'A' and 'A * 7' on the screen below these headings. Line 50 causes the computer to pause for two seconds before continuing to its next instruction. This enables children to use the two seconds to guess what is going to appear on the screen next. As such, it provides an extra stimulus for learning the table of sevens! (The other two programs above can be redesigned to run in a similar way.)

A useful BASIC instruction is 'INPUT N'. The computer obeys this instruction by waiting for a number to be typed, which is then put into store N. Let us consider the example of programming the computer to find the total of a list of numbers. We need a store N to receive the numbers as they are fed in, and another store, T, say, to keep track of the running total. The following program can be checked by going through the instructions step by step and filling in the appropriate order the boxes that represent the successive contents of the stores T and N. You might like to try it out for the following list of numbers: 12, 14, 23, 42, 18.

		T	N
10	LET T = 0	0	12
20	INPUT N	12	14
30	LET T = T + N	26	23
40	PRINT T		
50	GOTO 20		

Children can play a game based on this program. Instead of typing a given number to be fed into store N, a child chooses the number that he wishes the total to become. A second child must decide what number he will type into store N so that the required total will be printed on the screen. Suppose, for instance, that the last total printed on the screen was 92. If a child chooses 100 for the next total to be printed, the second child should type '8'. Children might experiment with negative numbers in this game. If the last total to be printed was 100, what will the next total be if the next N to be added is −100?

Note: The BASIC language described here is accurate for certain computers; but for others, some modifications are needed.

8. Computers as 'Pencils'

Computers can be programmed to 'draw' on a TV screen. The process is commonly called *graphics*. To obtain graphics by BASIC programming, some knowledge of coordinate geometry is needed. The instruction PLOT 10, 5 results in a small blob appearing on the screen at a point whose coordinates are $x = 10$, $y = 5$, referred to axes $0x$, $0y$ imagined along edges of the screen, as illustrated.

With a knowledge of coordinate geometry, it is possible to program the 'drawing' of shapes. For example, program A below results in a horizontal straight line and program B results in a parabola. Such programs are too sophisticated for most primary-level children to understand.

Program A
10 LET X = 0
20 PLOT X, 10
30 LET X = X + 1
40 GOTO 20

Program B
10 LET X = 0
20 PLOT X, X * X
30 LET X = X + 1
40 GOTO 20

To enable children to program graphics in a simpler way, another computer language has been designed, called Logo. Its inventor, Seymour Papert, describes Logo graphics as using computers as 'pencils'. For Logo graphics, a tiny 'turtle' appears on the screen, and it can be instructed to move in a straight line or to turn. The instruction FORWARD 50, for instance, causes the turtle to move 50 mm in the direction in which it is facing, and to leave a 'trail' on the screen of the path it has taken. The instruction RIGHT 60 causes the turtle to turn through 60° to the right of the direction in which it is facing. The instructions below, taken in order, cause the 'trail' illustrated.

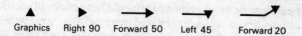

Graphics   Right 90   Forward 50   Left 45   Forward 20

With these instructions and another useful instruction, REPEAT, children can experiment to obtain a program that will draw a square. (The instruction END refers the computer back to the instruction REPEAT 4 until all four repeats have been carried out.)

```
TO SQUARE
REPEAT 4
RIGHT 90
FORWARD 50
END
```

The advantage of Logo is that graphics reflect natural movements; indeed, children will often move and turn their own bodies to help them decide how to instruct the turtle to move. You might like to decide what drawings will appear on the screen in response to programs C and D below:

Program C	*Program D*
TO . . .	TO . . .
REPEAT 3	REPEAT 360
FORWARD 50	FORWARD 1
RIGHT 120	RIGHT 1
END	END

Children can design complex shapes by combining programs for simpler shapes. For instance, in trying to obtain a house-like shape, they might combine the instruction SQUARE (which recalls the program TO SQUARE above) with the instruction TRIANGLE (which could recall program C above). The resulting drawing will not be a satisfying house-like shape unless an appropriate turning instruction is inserted between the instructions SQUARE and TRIANGLE:

```
TO HOUSE
SQUARE
RIGHT 30
TRIANGLE
```

9. Some Advantages and Drawbacks of Computers

Computers can be programmed to print out sentences and questions as well as calculations with numbers and graphics. Teachers can make or buy ready-made programs on discs or cassettes that can be plugged into a computer to make it print out tasks, games or questions. Children type their responses and the computer can be programmed to print out feedback to those responses. Such pre-prepared programs are called computer *software*. Computer software can provide exercises in mathematics, and they are reminiscent of the 'programmed learning' texts that were in vogue some years ago. Programmed learning was initially seen as an Open Sesame to painless mathematics learning, but it never reached the stage of replacing pupil–teacher contact, I am glad to say. I suspect that computer software will follow the same fate as programmed learning. The value of computers lies in their potential for following instructions rather than giving them.

There is no doubt that computing provides great motivation for children in mathematics. Even children of low mathematical attainment experience great delight in typing a program and inspecting the result as it appears on the screen. Designing a program is instructive, for it focuses attention on the operations to be performed rather than the calculations themselves. Feedback is immediate; children are free to learn from their errors. The recognition of errors is a constructive part of learning, and this fact is revealed relatively painlessly in the context of computing. However, the main importance of computers lies in their power (a) to store and organize vast quantities of information, and (b) to perform long or highly sophisticated calculations rapidly. With their limited mathematical knowledge, primary-school children cannot be expected to appreciate this. Because it is only with further mathematical knowledge that they will see the significance of computing, it is questionable whether their initial undoubted enthusiasm will be sustained. More serious is the conflict that exists between the computer language BASIC and the language of mathematics. The use of '=' in computing signifies 'replace by', and this conflicts with the use of '=' in mathematics to signify 'is the same number as'. The statement LET A = A + 3, so useful in BASIC, is meaningless in the context of mathematics. In algebra, children will learn that the equation $2a = a + 3$ has the solution $a = 3$; but the equation $a = a + 3$ has *no* solution.

At the beginning of this chapter I mentioned that because computers make such a significant contribution to modern life, children must be introduced to them at some stage. Indeed, we can hardly prevent this. As the price of a microcomputer constantly decreases, a computer keyboard that can be linked to a TV screen is more likely to be considered to be within the budget of household expenditure. Computers are now being supplied to primary schools as part of their normal resources. As long as they do not *replace* other resources, and as long as we do not expect primary-school children to appreciate the full potential of these machines, no harm is done, beyond, perhaps, taking the 'gilt off the gingerbread' in terms of children's later, more significant, need for them. Although computers can scarcely be regarded as a necessary classroom resource for primary mathematics, nevertheless they can stimulate children's interest in the subject.

Equipment Needed for the Activities in This Chapter

Simple electronic calculators with $\boxed{\text{M+}}$ and $\boxed{\text{RM}}$ keys.
A microcomputer, such as the BBC computer, Sinclair, Commodore Pet, Apple or Texas.
A TV set.

Suggestions for the Reader

1. Without using the routine procedure for long multiplication or long division, find several ways to perform these calculations: (a) 41 × 29; (b) 555 = 15 × □. Check your solutions on a calculator.

2. Use the memory key of a calculator to help you find the sums 1 + 2, 1 + 2 + 3, 1 + 2 + 3 + 4 and so on. Press the $\boxed{\text{RM}}$ key each time that you insert a new number into the memory and jot down the numbers revealed: 3, 6, 10 and so on. These numbers are called *triangular numbers*. Check that the sum of any two successive triangular numbers is a square number. Can you see why? The picture below might help. (Answer at the end of Chapter 21, page 248.)

```
  o           o           o             o
  o o         o o         o o           o o
              o o o       o o o         o o o
                          o o o o       o o o o
                                        o o o o o
```

3. On page 227, we met an activity using a calculator that led to the formulation of a test for divisibility by 3. Design a similar activity leading to the formulation of a test for divisibility by 9.

4. Design a computer program in BASIC to print out triangular numbers in order. You will need two stores (or 'boxes'): one for the total so far, and one for the new number to be added. (Answer at the end of Chapter 21, page 248.)

5. Design a Logo program to make a drawing of (a) a boat, (b) a spiral.

Answers to question 1, page 219
The largest rectangle is a square. The largest possible area is a circle.

21 Theories of Learning

Before I married I had six theories about bringing up
children. Now I have six children and no theories.

– The Earl of Rochester

In this book we have considered how children learn mathematics in
terms of (a) their experience with material objects, (b) the spoken
language that they use to describe this experience, (c) the pictures and
diagrams with which they represent it and (d) the mathematical symbols
by which they generalize it. The process is summed up by the mnemonic
'E–L–P–S'. In this final chapter, we shall consider theories of learning
constructed by four psychologists whose research has been very much
concerned with children's mathematical learning.

A theory of learning should provide an answer to the question how
children learn mathematics. In the final section of this chapter, we shall
look at the other side of the coin, and try to provide some answers to the
question why children *fail* at mathematics.

1. Piaget

Chapter 8 gave a brief introduction to the research methods of Piaget
and to his theory that cognitive development (i.e. the development of
modes of thinking in a child) is inextricably linked to biological development. Piaget claimed that cognitive development takes place in an
immutable sequence of steps, and that it is a purely biological process
that no amount of teaching can accelerate.

In addition to his theory of cognitive development, Piaget constructed
a theory of how learning takes place. Learning, according to Piaget, is
distinct from cognitive development. It takes place in relation to the
relevant stage of cognitive development, but it is achieved through
interaction with the environment. 'Penser, c'est opérer,' said Piaget. By
this he meant that thinking and learning involve taking the environment
apart, physically or mentally, and reconstructing it.

Piaget postulated three basic learning processes. They are: (a) the formation of mental concepts; (b) the adaptation of these concepts in the light of experience; and (c) the relating of concepts to form structures. We may attempt to illustrate these processes by returning to the example of Chapter 1, a child learning about the concept 'ball':

(a) The baby shows that he has a *concept* of his ball when he retrieves his ball from underneath a blanket placed over it. His senses did not tell him that the ball was there; his mind did.

(b) He shows that he has *adapted* his concept of 'ball' when he calls other objects 'ball', even if they are different from his own ball in size or colour. Now, 'ball' for him means not just his own ball, but a *class* of objects that *match* his own ball in some specific way.

(c) He shows that he has *related* concepts to form a structure when he tells us that 'balls roll'. This sentence relates the two concepts 'ball' and 'roll'.

Piaget claimed that *adaptation* is the essential ingredient of learning: 'Intelligence is adaptation' [1]. Just as living organisms adapt their behaviour according to the environment, so intelligent animals adapt their mental processes according to experience. Piaget claimed that we adapt in one of two ways: assimilation or accommodation.

Assimilation. This is the process of fitting our new experiences to our existing concepts. 'Intelligence is assimilation to the extent that it incorporates all data of experience within its framework' [1]. A child who has seen five cars and progresses to describing five kittens is *assimilating* a new experience into his concept of 'five'. On the other hand, in the process of assimilation a child can show that his concepts are unconventional. In Chapter 2 (page 17), we described Helen using the word 'bath' to describe a bowl. She was assimilating her experience to her concept of 'bath', which to her meant 'water container'.

Accommodation. Accommodation is a correcting process by which we either restrict or broaden our concepts. Helen had to *restrict* her concept of 'bath' to exclude bowls. On the other hand, children who have learnt that the symbol '5' represents 'five' have to *broaden* their concept of this symbol when they are faced with the numeral '54'. Now the symbol '5' represents 'fifty'.

We might call assimilation 'comfortable adaptation' and accommodation 'uncomfortable adaptation'. Accommodation sets up an imbalance between our existing concepts and our new experiences. You no doubt have a concept of 'banana', for instance. What will you feel if one day you find an object that resembles a banana in shape and taste, but is blue? Until then, a blue banana will have been inconceivable to you. But as a result of your experience, you will most probably broaden your concept of 'banana'. The child who has to accept that '5' sometimes means 'fifty' is in a similar position to you with your blue banana. His world is temporarily turned upside down. The process of learning seems to consist of periods of 'comfortable' assimilation and 'uncomfortable' accommodation. Perhaps this is why it is so often described as progressing in leaps rather than by a steady climb.

Piaget insisted that adaptation is a *necessary* accompaniment to learning. 'Each time you tell children something that they could have discovered for themselves, you prevent them inventing it and thereby gaining the restructuring process of assimilation and accommodation' [2]. An example of what he might have meant by this can be seen in Chapter 20 (page 224). If we *tell* children that they can multiply 11 by 100 by writing down 11 and adding two noughts, they have gained nothing but mystery. But if they discover this fact for themselves, they have gained an insight into the structure of our number system.

Most of the exercises suggested for children in this book have the aim of helping them to assimilate new experiences to their existing concepts. Some are aimed at helping them to accommodate concepts in the light of new experiences. You may find it instructive to consider which of the two processes you are aiming at if you construct exercises for children.

2. Skemp

The British psychologist, Richard Skemp, introduced the idea that concepts constructed by humans form a *hierarchy* [3]. The concept of 'red', says Skemp, is a *primary* concept, because it depends exclusively on data from our senses (the sense of sight). The concept of 'ball' also depends exclusively on sense data.

Skemp asserts that humans form *secondary* concepts in addition to primary ones. We cannot form a concept of 'two' until we have recognized that a pair of objects have something in common, such as 'redness' or 'ballness'. 'Two', according to Skemp, is a secondary concept, because it depends upon the recognition of primary concepts. Similarly, we cannot form a concept of 'colour' until we have recognized that objects may exhibit the sense data of 'red', 'yellow', 'blue' and so on. 'Colour', like 'two', is a secondary concept. The hierarchy of concepts continues to build up. We cannot form a concept of 'number' until we have already formed concepts of 'two', 'three', 'four' and so on. 'Number', according to Skemp, is a tertiary concept. 'Addition' is a fourth-degree concept. Mathematics, more than most other subjects, involves an extensive hierarchy of concepts. We cannot form any particular concept until we have formed all the subsidiary ones on which it depends.

Considering mathematics as a hierarchy of concepts can help us to organize the mathematical knowledge that we wish to teach, but it does not tell us how children can learn these concepts. Skemp has proposed a theory of learning that takes into account the important question of goals and motivation. Learning, he says, is a 'goal directed change of state of a director system towards states which make for possible optimal functioning' [4]. A director system, according to Skemp, is a part of an organism which directs and organizes its behaviour towards a goal. In the case of humans, we might consider it as a model for part of the brain. Its functioning is governed by emotions, such as: *pleasure*, which signals the approach or reaching of a *goal state*; *confidence*, which signals the ability to reach a goal state; *displeasure*, which signals a retreat from a goal state; and *frustration*, which signals the inability to approach or reach a goal state. Skemp illustrates these emotions by reference to the goal of finding the correct piece to insert in a jigsaw puzzle. Finding the correct piece is accompanied by pleasure; but if someone else interferes and shows us the piece, we may well feel frustration.

As well as goal states, says Skemp, there are *anti-goal states*, which we strive to avoid. The emotions associated with anti goal states are: *fear*, which signals their approach; *anxiety*, which signals the inability to avoid them; *relief*, which signals a retreat from them, and *security*, which signals the ability to retreat from them.

Faced with a mathematical problem, our director system registers it, and 'passes on the message' to our emotional system. The emotional system feeds back to our director system a message of confidence, such as 'This is an exciting goal; get on with it!' or a message of anxiety, such as 'This is an anti-goal; try to avoid it!' There is no doubt that emotion plays a dominant part in the way in which we learn. The sections that follow will be seen to take this into account.

3. *Bruner*

As mentioned in Chapter 8 (page 77), Jerome Bruner is one of the psychologists who has challenged Piaget's tenet that learning is completely subordinate to biological development. In contrast to Piaget, Bruner has claimed that 'any idea or body of knowledge can be presented in a form simple enough so that any particular learner can understand it in recognizable form' [5]. This attractive idea seems something of an overstatement. It seems unlikely, for instance, that differential calculus could be taught to four-year-olds in any form at all. At a more modest level, the programme described by Bruner himself to 'teach' the concept of conservation of liquid (see page 79) appeared to have no effect whatever on four-year-olds.

Bruner has constructed a theory of learning that is particularly interesting in the context of mathematics. He holds that learning consists essentially of concept formation, which is 'the multiple embodiment of an abstract idea in different physical forms' [6]. We need, says Bruner, a store of mental images on which to draw in order to form these abstract ideas. Our means of building concepts, he says, lie in the three *modes* of representing the world: (a) the enactive mode; (b) the iconic mode; and (c) the symbolic mode.

You will notice here a resemblance to the E–L–P–S sequence of learning referred to throughout this book. The enactive mode corresponds to our stage E (physical experience), the iconic mode to our stage P (pictures) and the symbolic mode to our stages L and S (spoken language and written symbols). Bruner does not, as we have done, subdivide the symbolic mode into two. But it seems essential to consider them separately in the context of mathematics. All children with normal hearing learn to speak. Learning to read and write symbols is a much less spontaneous process than communicating through speech.

Bruner's Theory of Instruction

Since learning is the end at which teaching aims, it seems appropriate to mention here Bruner's theory of instruction [5]. Bruner suggests that the essential points for teachers to consider are the following: (a) children's predisposition towards learning; (b) the way in which the knowledge to be learnt is structured; (c) the sequence in which the knowledge should be presented; and (d) the motivation and rewards provided.

Predisposition. The will to learn is deeply ingrained. We can hardly *prevent* children from learning, because they have an intrinsic curiosity. But this curiosity, says Bruner, needs to be channelled into what he calls 'guided discovery', which comes from carefully selected experience and its representation in language, pictures or symbols.

Structure of knowledge. Exercises that children are asked to perform should 'cry out', says Bruner, for simplification into conceptual form. As an example, we might look at the examples on page 48 of this book, that include the addition problems 3 + 2, 2 + 3, 2 + 4 and 4 + 2. These exercises might be said to 'cry out' for the concept that addition is commutative. The teacher's role, says Bruner, is to help children verbalize what they have done, so that they can develop the required concepts. Children might verbalize this concept of commutativity by saying, 'It doesn't matter in what order you add two numbers, you always get the same result.'

Sequence. The sequence of presentation of knowledge influences the ease with which children learn. There is no one 'best' sequence for mathematics (although you will find people who claim that there is!). There are different paths to the same goal, and because of individual differences it is important to build several. (For instance, a child who is used to doing the shopping may well learn the concept of place value through money; but a child who is unfamiliar with shopping is more likely to learn the concept through other experiences and apply the concept to money.) Bruner asserts that we need a *spiral curriculum*. At first, ideas are presented in language that is imprecise but honest. At a later stage, the same ideas must be revised and described more precisely. For example, the word 'square' will first be used by children to describe a primary concept – in response to the sense data they receive from a particular shape. Later they will associate the word 'square' with the existence of equal lengths, right angles, symmetry and so on. Robert, aged three, talks about 'square triangles'. I think he means isosceles right-angled triangles. But he is using imprecise language.

Motivation and reward. It is important, says Bruner, for children to feel that their work is leading towards a goal. The knowledge that they gain must be seen as a useful tool. We should motivate them by giving them an idea of what they will be able to achieve with their new knowledge. The most important reward for learning, says Bruner, is not praise from an adult, but intrinsic satisfaction. If children can correct their own work in mathematics – if an answer is right not because teacher says so, but because a calculator confirms it, or a measurement confirms it, or because a *pattern* confirms it – then they can begin to feel this sense of intrinsic satisfaction.

When considering motivation and reward, says Bruner, we should take into account children's readiness for learning. Will a particular piece of knowledge give children a feeling of what mathematics involves and enable them to 'travel beyond it'? Or will it make them feel that mathematics is a set of idiosyncratic rules? We might comment here that delight comes, paradoxically, from a *reduction* of complexity. When we are faced with such a reduction of complexity, we sometimes wonder why we did not discover it ourselves. What an extra delight if we did!

4. Dienes

It might be fair to sum up Zoltan Dienes's theory of learning by saying that he considers learning as a process of increasingly intricate *play* [7]. It is certainly an attractive idea, if not thoroughly convincing. Let us see what he means by play.

Dienes describes essentially *two* types of play: primary play and secondary play. Primary play, he says, is activity with materials aimed at gratifying immediate desires or instincts. Secondary play is activity performed with awareness, aimed at an end which is beyond the immediate gratification of desires. We might describe the activity of a baby trying to grasp his rattle as primary play. His end may be the pure satisfaction of grasping it. When he later uses the skill he has learnt of grasping it in order to make it sound, he might be said to be indulging in secondary play. Mathematical play, says Dienes, falls into these two categories. Primary play involves the manipulation and investigation of materials for its own sake. Secondary play involves trying to build with the materials, discovering patterns (or regularities, as Dienes calls them), and forming abstract conjectures or 'rules' concerning the patterns found. Secondary play may be followed by another period of primary play, with the rules themselves forming the 'material' which is investigated for its own sake. And so the process continues.

Secondary play, according to Dienes, may involve abstraction, symbolization or generalization. Let us see what he actually means by these terms.

Abstraction. Abstraction, according to Dienes, is the process of extracting what is common to a number of different situations and discarding 'noise' (see page 25). Abstraction, he says, requires the holding of several pieces of evidence in the mind. For instance, to label a given pair of objects 'two' requires the recall that other pairs of objects were labelled 'two'.

Symbolization. Like Bruner, Dienes does not distinguish between spoken symbols and written symbols. Symbols, says Dienes, are used to represent classes which have been assembled by the process of abstraction. We might interpose here the example of a child who has formed the abstractions 'two', 'three' and 'five', and who says that 'two toys and three toys are five toys'. This child might be encouraged to express his discovery in the written symbols '2 + 3 = 5' or in the spoken symbols 'two and three more is the same number as five'. If symbols are introduced too early, says Dienes, they can become an empty shell of *signs* with rules for manipulation, instead of an aid to thought. The child who has learnt to write '2 + 3 = 5' merely in response to 'two toys and three toys are five toys' will not be able readily to generalize this number sentence.

Generalization. According to Dienes, generalization is the process of *extending* a class to include new situations. For example, children who predict that 'two *things* and three more *things* will be five *things*' might be said to have generalized their experiences with two toys and three toys, two sweets and three sweets, and so on.

The Principle of Variability

Dienes claimed that we help children to abstract and generalize by varying as much as we can the aspects of their experiences that form 'noise', while retaining in these experiences the aspects of the abstraction that we wish them to form. For instance, if we wish them to form the abstraction 'two and three more is the same number as five', we should provide a rich variety of experiences with objects and measurements that exemplify this abstraction. However, Dienes qualified this advice. He noticed that young children generalize on a *narrower* front than adults; if we introduce too many variables on which to invite generalization, then children may become too distracted by the 'noise' of the varying situations. I would agree with this. For example, the exercise set to you on page 110 was meant to heighten your *own* appreciation of place value. I would not present this exercise to primary-level children, because the process of varying the numbers of tens and units is probably as much as they can manage conceptually. For you, the *base* was varied as well. (The 'umpty' numbers were actually counted and recorded using the base 'five' instead of the usual base 'ten'.)

5. Why Children 'Fail' at Mathematics

Why do some children 'fail' at mathematics? This question, so often asked, is almost unacceptably negative. If we know how children succeed at mathematics, then we ought to know what has been lacking in the experience of a child who fails. However, since this thorny question is so often asked, we shall attempt to answer it under the headings *rate of learning, anxiety, understanding* and *attitude*.

Rate of Learning

A fanatic follower of Piaget might claim that we can teach *nothing* to children, because their cognitive growth progresses at a predetermined rate, just as their bodily growth does. An equally fanatic follower of Bruner might claim that we can teach *anything* to anyone. The truth lies somewhere in between these two extremes. What is more, the truth is never the same for two different children, and here lies the challenge for the adult who tries to help children learn mathematics. Children learn not only in different ways but at different *rates*. Research has shown that we can expect the mathematical ability of seven-year-olds to vary roughly between the ability of an average five-year-old and an average nine-year-old; but we can expect the ability of eleven-year-olds to vary between the ability of an average seven-year-old and an average fifteen-year-old. If a child of eleven is asked to perform like an average eleven-year-old instead of at an actual lower level that he has reached, he will be confused; he may resort in desperation to 'rules' as a substitute for understanding.

Anxiety

Anxiety is akin to desperation. In section 2 of this chapter, we mentioned the attention paid by Skemp to emotion, and in section 3 the attention paid by Bruner to *motivation*. It is actually possible to become *overmotivated*. Many psychologists have shown that high anxiety *impedes* learning. This is why play is so important. Children do not run and climb *in order* to become agile; they do it for the intrinsic pleasure that it gives them. Nevertheless, they become agile as a *result* of their fervent practice of running and climbing. They will learn mathematics best if they consider it as something pleasurable for its own sake.

Understanding

Understanding is a *continuing* process. Throughout your own life, you will continually broaden or restrict your concepts, thereby increasing your own understanding of the world. (Perhaps, as a result of reading this book, your understanding of 'mathematics' has broadened!) Your ability to understand depends on your ability to *adapt*, as Piaget would have put it, or your ability to tolerate *variability*, as Dienes would put it. (For example, if you found the first of the 'Suggestions for the Reader' on page 110 intolerable, your understanding of place value may be limited to *base ten*. This is not a handicap in the everyday world, but it might limit your ability to understand further mathematics, such as the theory of polynomials.)

Children's understanding of mathematics, then, is progressive. We cannot be expected to know exactly which point each child has reached. For instance, a child who has understood that '28' means 'twenty and eight more' may or may not be able to extend that knowledge to the fact that '68' means 'sixty and eight more'. If he has not, he needs more experience in manipulating tens and units before switching his attention to a new mathematical concept. There is no easy solution for the adult who is trying to help this child.

Attitude

Research has shown that a child's attitude to mathematics seems to be consolidated by the age of eleven. Adults who say, 'I can't do maths', are usually found to have formed this opinion by the age of eleven. If you don't like something, you tend to avoid it and perhaps fear it. You form what is commonly called a 'blockage' to it. If only we can keep children's attitude to mathematics positive and inquisitive up to the age of eleven, regardless of their ability, we might prevent this 'blockage' that is so often formed to resist the pain of learning any further mathematics.

6. Conclusion

Teachers face the dilemma of 'getting children through the syllabus' while also allowing them the time needed to develop sound mathematical concepts. Although getting through the syllabus is an understandable aim, it is likely to prove inefficient in the long run. Even children who appear to be competent at performing mathematics at the level we have reached in this book may get 'stuck' very soon beyond this point if they have learnt to memorize 'tricks' as a substitute for conceptual understanding. My cello teacher used to say, 'If at some point you hear that you are playing out of tune, the likelihood is that you were playing out of tune before that point.' If you come to a point in mathematics where you feel lost, it is likely that your understanding was insufficient at an earlier point, even if it did not 'show'. If we let children's mathematics become 'out of tune', we are storing up problems for them in the future.

We come back to the ELPS saga. Perhaps this chapter has spelt out more than others the importance of emotion in mathematics learning. Children need the emotional stimulus of real materials and problems in which they feel interest and involvement. They need language to talk about and analyse these problems. Many teachers claim that teaching mathematics to others has helped them to understand it better themselves; children need similar opportunities. They also need pictures and diagrams to clarify the essentials of a problem at its outset. Finally, they need meaningful written symbols with which to solve and generalize a problem. The old Chinese proverb 'I hear and I forget,/ I see and I remember,/ I do and I understand,' is really about E, L and P. It says that experience is the most important aspect of understanding; pictures are a good aid to memory, and language is no good without the others.

Let me wish you 'Bon voyage' in introducing your children to the fascinating world of mathematics!

References

1. Piaget, J., *The Origin of Intelligence in the Child,* Routledge & Kegan Paul, 1953
2. Piaget, J., *The Science of Education and the Psychology of the Child*, Grossman, 1970
3. Skemp, R., *The Psychology of Learning Mathematics*, Penguin Books, 1971
4. Skemp, R., *Intelligence, Learning and Action,* Wiley, 1979
5. Bruner, J., *Towards a Theory of Instruction*, Norton, 1968
6. Bruner, J., *et al., Studies in Cognitive Growth*, Wiley, 1967
7. Dienes, Z., *An Experimental Study of Mathematics Learning,* Hutchinson, 1964

Answers to questions, page 236

2. The following picture should help to explain why the sum of any two successive triangular numbers is a square number.

4. 10 LET T = 0
   20 LET N = 1
   30 LET T = T + N
   40 PRINT T
   50 LET N = N + 1
   60 GOTO 30

371.91 ~~mon~~

371.9+44 ~~Rum~~

371.909417 IRE

371.904730941 Say

~~371~~

616.8553 M.L

~~371.914~~

Index

READ MORE IN PENGUIN

In every corner of the world, on every subject under the sun, Penguin represents quality and variety – the very best in publishing today.

For complete information about books available from Penguin – including Puffins, Penguin Classics and Arkana – and how to order them, write to us at the appropriate address below. Please note that for copyright reasons the selection of books varies from country to country.

In the United Kingdom: Please write to *Dept. JC, Penguin Books Ltd, FREEPOST, West Drayton, Middlesex UB7 OBR.*

If you have any difficulty in obtaining a title, please send your order with the correct money, plus ten per cent for postage and packaging, to *PO Box No. 11, West Drayton, Middlesex UB7 OBR*

In the United States: Please write to *Consumer Sales, Penguin USA, P.O. Box 999, Dept. 17109, Bergenfield, New Jersey 07621-0120.* VISA and MasterCard holders call 1-800-253-6476 to order all Penguin titles

In Canada: Please write to *Penguin Books Canada Ltd, 10 Alcorn Avenue, Suite 300, Toronto, Ontario M4V 3B2*

In Australia: Please write to *Penguin Books Australia Ltd, P.O. Box 257, Ringwood, Victoria 3134*

In New Zealand: Please write to *Penguin Books (NZ) Ltd, Private Bag 102902, North Shore Mail Centre, Auckland 10*

In India: Please write to *Penguin Books India Pvt Ltd, 706 Eros Apartments, 56 Nehru Place, New Delhi 110 019*

In the Netherlands: Please write to *Penguin Books Netherlands bv, Postbus 3507, NL-1001 AH Amsterdam*

In Germany: Please write to *Penguin Books Deutschland GmbH, Metzlerstrasse 26, 60594 Frankfurt am Main*

In Spain: Please write to *Penguin Books S. A., Bravo Murillo 19, 1º B, 28015 Madrid*

In Italy: Please write to *Penguin Italia s.r.l., Via Felice Casati 20, I-20124 Milano*

In France: Please write to *Penguin France S. A., 17 rue Lejeune, F-31000 Toulouse*

In Japan: Please write to *Penguin Books Japan, Ishikiribashi Building, 2-5-4, Suido, Bunkyo-ku, Tokyo 112*

In Greece: Please write to *Penguin Hellas Ltd, Dimocritou 3, GR-106 71 Athens*

In South Africa: Please write to *Longman Penguin Southern Africa (Pty) Ltd, Private Bag X08, Bertsham 2013*

READ MORE IN PENGUIN

SCIENCE AND MATHEMATICS

QED Richard Feynman
The Strange Theory of Light and Matter

'Physics Nobelist Feynman simply cannot help being original. In this quirky, fascinating book, he explains to laymen the quantum theory of light – a theory to which he made decisive contributions' – *New Yorker*

Does God Play Dice? Ian Stewart
The New Mathematics of Chaos

To cope with the truth of a chaotic world, pioneering mathematicians have developed chaos theory. *Does God Play Dice?* makes accessible the basic principles and many practical applications of one of the most extraordinary – and mind-bending – breakthroughs in recent years.

Bully for Brontosaurus Stephen Jay Gould

'He fossicks through history, here and there picking up a bone, an imprint, a fossil dropping and, from these, tries to reconstruct the past afresh in all its messy ambiguity. It's the droppings that provide the freshness: he's as likely to quote from Mark Twain or Joe DiMaggio as from Lamarck or Lavoisier' – *Guardian*

The Blind Watchmaker Richard Dawkins

'An enchantingly witty and persuasive neo-Darwinist attack on the anti-evolutionists, pleasurably intelligible to the scientifically illiterate' – Hermione Lee in the *Observer* Books of the Year

The Making of the Atomic Bomb Richard Rhodes

'Rhodes handles his rich trove of material with the skill of a master novelist ... his portraits of the leading figures are three-dimensional and penetrating ... the sheer momentum of the narrative is breathtaking ... a book to read and to read again' – Walter C. Patterson in the *Guardian*

Asimov's New Guide to Science Isaac Asimov

A classic work brought up to date – far and away the best one-volume survey of all the physical and biological sciences.